Florin Mușat

TESTE DE

Florin Muşat

Teste de limba engleză

EXIGENT

Teste de limba engleză
Florin Muşat

Editor: Fănica Alecu-Cocineanu
DTP: Ionuţ Tolontan

Descrierea CIP a Bibliotecii Naţionale a României
MUŞAT, FLORIN
Teste de limba engleză / Florin Muşat. - Bucureşti : Exigent, 2014
ISBN 978-973-1853-27-7

811.111(079.1)

Comenzile se pot trimite pe adresa:
E-mail: editura_exigent@yahoo.com
Tel: 021.260.04.76
Mobil: 0723.320.440

Cuvânt înainte

Teste de Limba Engleză reprezintă o colecţie de teste adresate nu numai studenţilor care se pregătesc pentru diferite examene – examenul de Bacalaureat sau examenul de admitere la facultate – dar şi tuturor celor care doresc să-şi verifice cunoştinţele de limbă engleză.

Teste de Limba Engleză este o carte completă care are ca obiectiv principal furnizarea unor explicaţii clare, simple, concise, putând fi utilizată de toţi cei care doresc să înveţe limba, indiferent de nivelul lor de engleză – de la începători, până la cei care au un nivel avansat de înţelegere. Această carte poate fi utilizată pentru studiu dar şi pentru recapitulare, pentru studiul individual sau studiul de grup.

Testele au o structură unitară, grupate pe diferite capitole, prezentând cititorilor conceptele gramaticale de bază ale limbii engleze. Fiecare temă este tratată separat, pe un capitol distinct, astfel încât oricine utilizează această carte să poată să lucreze pe o anumită temă.

Teste de Limba Engleză este o carte completă care se pretează la modalităţi variate de utilizare.

La sfârşitul testelor am inclus cheia exerciţiilor, o listă cu verbele neregulate precum şi un vocabular fundamental al limbii engleze, ce vor ajuta la rezolvarea şi verificarea diferitelor exerciţii.

Suntem convinşi că această lucrare cuprinzătoare se va dovedi indispensabilă tuturor celor care doresc să însuşească limba engleză corect din punct de vedere gramatical.

Autorul

Phonetics
(Fonetica)

Exercise 1.

Transcrieţi fonetic următoarele cuvinte.

a. **they**	ei, ele
b. **this**	acesta, aceasta, acest, această
c. **there**	acolo
d. **then**	apoi, după aceea
e. **mother**	mamă
f. **father**	tată
g. **though**	deşi, cu toate că
h. **thus**	astfel, aşa

Exercise 2.

Transcrieţi fonetic următoarele propoziţii.

a. This is a clock.
b. They are doctors.
c. It is there.
d. They are farmers.
e. This is a flower.
f. They are my friends.

Exercise 3.

Transcrieţi fonetic verbul **"to be"** la prezent, afirmativ, *formele literare*, **"*lungi*"**, utilizate în limba standard, mai ales în texte scrise, oficiale şi *formele contrase*, prescurtate, **"*scurte*"**, folosite în vorbire.

Forme literare

I am	eu sunt
you are	tu/dumneata eşti; voi/dumneavoastră sunteţi
he is	el este
she is	ea este
it is	el/ea este
we are	noi suntem
they are	ei/ele sunt

Forme contrase

Observaţi dispariţia primei vocale din forma verbului şi înlocuirea ei cu un apostrof, adică **'**

I'm	eu sunt, îs
you're	tu/dumneata eşti; voi/dumneavoastră sunteţi
he's	el e, -i
she's	ea e, - i
it's	el/ea e
we're	noi suntem
they're	ei/ele sunt

Exercise 4.

Urmăriţi transcrierea fonetică pentru perechile de cuvinte de mai jos şi alcătuiţi scurte propoziţii în limba engleză, realizând în acelaşi timp şi transcrierea fonetică.

then	[ðen]	thin	[θin]
thus	[ðʌs]	thank	[θæŋk]
they	[ðei]	three	[θri:]
there	[ðεə]	theme	[θi:m]
this	[ðis]	think	[θink]
though	[ðou]	theory	[θiəri]

Exercise 5.

Traduceţi în limba engleză şi realizaţi transcrierea fonetică.

1. El e fiul meu.
2. Ei sunt prietenii mei.
3. Ei sunt înalţi./Ele sunt înalte.
4. O idee interesantă.
5. Sunteţi înalt, domnule George?
6. Încântat/ă de cunoştinţă.
7. Numele meu este George.
8. E doar o coincidenţă.

Exercise 6.

Transcrieţi fonetic următoarele propoziţi.

1. I **have got** an American friend. — Am un prieten american.
   I've got an American friend.
2. You **have got** a good idea. — Ai/Aveţi o idee bună.
   You've got a good idea.
3. He **has got** a difficult problem. — El are o problemă grea.
   He'**s got** a difficult problem.
4. She **has got** a big car. — Ea are o maşină mare.
   She'**s got** a big car.
5. It **has got** four wheels. — Ea (maşina) are patru roţi.
   It'**s got** four wheels.
6. We **have got** a small farm. — Avem o fermă mică.
   We'**ve got** a small farm.
7. Thy **have got** a caring mother-in-law. — Ei au o soacră grijulie.
   They'**ve got** a caring mothe-in-law.

Exercise 7.

Scrieţi următoarele nume în alfabetul fonetic.

Exemplu: **CLAUDIA POPESCU**

C	[si:]	**P**	[pi:]
L	[el]	**O**	[əu]
A	[ei]	**P**	[pi:]
U	[ju:]	**E**	[i:]
D	[di:]	**S**	[es]

I [ai] **C** [si:]
A [ei] **U** [ju:]

1. Daniel Georgescu
2. Alina Cristoiu
3. Robert Popescu
4. Radu Florescu
5. Monica Teodorescu

Exercise 8.

În timp ce interogativul nu are decât o singură formă a verbului – cea lungă – o negaţie la prezentul verbului *"to be"* poate fi exprimată în trei forme – una lungă şi două scurte. Studiaţi tabelul de mai jos şi realizaţi transcrierea fonetică.

LONG FORMS	SHORT FORMS	
I am not	I'm not	-
You are not	You're not	You aren't
He is not	He's not	He isn't
She is not	She's not	She isn't
It is not	It's not	It isn't
We are not	We're not	We aren't
They are not	They're not	They aren't

Exercise 9.

Alegeţi pentru fiecare cuvânt transcrierea fonetică corectă.

1. <u>you</u>
a. [ju:]
b. [ju: ə]
c. [t□:l]

2. <u>we</u>
a. [hu:]
b. [wi:]
c. [ju:]

3. <u>relatives</u>
a. [k∂**uinsi**d∂ns]
b. [**di**fik∂lt]
c. [**rel**∂tivz]

4. <u>coincidence</u>
a. [k∂**uinsi**d∂ns]
b. [**di**fik∂lt]
c. [**rel**∂tivz]

Exercise 10.

Alegeţi pentru fiecare propoziţie transcrierea fonetică corectă.

1. He is short.	a. [ðei a: ʃ□:t]
2. She is short.	b. [ðei a: ʃ□:t]
3. They are short.	c. [ən 'intristiŋ ai'diə]
4. They are short.	d ['intristiŋ ai'diəs]
5. An interesting idea.	e. [hi: iz ʃ□:t]
6. An interesting project.	f. ['intristiŋ 'prɔdʒekts]
7. Interesting ideas.	g. [ən 'intristiŋ 'prɔdʒekt]
8. Interesting projects.	h. [ʃi: iz ʃ□:t]

Pronouns
(Pronumele)

Exercise 1.

Completaţi cu forma corespunzătoare a ***pronumelui personal***, alegând dintre: **he, she, they, we.**

Exemple:	Laura is my friend.	Laura este prietena mea.
	...... is my friend	...... este prietena mea.
	She is my friend.	**Ea** este prietena mea.
	Adrian and I are Romanians.	Eu şi Adrian suntem români.
	.... are Romanians.	...... suntem români.
	We are Romanians.	**Noi** suntem români.

1. Florin and Dan are farmers.	Florin şi Dan sunt fermieri.
... are farmers.	**Ei** sunt fermieri.
2. Magda is Romanian.	Magda este româncă.
... is Romanian	**Ea** este româncă.
3. Dana is my friend.	Dana este prietena mea.
... is my friend	**Ea** este prietena mea.
4. Adrian and Daniel are my sons.	Adrian şi Daniel sunt fii mei.
... are my sons.	**Ei** sunt fii mei.
5. Alina and Adriana are relatives.	Alina şi Adriana sunt rude.
... are relatives.	**Ele** sunt rude.
6. Dan and I are artists.	Eu şi Dorin suntem artişti.
... are artists.	**Noi** suntem artişti.
7. Paul is a driver.	Paul este şofer.
... is a driver.	**El** este şofer.
8. Diana is a doctor.	Diana este doctor.
... is a doctor	**Ea** este doctor.

Exercise 2.

Completaţi cu forma corespunzătoare, ţinând cont de cuvântul din paranteze.

Exemple: ………... often reads books.
She often reads books.

1. ………… is dreaming. (Gabriel)
2. ………… is green. (the window)
3. ………… are on the wall (the posters)
4. ………… is running. (the dog)
5. ………… are watching TV. (my father and I)
6. ………… are in the garden. (the flowers)
7. ………… is riding his bike. (Dan)
8. ………… is from Bucharest. (Andreea)
9. ………… has got a sister. (Dana)
10. Have ……. got a computer, Mary?

Exercise 3.

Completaţi următoarele propoziţii cu ***pronumele*** potrivit.

1. My friend Camelia loves chocolate. This chocolate box is for ....
2. My brother like Disney photo. The photo is for ....
3. My children Matt collects picture postcards. These postcards are for ....
4. My friends like music. The CD is for ....
5. I like skirt. This nice skirt is for ....
6. My daughter and I love flowers. These flowers are for ....
7. My nephew likes cars. The toy truck is for ....
8. My parents want to go to Italy next month. The guide book is for ....
9. Here is another guide books about France. I don't know what to do with ....
10. My husband loves France. It's for ....

Exercise 4.

Completați următoarele propoziții cu ***pronumele potrivit***.

1. .... have got some books.
2. The books are for ....
3. These are .... books.
4. The books are ....

Exercise 5.

Completați următoarele propoziții cu ***pronumele reflexiv*** potrivit.

1. I did the job ....
2. Let's do it ....
3. He .... didn't know it.
4. She .... broke the glass.
5. Control ....
6. I enjoyed .... very much
7. You hurt ....
8. I cut ....

Exercise 6.

Completați următoarele propoziții cu ***pronumele posesiv*** potrivit.

1. This is .... collar.
2. This is .... son.
3. They are .... brothers.
4. This is .... house.
5. Those are .... books.
6. This is ....
7. Those are ....
8. This is ....

Exercise 7.

Completați următoarele propoziții.

1. Adriana and Alexandru are concerned about .... welfare in this course.
2. Did Ionut or Cristi want .... hair cut?
3. Actors during early rehearsals often forget .... lines.
4. The committee has disagreed about .... next move.
5. At the end of the movies, each of the couples cleared up .... misunderstanding.

6. Each of the groups will have .... convention here.
7. If any one of the sisters needs a ride to church, ... can call me.
8. The books or the bag would be quite enough to carry, so don't tire yourself over ....

Exercise 8.

Alegeți varianta corectă.

1. I	a) are b) be c) am	writing a letter.
2. She	a) are b) am c) is	going to school by bus.
3. They	a) is b) isn't c) are	leaving for London.
4. Dan	a) isn't b) aren't c) be	eating his breakfast.
5. Dana and Florin	a) being b) are c) isn't	good friends.
6.	a) Is b) Are c) Am	they going home tonight?
7. It	a) isn't b) is c) aren't	raining today, is it?
8.	a) Is b) Are c) Isn't	this the way to the Theatre?

The Noun
(Substantivul)

Exercise 1.

Treceţi următoarele propoziţii la plural. Atenţie! Sunt patru modificări pe care trebuie să le faceţi. Primele patru propoziţii sunt rezolvate drept model.

1. I am a boy.
   ↓ ↓ ↓ ↓
   We are – boys.

2. It is a map. — They are maps.
3. He is a farmer. — They are farmers.
4. You are a doctor. — You are doctors.

1. She is a farmer. ....
2. It is a violin ....
3. I am a girl. ....
4. It is a tree. ....
5. He is an artist. ....
6. I am a driver. ....

Exercise 2.

Treceţi următoarele substantive la plural, adăugând formei de singular de mai jos **–s** sau **–es**, după caz.

1. clock	....	7. map	....
2. brush	....	8. tree	....
3. report	....	9. touch	....
4. cup	....	10. farmer	....
5. sandwich	....	11. driver	....
6. doctor	....	12. watch	....

Exercise 3.

Scrieţi forma la plural a următoarelor substantive neregulate şi traduceţi-le.

***Exemplu*:**	brush	perie		brushes perii
	flower	....	....	....
	car	....	....	....
	box	....	....	....
	economist	....	....	....
	sandwich	....	....	....
	violin	....	....	....

Exercise 4.

Completaţi propoziţiile de mai jos cu forma corectă de plural a substantivului subliniat.

1. This <u>man</u> is intelligent.	These .... are intelligent.
2. She is a nice <u>woman</u>.	They are nice ....
3. I have a <u>child</u>.	I have three ....

Exercise 5.

Traduceţi expresiile:

un buchet de flori	o felie de pâine	o cană de ulei
un mănunchi de banane	un pahar de apă	multă făină
o bucată de prăjitură	un pahar de zahăr	puţină făină
o legătură de chei	puţin zahăr	multe flori

Exercise 6.

Scrieţi pluralul la următoarele substantive:

girl, boy, house, book, pear, glass, chocolate, cup, television, apple.

Exercise 7.

Împărţiţi în cantităţi mai mici următoarele produse:

flour, sugar, oil, milk, wheat, bread, water, rice, corn.

Exercise 8.

Traduceţi în limba engleză.

1. Ai/Aveţi un copil?
Am trei copii.
2. El este bărbat.
Ei sunt bărbaţi.
3. Ea este o femeie.
Ele sunt femei.
4. Acest copil este inteligent.
Aceşti copii sunt inteligenţi
5. Acest bărbat este înalt.
Aceşti bărbaţi sunt înalţi.
6. Această femeie este frumoasă.
Aceste femei sunt frumoase.

Exercise 9.

Aşa cum deja stiţi există substantive care au de obicei formă de singular şi de plural, adică se pot număra şi substantive care denumesc materii sunt nenumărabile, adică nu se pot număra. Împărţiţi în două grupe următoarele substantive.

House	one house	two houses	o casă	două case
Oil	....	....	....	....
Sugar	....	....	....	....
Child	....	....	....	....
Water	....	....	....	....
Flower	....	....	....	....
Boy	....	....	....	....

Girl ....
Salt ....
Bread ....

Exercise 10.

În limba engleză sunt de genul neutru, substantivele ce denumesc obiecte neînsuflețite sau al căror sex nu interesează, precum și substantivele care au o singură formă pentru ambele sexe. Precizați pentru următoarele substantive forma de feminin și masculin.

Comun	Masculin	Feminin
Calf	....	....
Elephant	....	....
Cat	....	....
Pigeon	....	....
Bear	....	....
Goat	....	....

Exercise 11.

Traduceți în limba engleză.

a. Sunt cinci gâște pe iaz. (pond).
b. Un stol de porumbei zboară deasupra livezii.
c. Ursoaicele au grijă de puii lor.
d. Veverița are coadă lungă și blană maro.
e. Unele animale sălbatice sunt periculoase.

Exercise 12.

Identificați care din următoarele substantive sunt numărabile sau nu. Precizati și care dintre aceste substantive în funcție de context pot fi numărabile sau nu.

textbook	banana
applause	shopping
poetry	conduct
smoking	crystal
acid	progress
world	essay
thought	biology

Exercise 13.

Scrieți grupurile nominale corespunzătoare definițiilor. Prima propoziție a fost completată ca model.

a. a judge who is 57 years old = *a 57-year old judge*
b. a delay of two weeks =
c. a session of six months =
d. a person who gives law =
e. a person who makes troubles =
f. an embezzlement which amounts to a million of USD =
g. a person who breaks into a house to commit a crime =
h. the act of breaking into a house to commit a crime =
i. a report on a crime =

Adjectives
(Adjectivele)

Exercise 1.

Acest exerciţiu subliniază, o dată în plus, faptul că în limba engleză adjectivul nu se acordă cu substantivul pe care îl determină. Înainte de a rezolva exerciţiul, vă invităm să învăţaţi un număr de adjective.

important [im 'pɔ:tnt]	important, impotantă, importanţi, importante
big [big]	mare, mari
small [sm□:l]	mic, mică, mici
intelligent [in'telidʒnt]	inteligent, inteligentă, inteligenţi, inteligente
beautiful ['bju:təfl]	frumos, frumoasă, frumoşi, frumoase
good [gud]	bun, bună, buni, bune

Traduceţi următoarele propoziţii. Primele trei sunt traduse ca exemplu.

1. He is a good driver.	(El) Este un şofer bun.
2. She is an intelligent doctor.	(Ea) Este o doctoriţă inteligentă.
3. It is a beautiful picture.	Este un tablou frumos.
4. It is a tall tree.	....
5. He is an intelligent boy.	....
6. It is a big picture.	....
7. She is an important artist.	....
8. It is a beautiful flower.	....
9. She is a good driver.	....
10. They are big rings.	....

Exercise 2.

Completaţi spaţiile libere cu literele ce lipsesc cuvintelor din propoziţiile de mai jos.

1.Dan is go_d dr_ver.
2. It's an intel_igent ide_.
3. He's my s_n.
4. It's a be_utiful flo_er.

Exercise 3.

Completaţi spaţiile libere cu adjectivul corespunzător.

1. My cat is .... than yours.
2. This flower is .... than that one.
3. This is the .... newspaper I have ever read.
4. Non-smokers usually live .... than smokers.
5. Which is the .... animal in the world?
6. A holiday in the mountains is .... than a holiday by the sea.
7. It is strange but often a beer is .... than a coke.
8. Who is the .... man on earth?

9. The weather this winter is even ……………. than last winter.
10. He was the …………. thief of all.

Exercise 4.

Completaţi spaţiile libere cu adjectivul corespunzător.

1. His .... car was stolen.
2. Something smells ....
3. Their restaurant is very ....
4. What an .... story
5. My uncle is an .... scientist.

Exercise 5.

Traduceţi în limba română.

1. Their pictures aren't beautiful ....
2. Our children have interesting ideas. ....
3. My grandfather isn't at home. ....
4. Her brother is tall and blond. ....
5. His parents have a car. ....
6. Your coffee is ready. ....

Exercise 6.

Traduceţi în limba engleză.

rudele ei	....	ideea ei	....
bunica mea	....	unchiul lor	....
fraţii lui	....	mătuşa noastră	....
surorile tale	....	soţia mea	....

Exercise 7.

Completaţi cu ***my***, ***your***, ***his***, ***her***, ***our***, sau ***their*** propoziţiile din coloana din dreapta.

Exemplu:

You have a car. .... car is big. Your car is big.

1. They have two children. .... children are intelligent.
2. I have a daughter. .... daughter is nine years old.
3. You have two sister. .... sisters are architects.
4. We have a clock. .... clock is big.
5. David has a son. .... son is six.
6. Dana has two children. .... children are nice.

Exercise 8.

Completaţii propoziţiile cu adjectivele formate prin sufixarea substantivelor scrise cu majuscule. Folosiţi sufixele: ***-full, -ant, -ed, -ic.***

JOY a) The streets of the city were filled with …………. crowds celebrating New Year.

RADIANCE b) The announced, with a ………….. face, that she had passed the examination.

PLEASURE c) "I'll be on holidays in a week's time", she said looking ....

EUPHORIA d) "Now that the .... moments have past, let's get down to work!"

THRILL e) He's simply .... with his new Halloween costume.

Exercise 9.

Completaţi propoziţiile cu adjectivele corespunzătoare.

a. The General was a _ _ l _ old campaigner who had fought more battles than he could remember.
b. Traian had worked out a _ r _ _ _ _ way of avoiding the trap.
c. Be careful! He's very _ l _ and you never know what he's up to.
d. The British were very _ _ n _ _ _ _; they launched the attack in the early hours of the morning.
e. When the _ _ _ _ w _ old king was nearing his end, he chose his successor to the throne.
f. A _ I _ _ man once said that a fool and his money are soon parted.
g. All these heavy volumes were written by _ _ g _ people centuries ago.

Exercise 10.

Grupaţi adjectivele în funcţie de prepoziţiile care urmează. Lucraţi cu un dicţionar. Ce calităţi trebuie să aibă o femeie ca să reuşească în afaceri? Alcătuiţi propoziţii.

conducive, indignant, right, responsible, hostile, capable, bad/good, astonished, sensitive, discontented, doubtful, kind, ashamed, deficient, reluctant, angry, pleased, interested, thankful.

about	at	for	of	in	to	with

Exercise 11.

Completaţi următoarele propoziţii cu adjectivele posesive potrivite. Alăturat aveţi şi traducerea.

.... father is an arhitect.	Tatăl **meu** este arhitect.
.... wife ia a doctor.	Soţia **mea** este doctoriţă.
.... children are students.	Copiii **mei** sunt studenţi.
.... relatives are in Bucharest.	Rudele **mele** sunt în Bucureşti.
What is .... name?	Care este numele **tău/dvs.**?
Is .... mother-in-law at home?	Este soacra **ta/dumneavoastră** acasă?
Are .... children at home?	Sunt copiii **tăi/dumneavoastră** acasă?
Is .... uncle a driver, Mr. Florin?	Unchiul **dumneavoastră** este şofer, d-le Florin?
.... daughter isn't at home.	Fiica **lui** nu este acasă.
.... relatives are famous.	Rudele **lui** sunt celebre.
.... mother is an interesting woman.	Mama **ei** este o femeie interesantă.
Is Robert .... son?	Dan este fiul **ei**?
.... daughters are tall and blond.	Fiicele **ei** sunt înalte şi blonde.
I have a cat. .... fur is black.	Am o pisică. Blana **ei** este neagră.

.... sister is beautiful. — **Sora lor** este frumoasă.
.... brothers aren't in Bucharest. — **Fraţii lor** nu sunt în Bucureşti.

Exercise 12.

Grupaţi adjectivele în funcţie de prepoziţiile care urmează. Lucraţi cu un dicţionar. Ce calităţi trebuie să aibă o femeie ca să reuşească în afaceri? Alcătuiţi propoziţii.

conducive, indignant, right, responsible, hostile, capable, bad/good, astonished, sensitive, discontented, doubtful, kind, ashamed, deficient, reluctant, angry, pleased, interested, thankful.

about	at	for	of	in	to	With
					conductive	

The comparison of the Adjectives
(Compararea adjectivelor)

Exercise 1.
Traduceți următoarele expresii:

a) Adrian este mai înalt decât Dan, deşi este mai tânăr decât el.
b) Maria este mai mare decât mine.
c) Eu sunt mai mică decât Maria.
d) Tata este doctor. El este brunet şi foarte sobru.
e) Mama e subțirică şi blondă.

Exercise 2.
Traduceți în limba română.

a) I am younger than you.
b) She is taller than her sister.
c) We are faster than you.
d) You are fatter than you think you are.
e) He is older than his cousins.

Exercise 3.
Treceți următoarele adjective la toate cele trei grade de comparație.

Exemplu:	short	as short as not as short as shorter than	the shortest

short — thin
small — thick
tall — nice
big — light
fat — heavy

Exercise 4.
Treceți următoarele adjective la toate cele trei grade de comparație.

Exemplu:	beautiful	as beautiful as not as beautiful as more beautiful than	the most beautiful

intelligent — blasphemous
beautiful — creditable
arrogant — diabolical
aromatic — flattering
aristocratic — lockless

Exercise 5.
Înlocuiţi punctele de mai jos cu forma corectă a adjectivelor neregulate:

1. This book is …………..than the other one.
2. I need ………… milk for this cake.
3. She has ……….. flowers than me.
4. This is the ………… movie in the world.
5. You have the ………… mark at the test paper.
6. Dana has ………… money than her sister.
7. This apple is ……… than the yellow one.
8. He has the ………….. pencils in the class.
9. ………………. of the people in the world live in America!
10. The Pacific Ocean has the ……….. water on Earth.

Exercise 6.
Scrieţi comparativul şi superlativul de la următoarele adjective.

long	ugly
young	slim
easy	tiny
small	beautiful
big	tender
tall	difficult
bright	pleasant
fat	clever

Exercise 7.
Formulaţi comparativul şi superlativul următoarelor adjective neregulate.

good, bad, much, many, little.

Exercise 8.
Traduceţi în limba engleză.

a) Azi este mai cald decât ieri.
b) Camera mea este mai mare decât bucătăria.
c) Soţia ta este mai înaltă decât sora mea.
d) Unde este cea mai apropiată staţie de autobuz?
e) Cel mai bun copil în clasa noastră este Mihai.
f) Câinele meu este mai rău decât al tău.
g) Sora mea este mai mică decât mine cu 2 ani.

Exercise 9.
Traduceţi în limba română.

The more we study the more we know. The more we know the more we forget. The more we forget the less we know. The less we know the less we forget. The less we forget the more we know. So why study?

Exercise 10.

Completaţi spaţiile punctate cu adjectivele din paranteze la comparativ.

a) The sick man is getting ……… and ……… . (good)
b) The little boy runs …….. and ……… . (fast)
c) The storm becomes ………. and ……… violent. (much)
d) The ………. the building is, the ……….. flats it will have. (big, many)

Exercise 11.

Scrieţi comparativul de superioritate de la următoarele adjective.

a) tall
b) young
c) old
d) nice
e) beautiful
f) short
g) intelligent
h) fat
i) common

Exercise 12.

Scrieţi comparativul de inferioritate de la următoarele adjective, apoi alcătuiţi propoziţii.

a) creditable
b) thin
c) modern
d) flattering
e) thick
f) big

Exercise 13.

Completaţi spaţiile libere cu comparativul de superioritate de la următoarele adjective: ***good*, *bad*, *little*, *much*, *many***.

a) The drink is ………….. than the food.
b) I have ………….. bananas than you.
c) She has ………….. money than her brother.
d) I feel ……………. than yesterday.
e) Dana has ………. dresses than any other girl.

Exercise 14.

Puneţi în spaţiile libere superlativul de la următoarele adjective: ***beautiful*, *fat*, *modern*, *inteligent*, *nice***.

a) She is …………….. girl in the world.
b) This is …………… elephant that I have ever seen.
c) Marian is ………….. pupil in his class.
d) I'm buying the …………….. ring in the world.

Exercise 15.

Completaţi tabelul de mai jos cu formele care lipsesc.

	Positive	Comparative	Superlative
1			funniest
2		more	
3	tall		
4		crueller	
5	reliable		
6			the least
7		better	
8			the worst
9			the most sensible
10	intelligent		

Exercise 16.

Completaţi prepoziţiile ***of, in, on, under***.

1. Which is the most famous woman .... the world?
2. She is the best paid actress .... all.
3. He runs the most profitable company .... earth.
4. She is the most efficient .... my secretaries.
5. We'll be the happiest couple …………. the sun.
6. "Ladies and gentlemen, here she is the most beautiful woman …………. the world."

Exercise 17.

Aranjaţi adjectivele în ordinea corespunzătoare şi formulaţi propoziţii cu expresiile astfel obţinute.

a. a black / little / straw / amazing hat;
b. blue / enormous / bright eyes;
c. a thin / tall / Frenchman / young;
d. an attractive / woman / blond / long hair.

Exercise 18.

Citiţi CV-ul Danei şi al contracandidatului ei. Comparaţi în scris cele două CV-uri folosind unele dintre următoarele cuvinte. Folosiţi dicţionarul!

flexible, fashionable, experienced, young, fluent, skilled, proud, friendly, articulate, sensitive, daring, nice, intelligent, witty, creative.

Dana

Name:	Dana Ionescu
Age:	23
Status:	single
Training:	Institute of Politechnics
Research:	Scolarship in Toulouse (France); material lighter than air
Work experience:	- none
Skills and potential:	- computer literate;
	- English and French fluently;

	- enthusiastic, careful;
	- can adapt quickly to change;
Appearance:	- wears fashionable clothes;
Character, manners:	- sincere, conscientious;
	- at times, overconfident;
	- good organizer;
	- likes socializing;
	- even-tempered.
Sports and other interest:	- swimming;
	- all kinds of music;
	- SF literature.

Counter candidate.

Name:	Train Florescu
Age:	25
Status:	single
Training:	Institute of Politechnics
Research:	none
Work experience:	- 2 years with IAR Braşov
Skills and potential:	- computer literate;
	- excellent driver;
	- French and German quite well;
Appearance:	- handsome;
	- "clothes do not make the man"
Character, manners:	- a little impatient at times;
	- clear thinker;
	- friendly;
	- a good "team leader"
Sports and other interest:	- parachute jumping;
	- going to the theatre.

Exercise 19.

Realizaţi un portret caricatural folosind următoarele expresii idiomatice cu gradul comparativ.

as good as gold	bun ca pâinea caldă
as mad as a March Hare	nebun de legat
as thin as a rake/poker	slab ca un catâr
as black as pitch	negru ca tăciunele
as shy as a sheep	timid ca o fată mare
as blod as brass	neruşinat foc
as changeable as weather	schimbător ca vremea
as proud as a peacock	mândru ca un păun
as silent as a mouse	tăcut ca pământul
as tall as a lamp-post	înalt cât o prăjină
as obstinate as a mule	încăpăţânat ca un catâr

as poor as a church mouse	sărac lipit pământului
as meek as a lamb	blând ca un mieluşel
as wise as an owl	înțelept ca o bufniță
as silly as a goose	prost ca noaptea/o gâscă

Exemplu: My boyfriend is a good as gold. He is .... but sometimes .... He is always .... , but occasionally ....

Exercise 20.

Completați dialogul cu cuvintele care lipsesc.

A: I (1)........ girls are easier to raise than boys.
B: I don't (2)…………….. . I have two girls and, believe me, you're (3)……………
A: I'm (4)……………… . I (5)……………. (6)…………….. with you. Girls are quieter and prefer playing with dolls.
B: Dolls which (7)................. very expensive.
A: Come on, that's not a (8)…………. .

Exercise 21.

Scrieți gradele de comparație la următoarele adjective.

a. lazy ....
b. comfortable ....
c. resolute ....
d. wise ....
e. reliable ....
f. cruel ....

Exercise 22.

Puneți verbele din paranteză la gradul de comparație corespunzător.

a. Her solution was (good) of all.
b. She is (intelligent) person I've ever know.
c. He is (reliable) than she is.
d. Girls are (impulsive) than boys.
e. My little boy is growing (bright).
f. My father is not as (understanding) as my mother.
g. The (experienced) she is, the (good) for her.
h. I'm impressed. Your play is (interesting).

Exercise 23.

Completați propozițiile cu formele comparative ale următoarelor adjective: precious, wise, dark, yellow (2), deep (2), red (3), white (2), wild (2), mighty, dear. Folosiți cele trei forme ale gradului comparativ.

a. "His hair is as ………….. as the hyacinth-blossom, and his lips are as ……………. as the rose of his desire."
b. "It is ……… than emeralds, and ……….. than fine opals."
c. "My roses are as …………….. as the foam of the sea and …………… than the snow upon the mountain."

d. "My roses are as .... as the hair of the mermaid who sits on the amber throne and .... than the daffodil that blossoms in the meadow."
e. "My roses are as .... as the feet of the dove and .... than the great fans of coral that wave and wave in the ocean cavern."
f. "Love is .... than Philosophy ... and .... than Power."
g. "All night long she sang, and the thorn went .... and .... into her breast ... Bitter, bitter was the pain and .... and .... grew her song."

Exercise 24.

Completaţi chestionarul cu gradul superlativ al adjectivelor din paranteză.

a. Which is .... mountain in Scotland? (high)
b. Which is .... lake in the Lake District? (large)
c. Which is .... path in the Lake District? (long)
d. Which is .... valley? (quiet)
e. Which is .... threat for hikers? (great)
f. Which is .... temperature recorded in the area? (low)
g. Which is .... center for Lakelan walkers? (favourite)
h. Which is .... part of the walk? (steep)
i. Which park is .... to the public? (accessible)
j. Which is .... national Park in Britain? (big)

Exercise 25.

Completaţi corespunzător propoziţiile: ***of, in, on, under***.

a. Mount Ben Nevis is the highest .... the mountains in Britain.
b. The Thames in the most important river .... Britain.
c. Do you know which the wettest place .... Earth is?
d. "Mirror, mirror in the wall
Who is the prettiest .... all?"
e. She was the cruelest mother .... the Sun.

Exercise 26.

Completaţi propoziţiile cu adjective formate de la substantivele sau verbele din partea stângă.

a. Britain is known for it's .... weather	RAIL
b. The south of Britain is a .... region.	HILL
c. The Lake District is a .... area.	BEAUTY
d. We had a rest on a .... bench.	WOOD
e. The view was merely	IMPRESS
f. In spite of their appearance, woodlanders are .... people.	FRIEND
g. The road was not .... from the valley.	ACCESS
h. Thousands of .... stars studded the dark sky.	TWINKLE
i. We were .... with the incident.	AMUSE
j. He keeps telling the same story which no one considers	SURPRISE

Exercise 27.

Citiţi cu atenţie textul scris pe cartea poştală şi completaţi adjectivele care lipsesc. Alegeţi dintre următoarele adjective:

useful, topped, steepest, Georgian, most beautiful, larger, unpredictable, lucky, lazy, thrilling, comfortable, cold, changing, personal, marvelous, kind, overwhelming, relaxing, sunny, dearest, fine, best. Atenţie: sunt cinci adjective în plus!

My (1) …………….. Irina. The Lake District is the (2) ………………… place I've been to, despite the ever (3) ……………….. weather. It's always (4) ……………… and no matter how (5) …………….. a day it is, it could rain.
Anyway, the accommodation was (6) ……………… and the people I met, extremely (7) …………………; they provided me with all the (8) …………… information I needed.
I also visited Wordsworth's house. It's an old (9) …………… house built in 1754. It was (10) ……………… to see the poet's (11) …………… effects. I'll take another few days to wander about. If I'm (12) …………….. and the weather is (13) …………… , I'll take the open (14) ……………….. double-decker bus to have a tour to Keswick which is in the north. As you know me, I'm too (15) ……………… to hike.
I'll write you soon to share my new (16) …………… experience here.
Your (17) …………… friend, Elena.

Exercise 28.

Scrieţi o carte poştală asemănătoare respectând următoarea structură.

paragraph 1 – an introductory idea about the place;
2 – accommodation and people;
3 – one or two details about your programme;
4 – a decision for the future.

Exercise 29.

Reformulaţi enunţurile atenuând tonul incisiv.

a. The government shouldn't subsidize farming.
b. Country life is an old-fashioned way of living.
c. Country life is boring.

Exercise 30.

Completaţi particulele adverbiale corespunzătoare.

a. She just walked _ _ the beauty contest.
b. I walked_ _ the first woman and I asked her the same question.
c. Walking_ _ the conference room is not a mature behaviour.
d. He was too young and a coward and walked _ _ them.
e. I'm sure someone has walked _ _ my new pair of gloves.

Indefinite Pronoun/Adjective
(Pronume/Adjective nehotărâte)

Exercise 1.

Completaţi spaţiile libere cu ***some, any, no*** sau compuşii acestora.

1. I haven't seen .... in the hallway.
2. If .... calls, please tell them I'll be back after lunch.
3. He must be .... in the neighborhood.
4. There are .... meetings today.
5. I don't know .... about it. I've been away for two weeks.
6. .... must go and tell her the bad news.
7. They've talked to ....
8. I couldn't do it again for .... in the world.
9. There is more rain here than .... else in the country.
10. I can find them ....
11. He always brings me a little ....
12. I've seen .... in the hallway.
13. .... of them have already arrived.
14. Are there .... mistakes in the report?
15. She was speechless. She could say ....

Exercise 2.

Rescrieţi sintagmele de mai jos folosind "'s" sau "'".

a) a journey of an hour - ....
   a delay of half an hour - ....
   an absence of a year - ....
b) a cruise of three weeks - ....
   a war of thirty years. - ....
   a salary of two months - ....

Exercise 3.

Înlocuiţi sintagmele cu genitivul obţinut la exerciţiul precedent cu formele adjectivale compuse. Alcătuiţi propoziţii!

Exercise 4.

Parafrazaţi propoziţiile de mai jos cu: **It is certain, It is necessary, it is impossible, It is probable.**

1. You must be crazy. - ....
2. He can't be hungry. He has just had lunch. - ....
3. Weather may get worse. - ....
4. I might go to the mountains for the weekend. - ....
5. He need be kind to her to get what he wants. - ....
6. She may see him now. - ....
7. Although she is only 10, she can speak two languages fluently. - ....
8. They all can use a computer. - ....

9. You mustn't be late for classes. - ....

Exercise 5.

Reformulaţi propoziţiile de mai jos folosind verbele modale:

Exemplu: It is likely / It is possible that the doctor requires more blood tests.
The doctor may require more blood tests.

1. He is certain to have the dictionary.
He ....
2. It is impossible that Dona misses the meeting.
Dona ....
3. I'm absolutely sure that Ileana comes in time.
Ileana ....
4. The girl is hardly in the least going there.
The girl......................................
5. Maybe she is feeling better now.
She ....
6. There is a slight possibility they are here.
They ....
7. We have permission to leave earlier.
We ....
8. She is not able to translate the poem that fast.
She ....
9. Employees are obliged to observe the work hours.
Employees ....
10. It is necessary that we are accompanying her.
We......................................

Exercise 6.

Traduceţi în limba engleză.

1. Trebuie să-ţi amintesc de şedinţă?
2. Nu poţi să fi punctual?
3. Ceilalţi trebuie să sosească în orice moment.
4. Pot să iau loc lângă tine?
5. Lucrurile s-ar putea înrăutăţi.
6. Puteţi folosi biroul meu, eu plec acum.
7. S-ar putea să plece în străinătate.
8. Câte cuvinte pe minut poţi să baţi?
9. Nu trebuie să vii târziu la serviciu.

Exercise 7.

Alcătuiţi propoziţii care să exprime.

a. permisiunea de durată;
b. siguranţa cu privire la un fapt prezent;
c. abilitatea de durată;
d. posibilitatea în viitor;
e. obligaţia obiectivă;
f. necesitatea;
g. posibilitatea în prezent;

h. posibilitatea redusă în viitor;
i. imposibilitatea.

Exercise 8.
Completați verbele modale în mod corespunzător.

a. I don't know what to say. It .... be worse than I thought.
b. We .... rely on her. She is a tactful person.
c. Look at his red throat. It .... be a bad flu.
d. Read this book. It .... be useful for you presentation.
e. " .... I go out now?"
"Of course you ...."
f. This box is too heavy. You .... help me with it.
g. You .... say that. I know you are perfectly right.

Exercise 9.
Traduceți în limba engleză.

a. Pot să iau loc lângă dvs.?
b. Ar putea să facă un efort să vină la timp.
c. Nu pot fi prea departe. Au plecat acum 15 minute.
d. Nu pot să înțeleg ce vrei să spui.
e. S-ar putea să vină mai târziu.
f. Trebuie să te duci să-i vorbești.
g. "Trebuie să-ți mai explic încă o dată?"
"Nu, am înțeles."
h. "Am recunoscut cuvântul *tag*. Trebuie să fie în germană."

Exercise 10.
Citiți textul de mai jos și apoi explicați întrebuințarea verbelor modale.

Exemplu: can[1] - possibility

Lift Etiquette

Sharing a lift with others can[1] often prove to be simply an embarrassing experience. Human's might[2] get nervous if anyone apart from a close friend or loved one comes too close. In a lift you may[3] be in the company of a total stranger.

What could[4] you do?

Here there are a few ideas:

- Stare at your shoes. Don't start a conversation if you can't[5] continue it for three minutes.
- If you have a gift for telling jokes or chatting, you must[6] use it. Your jokes or remarks can[7] have an extraordinary effect.
- Don't forget careless chatting in lifts might[8] cost you your reputation.

2 ....
3 ....
4 ....
5 ....
6 ....
7 ....
8 ....

Exercise 11.

Completați dialogurile de mai jos cu următoarele cuvinte:

time	until	see	how about	with	me
you	invitation	timetable	like	call	fitness club,
I'd	does	suitable that's	would	unfortunately	
		pick you up		around	

a) A: How about going to the gym on Saturday morning?
B: I'd (1)........... that very much.
A: I'll (2)............. at half past ten. (3)................ it suit you?
B: Yes, (4)............. all right (5)................. me.
A: (6)................ you then.
B: See (7).............. .

b) A: I'm going to the (8)............. on Friday afternoon. (9).............. you like to join (10)............ ?
B: (11)............... love to, but (12)............. I have classes (13)........... half past six.
A: Oh, I (14)................ . Maybe some other (15)..................... .
B: At the beginning of next week my (16)................ is less loaded.
A: I'll (17).............. you on Monday morning then to arrange for a (18)........ hour.
B: Thanks for (19)............... .
A: See you (20)............... .
B: See you.

Exercise 12.

Completați ***who, which*** sau ***Ø***.

a. The boy can't forget the row _________ his parents had some time ago.
b. The people _______ were gathered in front of the government building waited for the prime-minister to come.
c. There must be an organization ___________ protects abused women and children.
d. He was the kindest man ___________ I have ever met.
e. There was a loud noise ___________ was coming from their flat.
f. Mother was very angry with children ___________ disobeyed her.

Definitive and Indefinitive Articles
(Articolul hotărât şi nehotărât)

Exercise 1.

Completaţi următoarele propoziţii acolo unde este nevoie cu articolul "*the*"

1. My grandfather likes .... chocolates very much.
2. I love .... flowers in your garden.
3. See you on .... Monday.
4. I always listen to .... radio in the evening.
5. Alex goes to work by .... car.
6. Don't be late for .... lunch.
7. Listen! Marius is playing .... guitar.
8. We often see our relatives over .... Easter.
9. She has never been to .... Moldavia before.
10. What about going to Italy in .... March?

Exercise 2

Citiţi titlurile de ziar şi trasformaţi-le în propoziţii complete.

Model: WINE FRAUD GOALED — A wine fraud has been goaled.
(or A wine fraud is in goal.)

a. SURVIVAL SKILL: GOSSIPING
b. STOLEN PAINTING FOUND IN LOST PROPERTY OFFICE
c. MURDER MASTERS SOLVED BY DOG
d. LAND SPEED RECORD BROKEN
e. MISSING YACHT SPOTTED OFF CAPE HORN

Exercise 3.

Completaţi următoarele propoziţii cu articolul "*a*" sau "*an*".

1. Lia has .... cat.
2. Let's listen .... song.
3. Emil needs .... new desk in her office.
4. I need .... blue pencil.
5. Andrei has .... new bike.
6. Peter has .... aunt in Budapest.
7. We listen to .... French CD.
8. She has .... exercise book in her school bag.
9. The speed of this car was 150 miles .... hour.
10. The finished .... unit.

Exercise 4.

Completaţi următorul text, cu articolele "*a*" "*an*" "*the*" acolo unde este necesar.

Wise people say that breakfast is …….. (1) most important meal of ……..(2) day. It is. When you have ……… (3) good breakfast in …….. (4) morning, you have more strength for ……… (5) whole day. When they have enough time, English ………. (6) people like to eat ……… (7) big breakfast. They have cereal, bacon and eggs, toast and ……… (8) marmalade. They drink tea or coffee. In Romania, people don't have ……… (9) lot of time in the morning so they don't have ………. (10) rich breakfast. They usually drink a cup of ……….. (11)coffee or tea and they eat ……… (12) sandwich in ………….. (13) big hurry. Diana likes ……….. (14) quick breakfast before work. She generally has toast and marmalade and tea or ………… (15) coffee. When she has plenty of time, she has cereal, fruit juice, bacon and eggs and tea or coffee. What do you usually have for ……………. (16) breakfast?

Exercise 5.

Traduceți următoarele propoziții în limba engleză.

1. Maria vorbește întruna.
2. Cel mic vrea să se joace.
3. Vreau să devin asistent manager.
4. Îmi place să am o mulțime de prieteni.
5. Ea o sună pe o prietenă bună.
6. Lucrez ca secretară la o firmă particulară.
7. Când îi dai înapoi dicționarul?
8. Relatarea despre Titanic este adevărată.
9. Pe masă se află un pahar și o farfurie, goale.
10. Ești un foarte bun dansator.

Exercise 6.

Inserați articolul potrivit: "*a*" "*an*" "*the*".

a. He has never admitted ________ error of marring her.
b. ________ philosophy is ________ basic course in all ________ universities.
c. It was ________ dessert of ______ chocolate ice cream.
d. ________ computer has changed ________ face of ________ world.
e. I'll be at __________ school until three o'clock.
f. He went to ________ town in the morning, so he must be at ________ University.
g. I've never liked ________ cream, but ______ cream for ________ dessert was very good so I helped myself twice.
h. How often do you go to ________ theatre?
i. Last year I had ______ worst experience in my life. I was skating in ______ Hyde Park when I stumbled over ______ kerb and broke ________ leg. I had to stay in ______ hospital for three days.
j. I read in "______ Evening Star" that there's ________ new film at ________ Odeon. It is based on ________ play by ________ Harold Pinter.
k. We set off from ________ Dover across ________ English Channel and into ________ France. After crossing Alps we arrived at ________ Lake Como in ______ north of ______ Italy.
l. We've received ________ invitation from ______ Browns.
m. ________ beautiful is ______ aesthetic category.

Exercise 7.

Corectați greșelile. În spațiul marcat scrieți articolul potrivit. Lucrați conform modelului.

a. She asked for the glass of fresh water. a
b. By the time they start to the school, girls. ___
c. Have an advantage that the boys don't have. ___
d. He was an editor who worked for "Observator." ___
e. I was annoyed at slowness of the coach. ___
f. He could speak neither the English nor French. ___
g. "Tom Sawyer" was the first book Mark Twain had printed. ___
h. He often went to the Zoo as he liked the animals very much. ___
i. Please, meet my friend; he is from USA. ___
j. He spent a lot of time drawing birds in the Andes. ___
k. They co-owned the Harrods. ___
l. The Mount Everest was climbed for the first time in 1953. ___
m. Some people think that the Kennedy's are doomed. ___
n. Severn is Britain's second important river. ___

Exercise 8.

Traduceți în limba engleză acordând atenție articolului hotărât și nehotărât precum și omisiunii acestuia.

1. A fost odată ca niciodată un rege și regele avea trei fii.
2. Ceaiul de pe masă nu este al tău.
3. Cei bogați locuiesc în acest cartier.
4. Englezilor le plac francezii?
5. Nu sunt avocat, sunt profesor.
6. Întotdeauna a știut să aprecieze frumosul.
7. În fiecare duminică bunica se duce la biserică.
8. Cum a fost călătoria cu trenul?
9. Oxford Street este un loc cu magazine recunoscute.
10. Vorbeau cu voce tare.
11. Au hotărât să facă o croazieră pe Mediterană.
12. Era murdar din cap până în picioare.
13. Ceaiul era băutura națională a englezilor.
14. A făcut avere vânzând produse de papetărie.

Exercise 9.

Traduceți în limba română acordând atenție articolului hotărât și nehotărât precum și omisiunii acestuia.

1. "I was staying at the time with my uncle and his wife."
2. "At least you are not a Scot, nor an Irishman, nor a Welshman."
3. "I have no taste for trade; I should only make a failure. In short I refused to become a merchant."
4. "The young O'Casey listened to the language of the poor, but looked not for the beautiful cadences."
5. "I've been to the Caucasus and I know what I'm saying."
6. "It was the Romania who, shortly after the invasion of Britain, ordered by the Emperor Claudius in 43AD, founded London. They built a bridge over the Thames and a town developed around the northern end of the bridge. Eventually, the Romans built a wall around London and the line of the wall roughly marks the area we call the City of London. Roman London was a large and important centre of trade, but when

the Roman legions left Britain in 409 AD, it went into decline. The Anglo-Saxon settlers, who came between 400 and 600 AD, did not live in the Roman cities, but in villages outside them."

Exercise 10.

Inserați articolul potrivit: "*a*" "*an*" "*the*"

(1) _____ psychologists working in (2) ______ new area of (3) _____ research are starting to realize that (4) _____ behavior is genetically controlled. Darwin himself believed that (5) _____ evolution was responsible for far more than just (6) ____ physical characteristics. He saw it as (7) ______ major influence in shaping (8) ____ people's psychology. He predicted that in (9) ____ distant future, (10) ____ psychology will be based on (11) ______ new foundation. To (12) _______ supporters of concepts like (13) ______ free will and (14) ______ personal responsibility such (15) _____ idea seems absurd.

Exercise 11.

Înlocuiți punctele cu articolul potrivit:

a) I have…..apple.
b) She is eating…….orange now.
c) Dana has……….house.
d) Dan is buying…………vegetables now.
e) Petre crosses……..big street every day.

Exercise 12.

Puneți articolul potrivit în locurile libere:

a) I have ……. big house and you have ………. big car.
b) He gives me ………… flower every day.
c) I want to buy ……….. oranges, please!
d) Dan, give me ………. pen, please!
e) Dana is leaving ……….. town now.
f) Have ……….. apricot ice-cream!
g) ………… sun is shining now.

Exercise 13.

Completați spațiile punctate cu articolele corespunzătoare (hotărâte sau nehotărâte):

- Father, […………] teacher does not know what […………] horse is.
- Why do you think so, Tom?
- You know, I drew [………….] horse yesterday and showed it to [……………] teacher and he asked me what it was.

Exercise 14.

Completați spațiile punctate cu articolele nehotărâte corespunzătoare:

… apple … hare … ape … boat
… orange … house … eye … umbrella
… herb … coat … horse… empire
… union … honour … ear … yard

Exercise 15.
Treceţi la formele de singular.

a) books, pencils and copy-books.
b) men, women and children
c) stories and essays
d) Europeans, Africans, Americans, Asians and Australians
e) hens and eggs

Exercise 16.
Treceţi la singular următoarele propoziţii.

a) Nouns are words.
b) Towns are big cities.
c) Horses are animals.
d) Roses are beautiful flowers.
e) Tables are pieces of furniture.

Exercise 17.
Treceţi la plural următoarele propoziţii.

a) A cat is an animal.
b) A fly is an insect.
c) A table is made of wood.
d) A chicken is a bird.
e) A cake is sweet.
f) A dictionary is a book.
g) A dog eats meat.
h) A bird can fly.
i) A fish can swim.
j) A man can walk.
k) A house is a building.
l) A plane is made of metal.
m) A fountain pen has ink in it.
n) A cow gives milk.

Exercise 18.
Traduceţi următoarele expresii.

a) Eu merg în fiecare săptămână la teatru.
b) Ea merge la discotecă în fiecare sâmbătă seara.
c) Ana joacă tenis acum.
d) Lui Adrian îi place să se plimbe prin parc.
e) Alexandra merge la cinema acum.

Exercise 19.
Alegeţi din WORD BOX numai cuvintele care se potrivesc şi scrieţi-le în locurile libere.

.... is a beautiful building in the centre of the town. There are a lot of .... in our town, too. I love to go to the .... , but I also like to .... I like to go in the .... with my friends. We always have a lot of fun.

WORD BOX

glass, museums, car, cinema, TV, theatre, Disco,
The National Theatre, park, Dan, football, basket.

Exercise 20.

Scrieți articolul corect:

a) ....concert is very nice!
b) I have .... apples.
c) She doesn't eat ……… orange every day, but she is eating one now.
d) Mother is baking .... cakes now.
e) .... river is very big.

Prepositions
(Prepoziția)

Exercise 1.

Alegeți *prepoziția* potrivită.

1. I'm looking forward ____________ visiting you in March.
   a) of b) at c) to
2. He was accused ___________ killing his wife.
   a) of b) with c) by
3. My daughter is very good ___________ telling stories.
   a) to b) in c) at
4. Will you stop complaining ___________ me?
   a) with b) about c) by
5. The bad weather prevented them ___________ continuing the trip.
   a) from b) to c) about
6. I'm sorry to say it, but she's not capable ___________ loving anyone but herself.
   a) to b) with c) of
7. She was not accustomed ___________ being treated badly.
   a) to b) with c) at
8. Are you interested ___________ finding the truth?
   a) on b) in c) about
9. We're not very enthusiastic ___________ going to a football march.
   a) to b) in c) about
10. What is mother preoccupied ___________ ?
    a) with b) of c) for

Exercise 2.

Completați *prepoziția* corespunzătoare. Alegeți cinci situații și alcătuiți propoziții.

1. to fall in love with somebody
2. to put the blame __________ somebody/something
3. it's typical __________ somebody
4. to be married __________ somebody
5. to head __________ somewhere
6. to complete __________ somebody
7. to get rid __________ somebody
8. to deal __________ somebody/something
9. to be popular __________ somebody
10. to participe __________ something
11. to be important __________ somebody
12. to wander __________
13. to be charged __________ something
14. to protect somebody __________ somebody else
15. to fight __________ something

Exercise 3.

Completați enunțurile cu una din *prepozițiile* corespunzătoare.

in, on, at, out, of

a. Maxime Patter is hard ______ work writing the script for the new film.
b. The music was terrible and the singer was ____ tune.
c. I can't tell what that is _____ the background of the picture.
d. Jane's new book is coming out _____ paper back next year.
e. Is there anything good _____ channel 4 this evening?
f. The school put on Hamlet _____ modern dress.
g. The critics found Joe's kind of writing rather _____ date.
h. In the last scene, all the actors are _____ stage.
i. The film stars Madonna _____ the part of Eva Perez.
j. Margaret's new sculptures are _____ display in the park.

Exercise 4.

Completați propozițiile cu ***prepoziția*** corectă.

1. .... these pictures you can see an n elephant.
2. Andreea is sitting .... a chair.
3. The boy is standing .... Carmen.
4. These photos were taken .... her boyfriend, who is a hobby photographer.
5. Santa and the girl are looking .... each other.
6. .... the girl, there is a Christmas tree.
7. There are more presents .... the tree.
8. .... the picture, I can see John and a girl.
9. Santa's big bag is lying .... the floor.
10. I got these photos .... my friend Smith.
11. So, these are pictures .... an elephant.
12. The boy has a present .... her hands.
13. Look .... these pictures.

Exercise 5.

Completați enunțurile cu una din ***prepozițiile*** corespunzătoare.

1. What are you doing .... the weekend?
a) at b) in c) on
2. I don't know yet. Maybe I'll go to the cinema .... Saturday.
a) at b) in c) on
3. That's interesting. I haven't been to the cinema .... so many years.
a) for b) since c) on
4. We could go there together .... the afternoon.
a) at b) in c) on
5. That would be great. But I would prefer to go there .... the evening. I am visiting my grandma .... Saturday.
a) at b) in c) on
6. That's okay. The film starts .... eight o'clock.
a) at b) in c) on
7. I can pick you up .... half .... seven. How long does the film last?
a) at b) in c) on
a) to b)past
8. It lasts .... two hours and forty-five minutes.
a) for b) to c) until

9. .... eight .... a quarter.......... eleven.

a) before b) by c) from

a) for b) past c) till

a) for b) past c) to

10. That's right. But I must hurry home .... the film. I have to be home .... eleven o'clock.

a) after b) before c) past

a) by b)since c) until

Exercise 6.

Completați propozițiile cu ***prepoziția*** corespunzătoare.

1. Smith comes to work ______ car but I prefer to come ______ foot.
   A. at / into
   B. beside / next to
   C. by / on
   D. in / next to
   E. at / in
2. Fred is the person standing ______ the window, ______ the woman with the long blonde hair.
   A. at / into
   B. beside / next to
   C. under / around
   D. in / next to
   E. at / in
3. She ran ______ the corridor and ______ the stairs to the second floor.
   A. from / into
   B. towards / over
   C. along / up
   D. by / on
   E. in / next to
4. The restaurant is ______ the High Street, ______ the cinema.
   A. through / in
   B. out of / in
   C. under / around
   D. in / next to
   E. up / along
5. I took the old card ______ the computer and put ______ the new one.
   A. through / in
   B. out of / in
   C. out of / between
   D. out of / into
   E. up / along

Adverbial particle
(Particula adverbială)

Exercise 1.

Folosind verbele şi ***particulele adverbiale*** date, formaţi ***verbe complexe*** pentru a completa corespunzător propoziţiile. Cifrele din paranteză indică faptul că aceeaşi particulă intră în combinaţie cu mai multe verbe. Atenţie la timpurile verbale.

VERBS: write, take, cut, play, lay, live, walk, speak, let, act, keep, get, make, turn, put.

PARTICLES: after, at, for (x2), forward, in, into off (x2), on, out (x3), through, up to.

a. I may lose this fight, but don't …………… me ………….. yet. I'll be back!
b. Maria really ………… her mother, she has the same eyes, nose and hair.
c. I like your article, but would you ………….. the references to environmental abuses?
d. The film about the underprivileged just ………….. people's sympathy.
e. The dining room is ………….. in a traditional manner.
f. He ……………. a famine and that's why his condition is rather weak.
g. The old man ………………. the boy and grabbed him by the collar (guler)
h. Next time will you ……………. yourself?
i. Don't ………… those fireworks indoors!
j. That was his chance to …………….. his fantasies.
k. I advised her to …………..…… while the weather is cold.
l. What ……..…. she ………….. when she said she knew our secret?
m. He wouldn't listen any more and ……………… the door.
n. The warehouses ……………. a modern flat building.
o. The new theory they …………….. is consistent with their previous research.

Exercise 2.

Citiţi cu atenţie sensurile verbului ***lay*** urmat de ***particulă adverbială.***

lay ***aside (by)***	= save for future needs
lay ***down***	= prescribe, indicate
lay ***in***	= provide oneself with (fuel, food, supplies)
pay ***into***	= (informal) attack violently (physically or verbally)
lay ***off***	= stop doing something unpleasant
lay ***out***	= plan and arrange; design
lay ***up***	= store, stock

Exercise 3.

Citiţi cu atenţi sensurile verbului "**turn**" urmat de următoarele ***particule adverbiale***.

- turn ***down***	= refuse to accept
- turn ***into***	= become, change into
- turn ***off***	= disconnect by means of a tap, suite
- turn ***on***	= connect, start the flow of power water
- turn ***out***	= prove to be, progress
- turn ***over***	= change position by rolling
- turn ***to***	= ask for help or advice
- turn ***up***	= appear, arrive by chance/suddenly.

Exercise 4.

Alegeți *particula adverbială* potrivită.

1. Mary slipped an interesting piece of information __________ her talk.
   a) away   b) on   c) into
2. Her hair was sticking ________________ from her fur cap.
   a) out   b) up   c) by
3. Granny's cat was run __________ by a neighbor's car.
   a) out   b) over   c) down
4. Although err aren't twins, people sometimes cannot tell me _________ my sister.
   a) from   b) off   c) upon
5. Mother is going to tell you __________
   a) off   b) on   c) off
6. We've run ____________ coffee. Will you go and buy some?
   a) off   b) out   c) out of
7. If I am slipping __________ on one single question, I'll miss the first prize.
   a) up   b) down   c) through
8. Stick ___________ the same language register.
   a) up for   b) at   c) to
9. I'll run __________ and see you this evening.
   a) off   b) over   c) in
10. With a spoonful of honey, the medicine will slip ____________ easily.
   a) up   b) on   c) down

Exercise 5.

Completați propozițiile cu verbul *slip* urmat de *particula adverbială* corespunzătoare. Atenție la forma verbală. Amintiți-vă că *p* final se dublează.

slip ***away/out/out of*** = leave quickly without attracting attention.
slip ***down*** = swallow smoothly and easily
slip ***in/to*** = mention a word, remark etc in conversation, speech
slip ***into/on*** = put on with a quick easy movement
slip ***through*** = pass through
slip ***up*** = make a mistake, blunder

a. You're not going to let a wonderful chance like that ____________ your fingers.
b. She ___________ of the room when no one was looking.
c. The ice-cream _______________ pleasantly.
d. Her uncle just _____________ a word and we understood the hint.
e. _______________ your swimming suit. The weather is hot today.
f. If she _____________ on only one question, her score wouldn't be perfect.

Exercise 6.

Înlocuiți cuvintele subliniate cu verbul ***work*** urmat de ***particula adverbială*** corespunzătoare.

work ***at*** = to give energy, thought to getting rid of or solving a problem, task
work ***away(at)*** = to give continuous effort, thought to
work ***in/into*** = to introduce, find a place for humor, romance etc. into

work ***off*** = to lose or get rid of something extra by working
work ***out*** = to solve, find an answer to a problem
work ***up*** = to develop, elaborate
work ***up into*** = to gradually change the shape or nature of wood, by thought, effort into something.

a. He ***is changing*** his notes on gender discrimination ***into*** a speech for the conference.
b. We'll have to ***find a solution*** to the employee's complaint.
c. He'***s been spending time and energy on*** his new intention.
d. If you want the story published, ***insert*** a bit of romance.
e. It has taken her months to ***get rid of*** the fat around her waist.
f. Designing clothes was something she didn't mind ***doing for a living***.
g. The dramatist ***devised*** an interesting conflict development.

Exercise 7.

Alegeți ***particula*** corespunzătoare.

1. I'll try to work __________ a mention of the help you gave.
   a) out b) in c) up
2. She's still not very good at speaking English, but is working _________ it.
   a) at b) up c) in
3. I'm afraid I can't work ___________ much enthusiasm for this scheme.
   a) off b) away c) up
4. I can't work __________ how to do it.
   a) in b) out c) off
5. I have three years to work __________ the debt.
   a) away b) up c) off

Exercise 8.

Inserați ***particula adverbială*** corespunzătoare.

a. I couldn't see who or what it was because it shot ___________ of the room.
b. International oil price has simply shot _____________.
c. They're trying to shoot ________________ a 50% increase of the profit.
d. He is afraid of competition, that's why he shoots ______________ any suggestion from younger managers.
e. Jim grabbed something from the table and shot ________________.

Exercise 9.

Răspundeți la următoarele întrebări folosind verbul complex ***send*** urmat de ***particula adverbială***.

send **back** = return something
send **away** = dispatch, post, send to another place
send **down** = expel from university for misconduct
send **for** = send somebody to fetch
send **in** = send something for official consideration to a place where it will be dwelt with
send **up** = destroy, blow up

a. Why hasn't the convoy arrived yet?
b. Why isn't doctor seeing her? She's got a fever.
c. How is your son doing at university? You must be proud of him.
d. How many people confirmed their attending the presentation?
e. I'm sure your children are going to good schools. Is the school far from house?

The verb "To be"
(Verbul „a fi")

Exercise 1.

Citiți cu atenție propozițiile și treceți formele literare in cele contrase ale verbului *to be* la prezent. Alaturat aveți și traducerea.

1. I am Alexandra Ionescu. — Eu sunt Alexandra Ionescu.
   .... Alexandra Ionescu.
2. She is Diana Predescu. — Ea este Diana Predescu.
   .... Diana Predescu.
3. They are my relatives. — Ele sunt rudele mele.
   .... my relatives.
4. He is Bogdan — El este Bogdan.
   .... Bogdan.
5. It is a flower. — Este o floare.
   .... a flower.
6. We are friends. — (Noi) Suntem prieteni.
   .... friends.
7. He is my son. — (El) Este fiul meu.
   .... my son.
8. It is a clock. — Este un ceas.
   .... a clock.

Exercise 2.

Completați punctele de suspensie cu formele corespunzătoare ale verbului "*to be*" la prezent, afirmativ. Utilizați formele literare: **am, are, is.**

Exemple:

She ... a girl. — She **is** a girl.
They ... my relatives. — They **are** my relatives.

1. They ... pictures.
2. He ... my son.
3. We ... farmers.
4. You ... Adrian.
5. I ... Alexandra Ionescu.
6. She ... an artist.
7. They ... girls.
8. You ... doctors.

Exercise 3.

Înlocuiți formele lungi cu cele contrase ale verbului "*to be*" la prezent, forma afirmativă.

Exemple:

They are pictures. — They ... pictures. They'**re** pictures.
I am Romanian — I ... Romanian. I'**m** Romanian

1. She is a farmer. — She ... a farmer.
2. I am Florin Ionescu. — I ... Florin Ionescu.
3. They are artists. — They ... artists.
4. We are doctors. — We ... doctors.
5. They are rings. — They ... rings.
6. You are a driver. — You ... a driver.
7. He is a boy. — He ... a boy.
8. They are flowers. — They ... flowers.

Exercise 4.

Completați cu forma corespunzătoare a pronumelui personal.

Exemple:

Alice is my friend. ...is doctor. **She** is a doctor.

Adrian and I are Romanian ...are boys. **We** are boys.

1. Maria and Alex are farmers ...are farmers.
2. Dana is Romanian ...is a girl.
3. Gina is my friend. ...is American.
4. Marius and Adrian are my sons. ...are tall.
5. Dana and Lisa are relatives. ...are interesting.
6. Crina and I are artists. ...are short.
7. Alex is English. ...is tall
8. Robert is American. ...is a doctor.

Exercise 5.

Transformați propozițiile afirmative de mai jos în întrebări, după exemplu.

Exemplu:

She is busy. Is she busy?

1. They are friends. ....
2. He is right. ....
3. It is three o'clock. ....
4. Lisa is an economist. ....
5. You are hungry. ....
6. It is a box. ....

Exercise 6.

Dați varianta negativă a propozițiilor de mai jos, utilizând forma lungă.

Exemplu:

She is hungry

She is not hungry.

1. My report is ready. ....
2. He is thin. ....
3. It's an interesting theory. ....
4. You are a good driver. ....
5. My son is short. ....
6. It's ten o'clock. ....

Exercise 7.

Dați varianta negativă a propozițiilor de mai jos, utilizând ambele forme scurte.

Exemplu:

He is busy. He's **not** busy.

He isn't busy.

1. They are my friends. ....

....

2. It is an interesting theory. ....

....

3. You are economists. ....
....
4. He is my friend. ....
....
5. It is six o'clock. ....
....
6. We are hungry. ....
....

Exercise 8.

Alegeți forma verbală corespunzătoare și scrieți-o în spațiul destinat.

1. My friend .... an economist.
a. am not b. isn't c. aren't
2. It ....five o'clock.
a. am not b. isn't c. aren't
3. You ....American.
a. am not b. isn't c. aren't
4. I ....hungry.
a. am not b. isn't c. aren't
5. My report................ready.
a. am not b. isn't c. aren't
6. They ....good drivers.
a. am not b. isn't c. aren't

Exercise 9.

Traduceți următoarele propoziții în limba engleză.

1. George și Diana nu sunt rude. ....
2. Ai dreptate. ....
3. Este Petre acasă? ....
4. Nu este ora trei, este ora patru. ....
5. Ți-e foame? ....
6. Este o cutie importantă. ....

Exercise 10.

Traduceți următoarele propoziții în limba engleză. Obișnuiți-vă să exprimați mereu subiectul alături de predicat.

1. Este Marius în birou?
2. Nu, nu este în birou.
3. Ești acasă?/Sunteți acasă?
4. Este (ea) inteligentă?
5. (Ea) Nu este inteligentă.
6. Sunt un bun dansator?
7. Da, ești un foarte bun dansator.
8. Sunt ei ocupați?/Sunt ele ocupate?
9. Nu, nu sunt ocupați/ocupate.
10. Cine ești?/Cine sunteți?
11. Sunt Roxana.
12. Este (ora) unu?
13. Nu este ora unu. Este (ora) două.

The verb „To Have" (Got)
(Verbul "A avea")

Exercise 1

Completaţi spaţiile libere cu forma corespunzătoare a verbului *"to have got"* la prezent. Utilizaţi formele verbale lungi. Apoi traduceţi propoziţiile în limba română.

Exemplu: She ... ... a beautiful daughter.
She **has got** a beautiful daughter. Ea are o fiică frumoasă.

1. He ... ... a car. ....
2. We ... ... four children. ....
3. I ... ... my report ready. ....
4. You ... ... an intelligent mother-in-law. ....
5. They ... ... a son and a daughter. ....
6. She ... ... a nephew who is a student. ....

Exercise 2.

Utilizaţi forma scurtă a verbului în locul celei lungi.

Exemplu: They have got three children. They'**ve got** three children.

1.You have got a good car. ....
2. We have got a big clock at home. ....
3. He has got two sandwiches. ....
4. I have got a big problem. ....
5. They have got an American car. ....
6. She has got a nice son. ....

Exercise 3.

Rescrieţi propoziţiile de mai jos utilizând forma scurtă a verbului.

1. I **have got** an American friend. Am un prieten american.
2. You **have got** a good idea. Ai/Aveţi o idee bună.
3. He **has got** a difficult problem. El are o problemă grea.
4. She **has got** a big car. Ea are o maşină mare.
5. It **has got** four wheels. Ea (maşina) are patru roţi.
6. We **have got** a small farm. Avem o fermă mică.
7. Thy **have got** a caring mother-in-law. Ei au o soacră grijulie.

Exercise 4.

Traduceţi propoziţiile de mai jos utilizând forma scurtă a verbului ***to have***.

1. Voi aveţi emoţii?
2. Eu nu am timp acum.
3. Tu ai nevoie de dicţionar?
4. Noi avem întâlnire.

5. Alina are treabă.
6. Ea are telefon ?
7. Mihaela are un prieten.
8. Ele au maşină.
9. Voi aveţi dicţionar englez-român ?
10. Tu ai manual de română ?
11. Alina şi Camelia au casă.
12. Mircea are carte?
13. Noi avem un creion.
14. Eu am un tablou.
15. El are un dicţionar.

Exercise 5.

Traduceţi propoziţiile de la exerciţiul anterior utilizând forma negativă a verbului ***to havea***.

Exercise 6.

Completaţi propoziţiile de mai jos cu verbele ***to be*** şi ***to have go***t.

a. ________ a cat.
b. We ___________ upset.
c. You ________ big.
d. He ________ very small.
e. She ________ a nice car.
f. You __________ a young sister.
g. I _________ a secretary.
h. They __________ a big house.
i. They __________ very happy.
j. It _________ ugly.

Exercise 7.

Completaţi propoziţiile de mai jos.

a. They __________ two sisters.
b. Dan _______ bicycle.
c. Florin ________ one cat called Puffy.
d. Mrs. Smith ________ a new cat.
e. I don't ________ much time.
f. We _______ a telly yet.
g. _______ Claudia ________ a kitty?
h. _______ you________ the time?
i. ________ Margaret ________ satellite TV?
j. It _________ much of a future.

Exercise 8.

Completaţi propoziţiile următoare cu verbele ***to be*** şi ***to have got***.

a. My sister´s name _________ Camelia.
b. Your sister _______ nine years old.
c. We ________ a nice house. It________ blue and yellow.
d. They _________ short and their childrens, too.

e. We ________ in the office now.
f. Marius _________ my best friend. He lives in Rome.
g. She _________ three brothers and a sister. They always play together.
h. We ________ in the classroom now.
i. My friend ________ two sisters.
j. Our grandparents ________ a big house in the country.
k. There _________ some trees in front of your house.
l. There __________ a tree near your house.
m. I _________ at home now, but I'll ________ there in ten minutes. Wait for me, please.
n. My friend and she __________ a new car in the garage.
o. She _______ a teacher, she works in that school.
p. They ________ two small houses in this village.
q. She hasn't got a bike, but they ________

Exercise 9.

Completați propozițiile următoare cu verbul ***to have*** la forma corectă.

1. Every man __________________ do military service in my country.
2. When do we _________________ pay for the next term?
3. Policemen __________________ wear a uniform.
4. A pilot __________________ train for many years.
5. Does Andreea ________________ work long hours?
6. I _______________ get up early on Saturday.
7. You ________________ have a visa to come to USA.
8. You _______________ to do it if you don't want to.
9. My sister ________________ to cook, because I cook for my family.
10. We __________________ pay.

Expressing Time and Date
(Exprimarea datei şi orei)

Exercise 1.
Traduceţi următoarele propoziţii în limba română.

1. It is eleven o'clock. ....
2. We are economists. ....
3. What's the time? ....
4. Are you still on British time? ....
5. What about a cup of coffee. ....
6. It is eight o'clock. ....

Exercise 2.
Scrieţi în litere ora la care au loc acţiunile de mai jos.

1. I get up at...................................in the morning. 6:30
2. I go to work at.. 7:45
3. I arrive at work at... 8:30
4. I have lunch at.. 1:30
5. I go home at...............................in the afternoon. 5:30
6. I go to bed at.......................................at night 10:45

Exercise 3.
Traduceţi următoarele propoziţii în limba română.

1. My daughter gets up at a quarter to seven every morning.
2. They live in Arad.
3. I have breakfast at half past eight o'clock in the morning.
4. We learn English every day.
5. He watches TV every evening.
6. I think my life is wonderful.

Exercise 4.
Traduceţi în limba engleză.

1. Eu mă scol la ora 7 dimineaţa.
2. Noi luăm cina la ora opt şi jumătate.
3. El învaţă în fiecare zi.
4. Ele locuiesc la Arad.
5. Sora mea se uită la televizor în fiecare seară, apoi citeşte o carte.
6. Eu mă culc la ora zece şi jumătate seara.

Exercise 5.
Scrieţi în limba engleză:

1. Este ora 1 şi 10.
2. Este ora 14 fără un sfert.
5. Este ora 21 şi 37 minute.
6. Este miezul nopţii.

3. Este ora 15 şi jumătate.
4. Este ora 20 fără 12 minute.
7. Este ora 16 fix.
8. Este ora 19 şi 30 minute.

Exercise 6.
Exprimaţi în litere:

a) 15:30
b) 20:21
c) 17:45
d) 19:52
e) 21:30
f) 07:27
g) 09:42
h) 10:20

Exercise 7.
Scrieţi în litere orele.

1) 15:30
2) 16:45
3) 20:20
4) 07.05
5) 09:27
6) 10:15
7) 14:20
8) 19.32
9) 22:40
10) 00:00 (24:00)

Exercise 8.
Traduceţi următoarele propoziţii în limba română.

1. It's a quarter to one. ....
2. It's a quarter past one. ....
3. It's half past one. ....
4. It's a quarter past four. ....
5. It's half past four. ....
6. It's a quarter to five. ....
7. It's half past five. ....
8. It's a quarter to six. ....

Exercise 9.
Exprimaţi data în ambele feluri învăţate:

1. Astăzi este 7 mai.
2. Astăzi este 9 iunie.
3. Astăzi este 4 ianuarie.
4. Astăzi este 3 februarie.
5. Astăzi este 8 martie.
6. Astăzi este 22 aprilie.
7. Astăzi este 25 iulie.
8. Astăzi este 30 august.
9. Astăzi este 31 septembrie.
10. Astăzi este 17 octombrie.
11. Astăzi este 19 noiembrie.
12. Astăzi este 11 decembrie.

Anul:

1700 → 17 00 → seventeen | hundred

1998 → 19 98 → nineteen | ninety-eight

1002 → 10 02 → ten | zero two

În acest fel citesc englezii anul.

Exercise 10.
Scrieţi anii următori în manieră englezească (în litere, ca mai sus).

a) 1900	e)2002	i) 2007
b) 1753	f) 1989	j) 2350
c) 1999	g) 1600	k) 2010
d) 2000	h) 1920	l) 2022

Exercise 11.
Scrieţi data în litere.

Astăzi este:

Z	L	A
12	12	1993
17	03	1995
23	05	1998
29	06	1999
01	01	2000
15	09	2002

Expressing quantity and probability
(Exprimarea cantității și probabilității)

Exercise 1.

Traduceţi următoarele propoziţii în limba română.

a. **Some of the people** understood what she meant.
b. He didn't take **any of my cassettes.**
c. They spend **most of the weekend** shopping.
d. I've read **a few of your articles** in The Times.
e. There were **lots of presents** all over the house.
f. **None of the people** was interested.
g. **Everyone of the shop-assistant** was busy.

Exercise 2.

Traduceţi următoarele propoziţii în limba engleză.

a. Poţi să-mi împrumuţi nişte zahăr?
b. Nu există şanse să găsim pisica.
c. Mă întâlnesc cu câţiva prieteni la restaurant.
d. N-am prieteni şi mă simt singură.
e. El nu are prieteni.
f. Aveţi nişte exemplare în plus?
g. Niciodată nu are bani.
h. A făcut-o singură, fără niciun ajutor.
i. Nu am mult timp liber zilele acestea.
j. Există mult şomaj în Marea Britanie?
k. Vor fi mulţi oameni acolo?
l. Ei au ridicat multe probleme noi.
m. Există pâine din belşug pentru populaţie.
n. Mulţi oameni au devenit conştienţi de costurile acestui avantaj.

Exercise 3.

Completaţi textul cu pronumele sau adjectivele nehotărâte pentru a afla cum se desfăşura comerţul în Anglia Victoriană (secolul al XIX-lea).

Town dwellers had to buy (1) ______ their food. (2) ________ of them grew their own food. (3) ____ of the poor people bought their food from local markets, but (4) _______ by (5) ________ shops became (6) ______ important. A middle-class wife could do (7) _________ of her everyday shopping without leaving home: (8) ___________ delivery body and tradesmen called for orders in the morning.

Gradually (9)_____________ shops in the bigger towns grew into larger stores. When the shop owners opened (10) _________ shops in other towns, they owned "chained stores". Street traders could sell almost (11) ________ in the street. (12) _________ could buy flowers from the sellers in the street. (13) ___________ morning you could seem them at street corners or at the market place. (14) __________ night the gas lamplighters went round (15) ____________ lamp-post to light the gas.

Exercise 4.

Completaţi propoziţiile folosind **a little/little, a few/few, many/much.**

a. Shoppers know ____________ about the degrading conditions of the overseas workers.
b. Workers in ____________ countries face health risks because of exposure to pesticides.
c. In places like Bangladesh and India, local people have ____________ land for growing rice.
d. ________________ of their land has been taken away from them for prawn (crevete) farms.
e. Although supermarkets profits are huge, workers earn very ____________ money per day.
f. ____________ overseas suppliers have adhered to the conduct code so far.
g. Unfortunately, politicians have supported these projects.
h. They object that the trade creates ____________ jobs for the local people.
i. Besides, the implementation of an ethical code implies ____________ work and money.
j. However, ____________ charities have organized campaigns to increase the public's awareness about this issue.

Exercise 5.

Citiţi situaţiile descrise şi scrieţi enunţuri (formule de comunicare) conform indicaţiilor din paranteză.

a. at your friend's you ask for a glass of juice (request)
b. there isn't any fruit in the fridge (suggestion)
c. you offer your guest a tray with tea biscuits (offer)
d. you want to know if you've received any news (asking for information)
e. you are annoyed because your sister never pays the bills as she says she is short of cash (complaint)
f. your 8-year-old son solved a Math's problem by himself (admiration)

Exercise 6.

Traduceţi în limba engleză.

a. Dacă sună cineva, spune-le că nu sunt acasă.
b. Nimeni nu ştie nimic despre această problemă.
c. Este toată lumea prezentă astăzi?
d. Cineva trebuie să-i spună vestea proastă.
e. Este cineva aici?
f. Cartea trebuie să fie pe undeva prin casă.
g. Băieţelul nu a putut fi găsit nicăieri.
h. Am căutat cartea peste tot, dar nu am găsit-o.
i. Spune-mi ceva ce nu ştiu.
j. Nu mi-a spus nimic despre necazul tău.

Exercise 7.

Studiaţi cu atenţie listele de preţuri. Scrieţi cel puţin cinci propoziţii prin care să completaţi preţurile din cele două supermarket-uri, A şi B (preţurile sunt in Lei).

		A	B
1	dry cheese	49.500/kg	57.000/kg

2	milk	8.300/l	8.500/l
3	juice	13.400/l	14.500/l
4	washing powder	18.900/900g	25.000/900g
5	note pad	7.900/piece	7.500/piece
6	chicken	31.950/kg	35.000/kg

Exercise 8.

Completaţi pronumele/adjectivele nehotărâte care exprimă cantitatea.

We have already highlighted (1) _________ of the ways in which Britain changed during the 20th century. The following shows (2) _________ other changes. There are now 20 million (3) _________ Britons than there were in 1901. They are richer and healthier and they live (4) _________ longer. This means that there are (5) _________ old people than ever before. At the same time, there are (6) _________ children being born. (…..) Today (7) _________ people work in shops and offices. People also spend (8) _______ time at work (9) week.

Exercise 9.

Citiţi afirmaţiile referitoare la călătoriile în spaţiu. În cele două coloane scrieţi propoziţii care să exprime diferite grade de probabilitate.

a. Holiday in space will be a common thing.
b. Spacecrafts will travel at speeds closer to the speed of light.
c. The human race will contact other beings from the outer space.
d. Moon will be a source of energy for the Earth.
e. Colonies on the Moon will solve the problem of over population.
f. A human being will land on the surfacc of Mars.

Exercise 10.

Scrieţi propoziţii care să exprime diferite grade de probabilitate referitoare la situaţiile descrise.

a. Launching satellites will be a common thing.
b. Unmanned missions will be sent further to the boundaries of our solar system.
c. Astronomy will be taught in kindergartens.
d. People will be trained in case of an alien invasion.
e. Experiments on space labs will deepen our knowledge about the Earth.

Exercise 11.

Completaţi propoziţiile cu substantivele care exprimă cantitatea dintr-un întreg.

a. John spread bread ___________ on the ground not to get lost.
b. Have you eaten the whole __________ of chocolate?
c. The stew (tocană) needs just one more __________ of salt.
d. Would you like a __________ of bacon with your eggs?
e. If I had a ________ of paper, I'd write a note for him.
f. I've got a __________ of dust in my left eye.
g. A ____________ of glass pierced into her heel.
h. The child stumbled over a _________ of earth.
i. The old woman was begging for a _____________ of bread.

The imperative
(Imperativul)

Exercise 1.
Traduceți în limba română.

1. Let's speak English! ....
2. They've got three children. ....
3. How old is your husband? ....
4. My mother-in-law is nice and caring. ....
5. Who are you? ....
6. Her friend is twelve years old. ....

Exercise 2.
Traduceți în limba engleză.

1. Hai să începem! ....
2. Copiii noştri nu sunt acasă. ....
3. Frații ei sunt economişti. ....
4. Câți ani are sora ta? ....
5. Vioara mea este mică. ....
6. Câți ani are mătuşa dumneavoastră? ....

Exercise 3.
Traduceți în limba română.

1. Let's get to know each other. ....
2. Let's be friends. ....
3. Let's speak English. ....
4. Let's start. ....
5. Let's think. ....
6. Let's eat. ....
7. Let's meet tomorrow. ....
8. Let's stop. ....

Exercise 4.
Alcătuiți propoziți utilizând imperativul ținând cont de faptul că:

a. You can use the imperative form ***to give an order.***
b. You can use the imperative ***to warn someone of danger.***
c. You can also use the imperative ***to make a request.***
d. You can use the imperative form ***to give an advice.***
e. You can use the imperative form ***to give an instruction.***
f. You can use the imperative form ***to make an invitation.***
g. You can use the imperative form ***to give friendly informal advice.***
h. You can use the imperative ***for all subjects.***
i. You can make ***a negative imperative.***
j. You can use the imperative ***'more polite' by adding 'do'.***

Exercise 5.

Completaţi propoziţiile cu următoarele cuvinte, astfel încât să obţineţi fraze clare.

a. Turn to ………..	1. me next month
b. Stand behind the ………………	2. the sofa
c. Shut ……………	3. two times a day
d. Go to the traffic lights and …………..	4. line, please
e. Come ……………	5. in
f. Tell me all ……………..	6. turn right
g. Put that ……………	7. down
h. Take your feet off ………..	8. page 4
i. Take one pill …………	9. about it
j. Come and see ………..	10. up

Exercise 6.

Transformaţi următoarele propoziţii imperative în propoziţii imperative negative.

a. Open the window!
b. Go to the theatre!
c. Buy a motorcycle!
d. Take off your coat!
e. Give me another drink!
f. Lend her some money!
g. Come in!

Exercise7.

Alcătuiţi propoziţii conform modelului.

Exemple: to go to the theatre — Let's go to the theatre.

a. to swim in the pool.
b. to walk in the forest.
c. to meet at school
d. to sky
e. to skate
f. to listen the music
g. to read a book

Exercise 8.

Alegeţi una din cele trei variante pentru a completa următoarele propoziţii.

1. _________ I'll help you.
   a. worry not
   b. don't you worry
   c. don't worry
2. _______ time before the exam
   a. don't you waste
   b. don't waste
   c. waste not
3. ________ up! We'll be late for the party.

a. don't hurry
b. hurry you
c. hurry

4. Please _______ your seats. Class will begin soon.
d. takes
e. take
f. you take

5. ________ your books. We'll need them in class today.
a. forget not
b. don't forget
c. forget

6. _______ early for work tomorrow.
a. arrives
b. do you arrive
c. arrive

Exercise 9.

Selectați propoziția imperativă.

A.
1. Good night.
2. When is your birthday?
3. Happy Anniversary!!

B
1. Am I prepared for the test?
2. I wish I had prepared for the test.
3. I am prepared for the test.

C
1. Are the lights turned on?
2. Let there be light!
3. The lights are on.

D
1. Maria, is this your book?
2. Maria, could you take this book with you?
3. Maria, please take this book with you.

Exercise 10.

Completați următoarele propoziții.

a. ________ down to the street.
b. ________ still!
c. ________ your book out of your schoolbag.
d. ________ to be on time.
e. ________ 259. This man feels bad.
f. ________ where you are.
g. ________ the door!

Present Simple Tense
(Timpul Prezent Simplu)

Exercise 1
Subliniaţi forma verbală corectă.

Exemplu:

She .... English every day.	a. speak	b. speaks
1. They ....TV every day.	a. watch	b. watches
2. He .... to work early.	a. go	b. goes
3. I .... a report every morning.	a. read	b. reads
4. We .... to bed early.	a. go	b. goes
5. Mother always .... in the afternoon.	a. cook	b. cooks
6. Roxana seldom .... English to her husband.	a. speak	b.speaks

Exercise 2.
Adăugaţi terminaţia **–s** sau **–es**, după caz, următoarelor forme verbale.

1. Andreea live... in Brăila.
2. He watch...TV in the morning.
3. Florina get... up early every morning.
4. Robert speak... English
5. Florin go... to work every day.
6. My mother-in-law arrive... at half past seven every morning.

Exercise 3.
Modificaţi următoarele propoziţii conform modelului:

Exemplu:

I always work in the afternoon.	He always **works** in the afternoon.
1. I get up early.	....
2. I live in a big house.	....
3. I speak English.	....
4. I watch TV in the evening.	....
5. I go to bed early.	....
6. I have lunch at half past one.	....

Exercise 4.
Completaţi spaţiile libere cu literele care lipsesc cuvintelor din propoziţiile de mai jos.

1. He has bre_kfast at ha_f past sev_n.
2. They l_arn English every d_y.
3. I wo_k in the mo_ning.
4. She al_ays gets up e_rly.
5. We t_ink life is wond_rful.
6. You hav_ din_er at nine o'clo_k in the _vening.

Exercise 5.

Traduceţi în limba engleză.

1. Mă scol întotdeauna la ora 6 dimineaţa.
2. De obicei eu gătesc micul dejun pentru familia mea.
3. Adesea bem cafea dimineaţa.
4. Andreea vorbeşte limba engleză în fiecare zi.
5. Rareori învăţăm noaptea.
6. Tu nu bei niciodată cafea seara.
7. Eu merg la lucru în fiecare zi.
8. Ne uităm la televizor în fiecare seară.
9. Mama mea găteşte în fiecare dimineaţă.
10. Noi dormim 8 ore în fiecare noapte.
11. Ei dau o petrecere în fiecare lună.
12. Noi ne întâlnim în fiecare zi.
13. Ea bea cafea în fiecare dimineaţă.
14. Eu citesc în fiecare zi.

Exercise 6.

Alcătuiţi un progam oficial în care să folosiţi Present Tense Simple.

Exercise 7.

Formulaţi întrebările pentru un chestionar care testează atitudinea faţă de practicarea exerciţiului fizic. Folosind *prezentul simplu*, alcătuiţi întrebări despre:

- practicing a sport;
- favorite games;
- favorite team;
- favorite sportsman/woman;
- spending free time;
- favorite type of holidays;
- activities at weekends;
- going to gym/fitness club,
- joining a club.

Exemplu: Do you practice any sport?
What sport do you practice?
How often do you go to the gym?

Present Continuous Tense
(Timpul Prezent Continuu)

Exercise 1.
Scrieţi forma în "*ING*" a verbelor:

to be	a fi	*to stand*	a sta în picioare	*to take*	a lua
to do	a face	*to listen*	a asculta	*to make*	a face
to have	a avea	*to become*	a deveni	*to belive*	a crede
to eat	a mânca	*to behave*	a (se) comporta	*to forget*	a uita
to drink	a bea	*to cut*	a tăia	*to leave*	a părăsi
to come	a veni	*to stop*	a (se) opri	*to go*	a pleca

Exercise 2.
Înlocuiţi punctele cu forma corectă a verbului **"TO BE"**.

1. I ....reading a novel now.
2. Dana.........................studying her lesson at the moment.
3. Dan and Liviu.......................talking on the phone now.
4. You ....explaining the lesson right now.
5. We.....................writing a composition at the moment.
6. It ....raining today.

to read	a citi
a novel	un roman
to study	a studia
to talk	a vorbi
to explain	a explica
to write	a scrie
to rain	a ploua
composition	compunere
today	astăzi

Exercise 3.
Formulaţi următoarele propoziţii folosind ***prezentul continuu***.

1. I / write a composition.
2. The girls / clean the classroom.
3. The teacher / ask questions.
4. Mother / cook dinner.
5. My brother / play football.
6. You / do your homework.

to clean	a curăţa
to ask	a întreba
dinner	a găti
to play	a se juca
to cook	a găti

Exercise 4.
Formulaţi INTEROGATIVUL şi NEGATIVUL la propoziţiile din exerciţiul anterior.

Exercise 5.

Răspundeţi la următoarele întrebări folosind răspunsul scurt (pozitiv sau negativ).

1. Are you listening to your teacher now?
2. Is she reading a novel now?
3. Are we going to school at the moment?
4. Is it raining now?
5. Are they coming home tonight?
6. Is he explaining the lesson now?

home	acasă
tonight	în seara aceasta

Exercise 6.

Răspundeţi afirmativ sau negativ la următoarele întrebări:

1. Are you a student?
2. Is she cooking dinner now?
3. Are you talking on the phone at the moment?
4. Are you doing your lesson?
5. Am I calling you now?
6. Are they teachers?

Exercise 7.

Completaţi punctele cu forma corectă a verbului ***TO BE*** şi daţi răspunsul corespunzător.

1. ....you going home tonight?
2. ....she reading a novel at the moment?
3. ....it raining now?
4. ....we your friends.
5. ....they drinking coffee now?
6. ....you eating cakes?

Exercise 8.

Completaţi propoziţiile următoare cu ***Prezentul Continuu***.

1. We usually go to school by bus, but ... (by car – today).
2. Mother usually drinks coffee in the morning, but ... (tea – this morning).
3. We usually study in the morning, but ... (in the afternoon – this year).
4. My father works in Bucharest, but ... (in Timişoara – for a fortnight – 2 săptămâni).

Exercise 8.

Formulaţi propoziţii.

1. .... , but - by car – today. [go to school]
2. .... , but - at 10 o'clock – today. [breakfast]
3. .... , but - I – today. [going shopping]
4. .... , but - they – mashed potatoes – today. [chips]
5. .... , but - on Saturdays – this week. [go for a walk]

Exercise 9.

Scrieţi prima parte a propoziţiilor.

1......................... , but I'm getting up late today.
2......................... , but she is buying today.
3......................... , but he is cooking dinner tonight.
4......................... , but he is flying this afternoon.

5........................... , but they are doing it this evening.

Exercise 10.

Alegeți varianta corectă.

1. I usually go to work by car, but
   a) I'm going
   b) I went by bus today.
   c) I go

2. Mihai usually has breakfast at 7, but
   a) she had
   b) she is having breakfast at 8 today.
   c) she have

3. Mother usually goes shopping on Saturday, but
   a) she is going
   b) she goes shopping on Friday this week.
   c) she go

4. Dan usually drinks coffee in the morning, but
   a) is drinking
   b) is drink tea today.
   c) drinks

Exercise 11.

Scrieți ce fel de acțiune exprimă ***Present Tense Continnous*** și dați exemple.

Exercise 12.

Scrieți continuarea propozițiilor.

1. I usually have breakfast at 8, but ….(at 7-today).
2. She usually goes to school by bus, but … (by car-today).
3. Petre usually comes home early, but … (late-this week).
4. Dana usually cooks dinner, but … (I-this week).
5. They usually play tennis on Sundays, but … (on Saturdays-this month).

Exercise 13.

Puneți verbele din paranteze la ***Present Tense Continuous***, pentru a exprima o acțiune viitoare, stabilită în prezent.

a) Laura (to go) to her sister this weekend.
b) Dana (to sing) at a pop concert next week.
c) I (to give) a test paper next month.
d) You (to fly) to Italy tomorrow.
e) She (to change) her house in a few days.

Exercise 14.

Priviți modelul și scrieți apoi care este programul dumneavoastră pentru săptămâna viitoare:

Exemplu: I'm having a test on Monday.
I'm going to the cinema on Tuesday.
I'm writing a lot of letters on Thursday.

Exercise 15.
Traduceţi în limba engleză.

a) Îmi cumpăr o bicicletă peste câteva zile.
b) Diana merge la petrecere sâmbăta viitoare.
c) Mâine vine verişoara mea de la Viena.
d) Laura îşi scrie temele mâine.
e) Dana merge la doctor peste 2 zile.
f) Andreea are un examen greu peste câteva zile.
g) Ana cântă la un concert pop mâine seară.
h) Tata repară maşina săptămâna viitoare.
i) Luăm cina la ora 6 p.m.
j) Andreea îl sună pe Florin poimâine.
k) Prietena ta te aşteaptă la gară mâine.
l) Alina studiază franceză anul viitor.
m) Mihai se trezeşte devreme mâine.
n) Alexandru face un picnic în weekendul viitor.
o) Maria se întâlneşte cu prietena ei vineri la ora două.

Exercise 16.
Traduceţi în limba română.

a) I'm going out to buy some ice-cream.
b) What time do you usually get up?
c) Everybody likes summer.
d) All the students in this class are reading in English well.
e) The park is looking beautiful in spring.
f) My friend is waiting for me at the corner.
g) The train arrives at the North Station at 6,30 p.m.
h) I have an appointment to my dentist at 5 p.m.
i) Why are you drinking from my glass?
j) I don't know what you mean.
k) During the week we generally get up early, but we are getting up late today.
l) My grandmother is coming to see me this afternoon.
m) He is flying to Arad tomorrow.
n) I hope to see you at the party.
o) "What are you doing there?" "I'm trying to find the key to the door."

Exercise 17.
Traduceţi în limba engleză.

a) Noi ne uităm la televizor în fiecare seară.
b) Acum luăm micul dejun. Mama bea cafea, eu beau suc de portocale şi tata mănâncă omletă.
c) Mihai este la el în cameră. Îşi scrie temele.
d) Prietenii tăi te aşteaptă la cafeneaua de după colţ.
e) Maria poartă o rochie frumoasă astăzi.

f) Tu nu ştii să prepari ceaiul, nu-i aşa?
g) Aşa este. Dar ştiu să prepar cafeaua.
h) De ce eşti aşa neîndemânatic azi?

Exercise 18.

Scrieţi forma în - *ING* a următoarelor verbe:

a) to make
b) to run
c) to cry
d) to swim
e) to build
f) to call
g) to travel
h) to stop
i) to hope
j) to blow
k) to fly
j) to come
m) to belive
n) to be
o) to buy

Exercise 19.

Completaţi punctele libere cu forma corespunzătoare a verbelor următoare: ***to eat, to do, to learn, to study***.

a) I ………… all the house work next week.
b) The children …………… at a hotel all this summer holiday.
c) He …………… only vegetables and fruit next month.
d) The pupils in the 3rd grade …………….. new words in English next month.

Exercise 20.

Traduceţi în limba engleză.

a) Merg la cumpărături săptămâna viitoare.
b) Ei îi vizitează pe bunici luna viitoare.
c) Copii organizează o petrecere mâine seară.
d) Părinţii mei merg la teatru duminică.
e) Vecinii noştrii zugrăvesc casa mâine.

Exercise 21.

Traduceţi în limba română.

a) My friends are having a party tomorrow night.
b) All the students are working on a new project next month.
c) The band is performing on Saturday evening.
d) Maria is wearing a silk dress at the party.
e) The girls are going for a walk at week-end.

Exercise 22.

Corectaţi greşelile din propoziţiile următoare:

a) She are going on a trip next week-end.
b) They study for the exam now.
c) The theacher teaching a new lesson.
d) My mother is make a cake.
e) The children are playing football now?

Exercise 23.

Spuneți ce acțiune exprimă timpurile folosite în propozițiile de mai jos:

a) I **go** to work every day.
b) She **goes** to the theatre every Saturday night.
c) **I'm not doing** my homework now because I'm watching TV.
d) **I'm having** breakfast now.
e) **She's going** to the seaside next week.

Exercise 24.

Alegeți varianta corectă:

1. Maria	a) has b) expects c) is expecting	a baby in 9 months.
2. Dana	a) is b) are c) is expecting	going to the theatre now.
3. We are having	a) dinner b) supper c) breakfast	at 7.30 a.m.
4. Can you	a) say b) spend c) spell	your name, please?
5. She doesn't know you	a) is she? b) isn't she? c) does she?	

Exercise 25.

Înlocuiți punctele cu verbele potrivite la timpul gramatical potrivit.

1. What .... your name?
2. How old ....you?
3. .... you usually have lunch at 2:30 p.m?
4. I .... waiting for you here.
5. .... she like the cake?
6. .... mother .... dinner now? Yes, she is.
7. What color .... this pen?

Exercise 26.

Puneți verbele la timpurile potrivite.

1. I (***leave***) this town tomorrow night.
2. I (***know***) your name.
3. She usually (***go***) there at 8 o'clock.
4. We (***travel***) abroad next summer.
5. They (***be***) very tall.

6. She (***look***) very nice in that dress.
7. Irina usually (***go***) to work by car, but she (***go***) by bus this week.

Exercise 27.

Traduceți următoarele expresii:

a) Interviu pentru un loc de muncă.
b) Ce rochie frumoasă porți!
c) Eu de obicei port haine sport.
d) Eu am o rochie elegantă.
e) Tu arăți superb în această rochie.
f) Sunt sigură că obții postul cât ai bate din palme.
g) Sunt puțin încordată.
h) Este o reclamă T.V.
i) Acum înțeleg de ce ești tensionată.
j) Tu arăți astăzi absolut încântător.
k) Baftă!

Exercise 28.

Formulați întrebări astfel încât să răspundă cuvintele subliniate.

a) I'm wearing *a smart dress*.
b) She is looking *very nice* today.
c) Maria is going *to a job interview*.
d) It is *a T.V. advertising*.
e) She is going to the seaside *tomorrow*.

Exercise 29.

Faceți comentarii la propozițiile următoare, folosing ***Present Tense Continuous.***

Exemplu: Mother is in the kitchen.
She is cooking dinner.

a) Father is in the garage.
b) Grandfather is in the garden.
c) The children are in the park.
d) Dana is in the front of the T.V.
e) Mr. Popescu is in the office.

Exercise 30.

Ce faceți pe perioada vacanței? Folosiți ***Present Tense Continuous*** pentru a răspunde:

Exemplu: buy – postcards
I'm buying a lot of postcards while I am on my holiday.

a) eat – sweets
b) write – letters
c) catch – fish
d) read – books
e) watch – movies
f) have – fun

Exercise 31.

Acesta este programul Danei pentru săptămâna viitoare. Alcătuiţi propoziţii folosind ***Present Tense Continuous.***

Exemplu: Monday – exam
Dana is having an exam on Monday.

a) Sunday	trip to Sinaia meet her sister there
b) Monday	test in mathematics cinema
c) Tuesday	go to school go swimming
d) Wednesday	test in English play tennis
e) Thursday	visit her aunt shopping in town
f) Friday	Tea at Maria's cinema
g) Saturday	party at Jane's go to bed late

Exercise 32.

Reformulaţi fiecare propoziţie folosind câte unul dintre verbele de mai jos, urmate de un adjectiv.

to seem	a părea
to look	a arăta, a privi
to smell	a mirosi
to taste	a gusta, a avea gust de
to sound	a suna

Exemplu: The steak has a great smell! — Friptura are un miros nemaipomenit!
The steak <u>smells</u> great. — Friptura <u>miroase</u> nemaipomenit.

a) This cake has a sweet taste.
b) Your teacher has a nice look.
c) This problem seems to be difficult.
d) This coffee has a bad taste.
e) This soup has a delicious smell.
f) This song has a bad sound.
g) The apple is very fresh.

Exercise 33.
Puneți verbele la timpul potrivit și adăugați "**like**"

Exemplu: your dress – fell – cotton.
Your dress feels <u>like</u> cotton.

a) Your teacher – look – model.
b) This car – look – frog.
c) This blouse – feel – silk.
d) Your piano – sound – a broken box.
e) This cake – taste – cinnamon.

Exercise 34.
Puneți verbele din paranteze la ***Present Tense Continuous***.

a) I (think) about the concert now.
b) Raul (see) the manager tomorrow. He (have) an interview.
c) What are you doing? I (taste) the soup.
d) You (be) extremely rude today.
e) I (expect) a phone call from Maria today.
f) What are you doing? I (fell) this material to see if it is cotton.
g) What are you thinking about? I (think) about the holiday.
h) We (have) a test tomorrow and we (study) now.

Exercise 35.
Puneți verbele din paranteză la ***Present Tense Continuous.***

a) I ……………….. music now. (to listen to)
b) My father …………… a letter at the moment. (to write)
c) The Popescu ………………. dinner now. (to have)
d) My friend ………………… the piano now. (to play)
e) You ………………….. you homework now. (to do).

Exercise 36.
Scrieți continuarea următoarelor propoziții folosind ***prezentul continuu***.

a) I usually drink coffee, but …………………. today.
b) They read stories every evening, but ………………….. this evening.
c) We go to the mountains every summer, but ………………….. this summer.
d) I go to school by bus, but …………………… today.
e) My neighbors go to the theatre every weekend, but ……………….this weekend.

Exercise 37.
Puneți verbele din paranteză la ***Present Tense Continuous.***

a) We ………….. on a trip next week. (to go)
b) He …………….abroad next month. (to travel)
c) Maia and Bogdan ……………………. Next Sunday. (to get married)
d) They ………………….. for Vienna on Friday afternoon. (to leave
e) My cousins ………………….. to visit me next winter. (to come)

Exercise 38.

Traduceţi în limba engleză:

a) De obicei poartă pantaloni, dar azi poartă o rochie.
b) Ne uităm la un film de groază acum.
c) Mâine seară, prietenii mei ies în oraş.
d) La sfârşitul săptămânii, domnul şi doamna Dumitrescu mănâncă la restaurant.
e) Săptămâna aceasta gătesc şi fac curat în casă pentru că mama este plecată.

Exercise 39.

Corectaţi greşelile din propoziţiile următoare.

a) She is makeing a cake now.
b) My father is repair the car now.
c) The children is playing in the sand.
d) The baby isn't crying, he is sleeping now.
e) My grandfather reads them newspaper on the moment.

Revision of the Present Simple and Continuous Tense
(Recapitulare Timpul Prezent Simplu şi Continuu)

Exercise 1.

Uniţi propoziţiile cu explicaţia corespunzătoare întrebuinţării timpurilor prezente.

1. Technology is currently ***continuing*** to advance.	a. unreal situation in the present
2. Computers ***have revolutionized*** many industries.	b. an established fact
3. If systems ***were*** to shut down, it would be dangerous.	c. describing a trend or development
4. Office workers ***are*** no longer ***needed***.	d. present result of an action started in the past
5. People who ***work*** in isolated places can use mobile phones to communicate.	e. a state of affairs which has a certain influence

Exercise 2.

Citiţi textul cu atenţie şi eliminaţi cuvântul care este în plus. Lucraţi conform modelului.

Model: He has been here for ten years ago.
He has been here for ten years.

a. Talking in the library is not being allowed.
b. What time are you been expecting them?
c. I insist that you are leave immediately.
d. I can't imagine what her husband is looking like.
e. Andreea is being talking to Veronica at the moment.
f. They have been finished their work.
g. When you will meet Mihai, don't forget to tell him the news.
h. He doesn't mind to lending him books.
i. How long is he be staying in Rome?
j. I have ever never met such a boring person before.
k. He has had been studying Chinese for two years.
l. The meeting does start sat 10 o'clock sharp.
m. Unless you not let them know, there will be trouble.
n. You can go out after you will have done your homework.
o. Lidia behaves as if she were been a queen.
p. We're having had a nice cup of tea.

Exercise 3.

Reformulaţi propoziţiile astfel încât să folosiţi cuvântul dat. Atenţie la timpurile prezentului. Prima propoziţie a fost formulată ca model.

a. There's a party at Mary's place next week.
having.
Next week ***Mary is having*** a party at her place.
b. I started working here three years ago.

for
I've .... three years.

c. Our meeting is tomorrow.
a
We .... tomorrow.

d. I haven't had a Chinese meal for ages.
since
It's .... a Chinese meal.

e. The arrival time of Helen's flight is 8:00
at
Helen's flight .... 8:00.

f. Oh, no! My wallet is missing.
lost
Oh, no!I .... wallet.

g. Do you have any plans for Saturday evening?
doing
What .... Saturday evening?

h. Is this car yours?
you
Do .... car?

i. I would like you to be here!
wish
I .... here.

j. Excuse me, is somebody serving you, sir?
being
Excuse me, ..., sir?

Exercise 4.

Puneți verbele din paranteză la modul şi timpul corespunzător, diateza activă sau pasivă.

They can hardly walk or talk, but some babies (1) ___________ (put) their parents to shame by dealing seriously with computers. Andreea Smith, for example is obviously something of a computer whiz-kid. She (2) ___________ (stare) closely at the screen while her parents (3) _________ (fly) across the keyboard. There is nothing strange in that except the fact that Andreea is only twenty months old. She is one of the youngest in a class of children who (4) _________ (learn) to use computers before they (5) _________ (walk) or (6) ___________ (talk) properly. She (7) ___________ (follow) in her three and a half year-old sister Christine's footsteps. Bianca's mother (8) __________ (say): "People (9) ___________ (laugh) when I say I (10) ____________ (take) the girls to computer classes. She (11) ___________ (not, hide) the fact that she thought it was a bit dangerous in the beginning. Just now she (12) ___________ (change) her whole view on computer learning." I (13) ___________ (think) it's an excellent introduction to education and basic learning of numbers and words. It's really good. I wish I (14) ____________ (know) how to use a computer. If I (15) __________ (do), I would find a better job", she admits. For such a small child, Bianca (16) ___________ (get) familiar with computer sat a surprising rate. The classes (17) ___________ (run) in Liverpool by Dr. June Jofnson who picked up her computer expertise while studying for her Doctorate degree.

Exercise 5.

Puneți verbele din paranteză la modul, timpul şi diateza corespunzătoare.

a. Computers (change) our lives.
b. The project (coordinate) by a Commission.
c. The Internet (offer) unlimited access to information.
d. Scientists (resort) to latest technology to make up an inventory of human genes.
e. I see the computer is on. What (type)?
f. She (run) the school for the past five years.
g. If it (be) true, human, knowledge would be totally revised.
h. When (expect) your guests to come?
i. The symposium (being) on 14th June.
j. Next weekend the Smiths (go) on a holiday.
k. The agenda of the meeting (change) by the chairman himself.

Exercise 6.

Acestea sunt activităţile zilnice desfăşurate de un cursant la o şcoală unde se predă limba engleză ca limbă străină. Alcătuiţi un text de zece propoziţii folosind forma de prezent adecvată şi conjuncţiile enumerate. Prima propoziţie a fost formulată ca model.

then, next, after that, in the ....., after + noun, when, later

a. They have breakfast at 8 o'clock. Then ....
....
....
....

Exercise 7.

Dacă optaţi pentru un curs de limba engleză în Marea Britanie, aveţi posibilitatea să locuiţi la o familie de englezi. Imaginaţi-vă că la sfârşitul unei zile aveţi următorul dialog cu gazda dumneavoastră. Puneţi verbele din paranteză la timpul prezent potrivit.

Host:	.... you .... (have 1) an interesting day?
Student:	Yes, I have indeed. I (make 2) a new friend. She (come 3) from Japan and (learn 4) English to get a scholarship here.
Host:	What (be 5) she interested in?
Student:	Fashion. Her parents (own 6) a textile factory. Look what I (have 7) here. An origami elephant. She (teach 8) me to do it.
Host:	It's wonderful. You (be 9) here for several days now and you (not tell 10) me why you (attend 11) an English course in our town.
Student:	Because I (discover 12) that English is an excellent means of communication. It also (help 13) me in my job.
Host:	I see. How long ………….. you …………… (study 14) it?
Student:	Since primary school.
Host:	Quite a long time. Tell me, ………. You …… (make 15) plans for tonight?
Student:	Actually, yes. I (work 16) on a project with my group mates and there (be 17) some topics I have to look though.
Host:	OK, then. Let me known if I can be of any help. I (watch 18) TV in the living room.
Student:	Thank you. You (be 19) so kind to me.

Exercise 8.

Traduceți în limba română folosind ***prezentul simplu/continuu sau prezentul perfect simplu/continuu.***

a. Dl. Popescu predă engleza. El predă engleza de 10 ani.
b. Ce cărți ai citit pentru lucrarea despre noi metode de predare a limbii străine?
c. Particip la acest curs din primăvară. Particip ca să îmi îmbunătățesc cunoştinţele de engleză.
d. Împrumut deseori casete video când nu sunt subtitrate.
e. Ea vorbeşte engleza fluent. Acum vorbeşte cu un client.
f. Din ce în ce mai mulți oameni vorbesc engleza pentru a comunica mai uşor.

Exercise 9.

Rezolvați exercițiul următor după model, folosind ***Present Tense Simple*** sau ***Present Tense Continuous*** la locul potrivit.

Exemplu: She / to travel abroad / **every** summer. She / to make a reservation / **now**.
She travel**s** abroad every summer. She **is** mak**ing** a reservation now.

a) I / to call a friend / now.
b) Dana / to want / an apartment.
c) Toni / to cook dinner / now.
d) Paul / to go to the theatre / every week.
e) Elena and Mihai / not to go to the party / now.
f) You / to like sweets / very much.
g) The children / to play tennis / every day.
h) The girls / to go for a walk in the park / now.

Exercise 10.

Folosiți ***Present Tense Continuous*** și ***Present Tense Simple*** pentru a înlocui spațiile punctuate.

1. I …………….. the water in a kettle. (to boil)
2. The tea …………….. now. (to boil).
3. This shop ………………… at 8 o'clock every day. (to open)
4. I ……………. the book to read the lesson now. (to open)
5. They …………… to a talk show on T.V. now. (to listen)
6. I don't understand what you …………….. . (to mean)
7. I ……………… them to the station tonight. (to see)
8. She ………………… good all the time. (to smell)
9. Toni ……………. the perfume to see if she likes it or not. (to smell)
10. She …………… a nice girl. (to be)
11. He usually behaves well, but he …………….. extremely rude today. (to be)
12. I ………………. what you mean! (to understand)
13. She ……………… lunch now! (to have)
14. Dana ……………… something to show me. (to have)
15. Can you answer the phone? No, I …………………. a bath now. (to have)
16. Your friends …………………. for you at the corner. (to wait)
17. I …………. about my summer holiday. (to think)
18. I …………. you are late again. (to think)
19. I …………. this apple to see if it is fresh or not (to feel)

20. She .... all right now. She is not sick anymore (to feel)
21. You .... at me, aren't you ? (to look)
22. You .... very nice in this dress. (to look)
23. It ....like we have to go back home. (to look)
24. This girl .... like a model. (to look)

Exercise 11.

Puneţi în spaţiile libere ***Present Tense Simple*** sau ***Present Tense Continuous***, după caz.

a) Tomi .... (have) her birthday party today.
b) She .... (prepare) a lot of nice things to eat now.
c) She .... (wear) a beautiful silvery dress.
d) Her friends .... (ring) the door bell.
e) Tomi .... (open) the door and .... (invite) them in.
f) She .... (open) the presents in a big hurry.

Exercise 12.

Folosiţi ***Present Tense Simple*** sau ***Present Tense Continuous*** pentru a formula propoziţii:

a) o activitate obişnuită, regulată;
b) o activitate desfăşurată pe o perioadă limitată de timp;
c) câteva adevăruri general-valabile;
d) o activitate care se desfăşoară în momentul vorbirii;
e) un anunţ care se face de obicei la radio sau la televizor;
f) o acţiune programată în prezent pentru un timp viitor;
g) cum preparaţi ceaiul;

The YES/NO, TAG and WH Questions

A. The YES / NO Questions

***Exemple*:**

1. Are you Maria?	1. Tu eşti Maria?
Yes, I am	Da.
No, I am not.	Nu
2. Is it raining now?	2. Plouă acum?
Yes, it is.	Da, plouă.
No, it isn't.	Nu, nu plouă.
3. Are they going to school now?	3. Ei merg la şcoală acum?
Yes, they are.	Da, merg.
No, they aren't.	Nu, nu merg.

B. Tag Questions – Întrebările disjunctive

Exercise 1.

Scrieţi întrebarea disjunctivă corespunzătoare pentru propoziţiile de mai jos.

1. It isn't raining,…………………………….?
2. I'm not drinking coffee,………………...?
3. Mother is cooking diner,……………..…?
4. Diana isn't coming home tonight,……....?
5. He is eating a cake,…………………..…?
6. You are not doing your homework,…….?
7. They are listening to music,……………?
8. We are going to the mountains,………...?
9. She isn't eating breakfast,……………....?
10. She is leaving Bucharest,……………...?

Exercise 2.

Puneţi verbul **TO BE** la forma corectă.

1. The sun [……………] shining, isn't it?
2. Laura [……………] drinking coffee, is she?
3. The dog [……………..] running fast, isn't it?
4. You [……………] waiting for me, are you?
5. They [……………] buying flowers, aren't they?
6. Paul […………..] driving very well, is he?
7. It […………….] raining now, is it?
8. She […………] cooking very well, isn't she?

Exercise 3.

Formulaţi întrebări disjunctive la următoarele propoziţii:

1. It is raining,…………………………..?
2. She doesn't know you,………………..?
3. Florin isn't working,………………...?

4. Dana is having dinner,……,…....…....?
5. You don't need this book,……….…...?

Exercise 4.
Adăugați întrebări disjunctive la următoarele propoziții afirmative.

1. They are coming by car,....................................?
2. You're watching TV,……………….…….…...?
3. It's raining,……………………………..……?
4. The washing-machine is working,…………..….?
5. You're feeling better,…………………………...?
6. I'm working now,………………………………?
7. That man is carrying an umbrella,…………….?

Exercise 5.
Puneți forma corectă a verbelor TO BE / TO DO în următoarele propoziții:

1. They [………..] having dinner, [……………]?
2. Mihai […………] usually has porridge for breakfast, [……………]?
3. You […………..] having lunch now, [……….]?
4. You [………….] usually have lunch in a Fast food, […………]?
5. He […………] preparing our Sunday lunch now, [……………]?
6. He […………] cooking Brussels spouts, […………]?

Exercise 6.
Adăugați ***Tag Questions*** la următoarele propoziții:

a) You didn't want to see me, …………….. ?
b) She worked in the garden a few days ago, ………………?
c) Alina didn't finish her homework, ……………….?
d) You didn't go to school yesterday, ………………?
e) She wanted to buy that dress, …………….. ?

C. "WH" Questions – Special Questions

Exercise 7.
Răspundeți la următoarele întrebări în scris.

1. Where are you going? ....
2. What are you doing? ....
3. Which cake is good? ....
4. Who is coming? ....
5. Where are you waiting for me? ....

Exercise 8.
Răspundeți în scris la următoarele întrebări.

1. Where do you live? ……………………………………
2. What are you writing now? ……………………………………
3. Who do you love? ……………………………………

4. Where are you waiting for Dana? ....
5. What do you do every day? ....
6. Who is going with you? ....
7. Where do you meet him every day? ....
8. Why are you crying? ....
9. Why do you write it every week? ....
10. Where is the baby sleeping? ....

Exercise 9.

Formulaţi întrebări speciale folosind expresiile de mai jos.

1. creionul este în mâna mea.	(Where..)
2. computerul este pe birou.	(Where....................; What.....................)
3. copilul desenează o casă.	(Who......................; What.....................)
4. ei se grăbesc	(Who......................; Where...................)
5. el găteşte	(Who......................; What.....................)
6. ea dansează	(Who......................, What.....................)

Exercise 10.

Răspundeţi la următoarele întrebări.

1. Where do you usually have dinner?
2. What do you usually have for breakfast?
3. When do you usually have lunch?
4. Are you having lunch now?
5. What are you having for lunch?
6. What are you cooking for dinner?
7. What do you usually have for five o'clock tea?

Exercise 11.

Puneţi întrebări astfel încât să răspundă cuvintele subliniate.

1. <u>Florin</u> is cooking <u>dinner</u>. [Who, What]
2. Florin usually has <u>cereal</u> for breakfast. [What]
3. <u>They</u> have <u>lunch</u> <u>at 12 o'clock</u> every day. [Who, What, When]
4. <u>Mother</u> <u>is cooking</u> <u>mashed potatoes and roast</u> for lunch. [Who, What]

Exercise 12.

Formulaţi "***wh questions***" ale căror răspunsuri sunt cuvintele subliniate.

Exemplu: ***Who*** looked after their younger sisters and brothers? (Girls did)

Little Mothers

In working class families, girls (a) looked after their <u>younger sisters and brothers</u> (b) while their mothers were busy. On the threshold of some houses <u>in the East End</u>(c) of London one could see "a little mother" of <u>eight</u> (d). She would <u>nurse</u> (e) a <u>newly born baby</u> (f), <u>hush</u> (e) it to sleep or <u>rock</u> (e) it. When it cried, the little mother would soothe it <u>by kissing</u> (g) the little face again and again. <u>Most of the times</u>(h) her attention was drawn by a prank of a four year-old brother who was also under her care. By the time she married and had her own children she was a woman fed up <u>with motherhood</u> (is).

Exercise 13.

Puneți întrebări astfel încât să răspundă cuvintele subliniate:

1. I want this book.
2. She is waiting for Adrian at the theatre.
3. Mother is cooking dinner tonight.
4. Adriana is having an exam tomorrow.
5. The dog is running to the gate.

Exercise 14.

Traduceți în limba engleză următoarele întrebări și dați răspunsuri tot în limba engleză.

1. Unde te duci?
2. Câți ani ai?
3. Cum te cheamă?
4. Unde locuiești?
5. Unde este Alina?
6. Mergi la teatru acum?
7. Vrei să iei cina cu mine?
8. Nu te cunoaște, nu-i așa?
9. Vrei cartea aceasta?
10. Ce culoare are părul tău?

Exercise 15.

Puneți întrebări astfel încât să răspundă cuvintele subliniate.

a) I go *to work* every day. (were)
b) *I'm having dinner* now. (what)
c) I usually get up *at 7^{30} in the morning.* (when)
d) She works as a secretary *at a private company*. (where)
e) Maria is happy *because she got the job.* (why)

Exercise 16.

Formulați întrebări, astfel încât să răspundă cuvintele marcate.

a) Mircea lived **in a big house** last summer.
b) **Dan** walked to the beach yesterday.
c) Paul played **football in the schoolyard** two days ago.
d) I visited **my friends** yesterday.
e) I decided **to visit them again**.

Exercise 17.

Citiți textul și fromulați întrebări ale căror răspunsuri sunt cuvintele accentuate.

The motorist (1) of the 21st century is already prepared for the day's disk drive. ***From the breakfast table*** (2) a remote control has opened the garage door, unlocked the car and set air conditioning. He doesn't need the old road atlas to work out a route. A video disk is on hand ***to provide step-by-step instructions*** (3) ***either on screen or by voice, or both.*** The disk stores enough ***information's*** (5) to offer a choice of routes and print out maps of regions, towns or individual streets. ***During the journey*** (6) the car radio will be automatically interrupted ***to let the driver know*** (7) about traffic problems-fog, accidents.

Exercise 18.

Imaginaţi-vă că vreţi să cumpăraţi un video player. Ce ar trebui să ştiţi? Folosiţi cuvintele ajutătoare şi alcătuiţi răspunsuri conform modelului.

Model: What would you need to know?
I would need to know how much the hardware costs.

a. cost – the hardware
b. have – tracks
c. be compatible – image support system
d. be – advantages/disadvantages of the tape system
e. can – record off TV
f. can use – a camera for personal filming
g. be – sound quality
h. recommended – an expert
i. can buy – that latest generation of VCR (Video Cassette Recorder)
j. be installed – the VCR

Exercise 19.

Adăugaţi întrebări disjunctive (*tag questions*). Prima propoziţie a fost completată ca model.

a. The Earth is being squeezed dry, isn't it?
b. There are some alternatives to the global shortage of fuel, ………………. ?
c. The Centre for Alternative Technology supports Mr. Glenville's answer, …………………?
d. 1973 was the year of the first oil shock, ………………….. ?
e. Mr. Glenville didn't pick up the place by accident, ……………..?
f. The energy they use at the Centre is renewable, …………………?
g. People at the Centre don't spare themselves the industrial comfort, ……………….?
h. Mr. Glenville has a vast knowledge in alternative technologies, ……………..?
i. People can benefit from alternative technology, ……………….?
j. The funds were raised from private donations, ………………..?
k. There isn't any other similar Centre in Europe, ………………..?
l. Listeners will be interested to visit the Centre, …………………?

Exercise 20.

Formulaţi întrebări astfel încât să răspundă cuvintele subliniate.

1. She is sleeping <u>in the bedroom</u>. (Where)
2. I go <u>to work</u> very day. (Where)
3. Florin is playing tennis <u>in the park</u>. (Where)
4. She loves Dan <u>because she is nice</u>. (Why)
5. The baby is crying <u>because he is hungry</u>.(Why)
6. I'm writing <u>a letter</u> now. (What)
7. They are leaving for Paris <u>tomorrow</u>. (When)
8. I have lunch <u>at 12</u> every day. (When)

Past Simple Tense
(Timpul Trecut Simplu)

Exercise 1.
Alegeţi din următoarea serie de verbe doar pe cele regulate şi scrieţi-le la ***Past Tense Simple***:

to work, to learn, to cry, to fly, to try, to do, to have, to be.

Exercise 2.
Scrieţi verbele din paranteze la ***Past Tense Simple***:

a) She (do not) her homework last night.
b) Adina (try) to solve the problem yesterday.
c) Alin (study) in the library last week.
d) Dan (walk) in the park two days ago.
e) I (watch) TV every night last week.
f) … you (listen) to that new song?
g) We (play) tennis the whole afternoon yesterday.

Exercise 3.
Scrieţi ***Past Tense Simple*** la următoarele verbe şi formaţi propoziţii:

a) to walk, b) to play, c) to work, d) to talk, e) to listen, f) to look, g) to try, h) to do.

Exercise 4.
Formulaţi întrebări astfel încât să răspundă cuvintele subliniate:

a) I looked into a magazine **last night**.
b) You watched **TV** the whole day yesterday.
c) Dana played **tennis** last week.
d) She talked to her for an hour **the day before yesterday.**
e) I didn't look at you **a few minutes ago.**

Exercise 5.
Scrieţi 10 verbe neregulate la ***Infinitive*** şi la ***Past Tense Simple***.

Exercise 6.
Traduceţi următoarele propoziţii:

a) Eu nu am muncit luna trecută.
b) A studiat ea în bibliotecă seara trecută?
c) Dana a încercat să vorbească cu el cu o săptămână în urmă.
d) L-am oprit lângă semafor acum o oră. (cu o oră în urmă).
e) Eu nu am jucat tenis anul trecut.

Exercise 7.
Traduceţi în limba română.

a) He played the piano for two hours last night.
b) I didn't study French last year.
c) He talked to her once, about two years ago.
d) I didn't want to wake him up.
e) She watched TV last Saturday.

Exercise 8.

Adăugaţi *TAG QUESTIONS* la următoarele propoziţii, conform exemplului:

Exemplu: You didn't do your homework, did you?
She worked in the garden yesterday, didn't she?

a) You wanted to buy the flower, …………………..?
b) She didn't try to help him, ……………… ?
c) He talked to her yesterday, …………………?
d) You didn't listen to the music last night, ………………?
e) Dana played the piano on Sunday, ………………?

Exercise 9.

Formulaţi întrebări astfel încât să răspundă cuvintele subliniate:

a) I didn't see you **last night**.
b) She worked **in the garden last weekend.**
c) You walked to **your office** last month.
d) **He played the piano** the day before yesterday.
e) **I listened to music** two hours ago.

Exercise 10.

Traduceţi următoarele propoziţii:

a) Deodată, Mirela spune:
b) Putem să aruncăm o privire, dacă vrei.
c) Uite o masă acolo.
d) Aici sunt întotdeauna haine drăguţe.
e) Îmi plăcea la nebunie îmbrăcămintea sport.
f) Obişnuiam să port tot felul de haine din bumbac rezistent.

Exercise 11.

Alegeţi din verbele următoare doar pe cele regulate şi scrieţi-le la ***Past Tense***:

to write, to go, to do, to learn, to invite, to listen, to talk, to have, to wait, to work, to dream, to cut, to read, to watch, to look.

Exercise 12.

Alcătuiţi propoziţii cu verbele regulate de mai sus la ***Past Tense Simple***.

Exercise 13.

Puneţi verbele din paranteze la timpul potrivit.

a) I (*do not*) watch TV last night.

b) Dana (*to cook*) dinner two days ago.
c) Mother (*to invite*) my aunt to dinner yesterday.
d) Andra (*to use*) to wear sports clothes a few years ago.
e) Mirela (*to watch*) her favorite shows a TV last evening.
f) We (*to visit*) our grandmother last Sunday.
g) Florin (*to solve*) the math problem very quickly yesterday.

Exercise 14.

Puneţi verbele din paranteze la timpul potrivit şi adăugaţi adverbe de timp trecut la final.

Exemplu: I (to work) in the garden ....
I **worked** in the garden **yesterday afternoon**.

a) I (to phone) my mate ....
b) She (to travel) in the country ....
c) Dana (to live) in Slatina ....
d) He (to play) tennis ....
e) I (to receive) a letter ....

Exercise 15.

Formulaţi întrebări astfel încât să vă răspundă cuvintele marcate.

a) I washed **the dishes** yesterday.
b) **It rained** yesterday morning.
c) My mate phoned me **last night.**
d) **Mother** prepared breakfast yesterday.
e) **Dan cleaned his room** last week.

Exercise 16.

Răspundeţi în scris la următoarele întrebări.

a) What time did the rain start?
b) When did the rain start?
c) Did you climb the mountain?
d) Where did you stop for lunch?
e) Did you listen to music in the evening?
f) What interesting places did you visit?

Exercise 17.

Traduceţi în limba engleză.

a) Noi ne-am mutat într-o casă nouă luna trecută.
b) Paul l-a ajutat pe fratele lui ieri.
c) Dana a ajuns târziu la şcoală vinerea trecută.
d) Copiii au vizitat Muzeul Satului.
e) Eu m-am uitat la televizor seara trecută.
f) Alina a cântat la pian ieri după-masă.
g) Simona a studiat franceză la şcoală anul trecut.
h) Tim a vorbit cu Mihai seara trecută.

Exercise 18.

Traduceţi în limba română.

a) I didn't want to watch that movie.
b) She arrived at school at 9 o'clock yesterday.
c) You didn't see me at school.
d) Diana helped me with this problem.
e) I visited my grandmother yesterday.

Exercise 19.

Scrieţi 10 verbe regulate la ***Past Tense Simpl***e şi formulaţi propoziţii cu ele.

Exercise 20.

Folosind lista cu verbe neregulate, completaţi tabelul.

The Infinitive Form	**The Past Tense Form**
go	
have	
	left
	told
lose	
say	
write	
	met
teach	
will	
stand	
	ran
	set
	sang
sell	
	read
make	
speak	
	ate
	drank
	felt
drive	
	broke
fall	
	brought
catch	
buy	
choose	
	was

Exercise 21.

Transformaţi propoziţiile de mai jos în propoziţii negative.

a. White Fong left his kennel.
b. He saw five women.
c. His Indian master sold him for gold dust.
d. White Fong fought a ferocious bear.
e. He felt friendship for Beauty Smith.

Exercise 22.

Transformaţi propoziţiile de mai sus în propoziţii interogative.

Exercise 23.

Adăugaţi întrebări disjunctive şi daţi răspunsuri scurte de tipul: Yes/No!

a. The story didn't begin in California, ... ?
b. White Fang lived in the Indian camp, ...?
c. His Indian master took him to Fort Yukon, ...?
d. He didn't sell White Fang for a lot of money, ...?
e. His new master wasn't a nice man, ...?

Exercise 24.

Traduceţi în limba engleză.

f. Sunt cinci gâşte pe iaz. (pond).
g. Un stol de porumbei zboară deasupra livezii.
h. Ursoaicele au grijă de puii lor.
i. Veveriţa are coadă lungă şi blană maro.
j. Unele animale sălbatice sunt periculoase.

Exercise 25.

Formulaţi întrebări folosind cuvintele ajutătoare şi apoi răspundeţi.

Exemplu: What time [***get up***] yesterday?
What time did you get up yesterday.
I got up at 7 a.m.

a. When [go to work] last Monday?
....
....

b. Who [meet with] three days ago.
....
....

c. What book [read] last week?
....
....

d. Where [spend your holidays] last year?
....
....

e.What [be the last cassette] bought?
....
....

Exercise 26.

Completând spațiile libere cu formele de trecut ale verbelor următoare, veți afla cum Dick Whittington a devenit primarul Londrei datorită pisicii sale.

fell, buy, hear, belong, be, want, line, find, go, sleep, wake, give, come, set, take, send, become, get, marry, knight.

Once upon a time, there (1)………….. in a village an orphan boy, Dick Whittington. The villagers (2)…………….. sorry for him. They (3)……………. him food and clothes. One day, he (4)………………. about the great city of London. People (5)……………… it (6)……………… paved with gold. Soon after, he (7)……………… there. He (8)…………… to find a golden street. After three days with no luck, he (9)……………. a door way in which he (10)……………….. . The door (11)………………. to a rich merchant. He (12)……………… him a job and a room to sleep in. The room (13)……………… holes. Mice (14)……………… in the night and (15)…………….. him. Alice, the merchant's daughter (16)……………… Dick. One day, she (17)…………… him a penny. Dick (18)…………….. a cat and (19)…………….... it to his room. The cat (20)………………… rid of all the mice. Later, the merchant (21)………………… out on a voyage to North Africa. Each Servant (22)………………… something to take their profit when the ship returned. Dick (23)……………… his cat.

Dick was unhappy and it occurred to him to become the Mayor of London.

Meanwhile, the Africa King (24)……………. rid of the mice and rats in his palace with the help of Dick's cat. The King (25)………………. the cat for jewels and gold. Dick (26)…………….. rich and (27)…………… Alice soon afterwards. The king (28)………………… him as Sir Richard Whittington. He (29)……………… Lord Mayor of London three times.

Exercise 27.

Înlocuiți verbele îngroșate cu *"give + particulă"* (*back, in, off, ont, up*).

a) The officer **was distributing** pictures of the missing child.
b) The garden **emits** a wonderful smell in spring.
c) She **stopped** drinking as she was ill.
d) There was one issue my father was not willing to **surrender** to.
e) I'm **bringing back** the tapes tomorrow.

Exercise 28.

Traduceți în limba engleză.

a) Cred că are dreptate.
b) Tocul ferestrei era foarte îngust.
c) Nu pot să pricep ce spui.
d) Băiețelul a întins mâna după înghețată.
e) Încearcă să prinzi mingea!
f) Eram țintuită locului de frică.
g) Prizonierul zgâria numărul zilelor pe zid.
h) O echipă de salvare (rescue team) a căutat supraviețuitori.

Past Continuous Tense
(Timpul Trecut Continuu)

Exercise 1.

Transformați propozițiile de la timpul ***present continuu*** la timpul ***trecut continuu.*** Înlocuiți adverbul "***now***" cu o expresie de timp trecut.

a) Dona is standing in front of the building now.
b) The little girl is whining now.
c) The kitten isn't running at the moment.
d) The little girl is reaching out her hand now.
e) Is the woman screaming?

Exercise 2.

Puneți verbele din paranteză la ***timpul trecut***.

a) Dona (*talk*) to Alex about the happening.
b) She (*stand*) then looking at the little girl.
c) She (*not do*) anything to draw the people's attention.
d) No one else (*pass by*).
e) The little girl's mother (*try*) to catch her.

Exercise 3.

Transformați propozițiile de la exercițiul anterior în propoziții interogative.

Exercise 4.

Citiți programul unui turist care a stat pentru o zi, la Hotelul Lido. Scrieți ce a făcut în intervalul de timp menționat pentru fiecare activitate.

Exemplu: He got up at 9.
He was having breakfast in the hotel from 9 to 9.30.

<u>*Staying at Lido Hotel*</u>
Get up 9.00
Breakfast in hotel 9.00 – 9.30
Visit Art Museum 9.30 – 11.30
Shopping 11.30 – 13.30
Back to hotel 13.30
Lunch, rest at hotel 13.30 – 16.00
Tea at hotel 16.00 – 16.30
Leave hotel 16.30
Walk 16.30 – 18.30
Back to hotel 18.30
Shower and change 18.30 – 19.30
Dinner at hotel 19.30 – 21.00
Party at hotel 21.00 – 23.30
Get to bed 23.30

Exercise 5.

Transformaţi cele două propoziţii într-o frază. Folosiţi ***when, while, as,*** ca elemente de legătură.

Exemplu: The little girl was reaching onto her hand. Her mother appeared.
The little girl was reaching onto her hand **when** her mother appeared.

a) Dona came in. Alex was talking over the phone.
b) Dona was walking. She heard a whine.
c) Dona was telling the story. Alex interrupted her.
d) She turned round. Some one was looking at her.
e) She was standing speechless. The man came to her.

Exercise 6.

Uniţi acţiunile din coloana A cu cele din coloana B, pentru a exprima simultaneitatea a 2 acţiuni în curs de desfăşurare, în trecut.

Exemplu: Len was asking questions **while** Dona was telling the story.

A / Alex	B / Dona
1. ask questions	1. stand by the window
2. eating a sandwich	2. read a magazine
3. watch TV	3. feed the children
4. jog	4. tell the story
5. do crosswords	5. cook dinner
6. make a phone call	6. have a cup of coffee

Exercise 7.

Formulaţi întrebări folosind cuvintele sugerate şi apoi răspundeţi. Atenţie la întrebuinţarea ***trecutului simplu sau continuu***.

Exemplu: *When/mother/watch TV*
Q: When did mother watch TV?
A: Yesterday mother watched TV.

a) What/TV/show.
Q: ....?
A: ....?
b) What/father/do
Q: ....?
A: ....?
c) Who/ask/help
Q: ....?
A: ....?
d) Where/David/climb
Q: ....?
A: ....?
e) What/David/do
Q: ....?
A: ....?

f) How/David/straighten/aerial
Q: ....?
A: ....?

g) Why/TV/work, not
Q: ....?
A: ....?

Exercise 8.

Scrieţi redarea unei întâmplări personale.

Menţionaţi:
- locul şi timpul
- amănunte despre atmosferă (It was getting dark, it was raining, the sun was shining, etc.)
- acţiunea 1: - when
  - while - I saw
  - I heard, etc.
- amănunte descriind acţiunea 1 (The man was wearing... screaming, etc.)
- acţiunea 2, etc.
- amănunte
- finalul

Exemplu: One day I was walking in the street. It was getting dark. Passers-by were passing by me hurriedly. When I came to a street corner ....

Exercise 9.

Uniţi verbele din coloana A cu sinonimele lor din coloana B. Alcătuiţi propoziţii.

A	B
1. give up	a. distribute
2. give off	b. return
3.give in	c. emit
4. give out	d. stop doing
5. give back	e. surrender

Exercise 10.

Alcătuiţi propoziţii care să exprime:

a) un obicei din copilărie;
b) două acţiuni în curs de desfăşurare în acelaşi timp, în trecut;
c) activitatea unui membru al familiei când aţi venit ieri acasă;
d) o activitate în curs de desfăşurare într-un interval de timp trecut:

Exercise 11.

Traduceţi în limba engleză.

a) Îmi făceam bagajul când a sunat telefonul.
b) În timp ce îmi făceam bagajul, mama îmi pregătea sandvişurile.
c) Mă uitam la TV când am auzit un zgomot.
d) Am vrut să mă uit la TV, dar acesta nu funcţiona.
e) L-am rugat să mă ajute, dar învăţa pentru examen.

Exercise 12.

Găsiți șapte cuvinte care denumesc clădiri care pot fi întâlnite într-un oraş. Cu literele care au rămas se poate formula o propoziție din 5 cuvinte. Ați descoperit-o?

S	T	T	R	E	L	A	T	M
A	T	H	E	A	T	R	E	U
S	R	A	G	E	N	C	Y	S
T	E	I	D	P	T	I	C	E
H	O	S	P	I	T	A	L	U
I	Y	U	C	A	U	H	C	M
B	S	C	I	N	E	M	A	A

Exercise 13.

Rescrieți textul de mai jos la ***timpul trecut***!

Atenție!

Present simple ⟶ past simple, present continuous ⟶ past continuous

For the majority of spectators, it is not the best runners who interest them, but the silliest. For instance, there is a waiter who is carrying a tray with a bottle of mineral water. Another competitor, a policeman, is dressed as a bishop; he is raising money for a children's hostel. A team of three men and two women run dressed as tigers to raise money for endangered species. The non-profit organizations which are taking part in the Marathon can more or less raise funds of five million each.

Although it is very difficult to run across London in a silly costume, the competitors enjoy themselves.

There is a real carnival atmosphere: the runners laugh, dance and, sometimes, fall over. This year's Marathon is a record because 30.000 competitors are participating in the event.

Of course, there are other similar races organized by other important cities in the world. However, they cannot claim their runners are those happy as the London ones are.

Exercise 14.

Uniți propoziția cu explicația corespunzătoare.

1. He went on a safari holiday last summer.
2. They were traveling in Italy when they had the car accident.
3. Maria had been to Italy three times before she took him there.
4. When I was young I used to spend my summer holiday at my grandparents.
5. They had been looking for a flat for three months before they decided to buy a house.
6. This time last year he was working for an oversea branch of the company.
7. The sun was shining and the wind wasn't blowing.
8. If you had come earlier, you would have had the change to see her.
9. She promised she would tell him the whole truth.

a. simultaneous past actions which describe a scene.
b. a past action completed before another past action.
c. a past action to happen after another past action
d. a complete action which happened at a certain past time
e. a past action in progress interrupted by another past action
f. an unreal situation the past in

g. a past habit
h. an anterior past action in progress
i. an action in the middle of happening at a moment in the past.

Exercise 15.

Completați auxiliarul corespunzător, la ***diateza pasivă sau activă***.

a. When I __________ got home I found a note on my desk.
b. I __________ making my way through the tourists who crowded the square that square that's why I __________ realize what __________ going on.
c. My flight __________ been delayed because of the fog and I found myself trapped in the airport.
d. We had __________ having problems and I __________ want to admit to it.
e. She told me everything __________ be alright by the end of that year.
f. I will always remember that dinner. It __________ served irreproachably.
g. I __________ only been there for a few minutes when a young lady came up and asked if she __________ allowed to seat next to me.
h. As I left building I wondered whether I __________ ever go back there again.
i. Our anniversary __________ always been celebrated without any fuss, but suddenly we decided to happened it differently.

Exercise 16.

Corectați greşelile.

a. We have met last year when I was on holiday in Bucharest.
b. They said they will come in time for the show.
c. She was studied when I rang her up.
d. Florin didn't used to call on unexpectedly.
e. He had been thought over and over again till he made up his mind.
f. Hardly had they known each other than he proposed to her.
g. The professor examined a candidate when the secretary came in.
h. If only he knew about the danger, the damage could have been avoided.

Exercise 17.

Puneți verbele din paranteză la un timp ***trecut corespunzător***.

At first I (notice) that two fire engines (be) parked outside my block of flats. Their ladders (be) raised as far as the third floor, below my flat. While I (rush) towards the building I (become) aware of the group of onlookers who (stand) around the entrance. As soon as I (come) closet o them, they (recognize) me. After they (greet) me I (ask) what (happen). They (tell) me the flat below mine (catch) fire but the fireman (manage) to put it out. While I (head for) my flat I (meet) a man who (carry) a TV set. He (ask) met o help him load it into his van. I (know, not) who he (be). After we (put) the TV ser in the van I (enter) the building and (go) towards my flat. When I (reach) it I (see) the door (be) open. When I finally (enter) my flat I (notice) my television (miss). I (help) just a burglar to steal my television.

Present Perfect Simple Tense
(Timpul Prezent Perfect Simplu)

Exercise 1.

Pentru a învăţa mai uşor verbele neregulate grupaţi-le în următoarele categorii:

a) ***verbe cu 3 forme diferite:***	be	was were	been
	do	did	done
b) verbe cu două forme identice:			
i) trecut şi participiu trecut:	have	had	had
ii) infinitiv şi participiu trecut:	come	came	come
c) ***verbele cu o singură formă:***	cut	cut	cut

Exercise 2.

Completaţi formele ***HAVE*** sau ***HAS***, după caz:

a) "What would you have Alex?"
"Nothing, thank you. I …………….. already eaten a cheeseburger."
b) "What ……………… happened?!
c) "100 km/h! …………… you driven that fast?"
d) "Look at your knee! You …………… not ridden your bike carefully!"
e) "Speed up! The traffic lights ………….. turned green!"

Exercise 3.

Completaţi propoziţiile cu formele corecte ale ***participiului trecut***:

a) Dona has (drive) fast.
b) Alex and Dona have (take) a taxi.
c) The teenagers have (get) in the bus noisily.
d) They have (run) down the street.
e) Dona has (come) across a car accident.

Exercise 4.

Completaţi: ***already, yet, just*** şi ***recently***.

a) She has ………….. entered the restaurant.
b) The passers-by haven't crossed the street ………….. . The lights are red.
c) The bus has …………… gone. You missed it.
d) The policeman has …………… fined 3 careless drivers.
e) Mother hasn't taken a driving lesson ………….. .
f) The traffic hasn't been crowded …………….. .

Exercise 5.

Citiţi exclamaţiile de mai jos. Explicaţi într-o propoziţie ce s-a întâmplat folosind ***prezentul perfect simplu*** pentru a exprima rezultatul prezent al unei acţiuni efectuate în trecut.

Exemplu: "Ah!" - She has hurt hereself.

a) "My God!"
b) "Thank you!"
c) "Well!"!
d) "Welcome!"
e) "Good luck!"
f) "Tonch wood!" ("Bate-n lemn!")
g) "Cheers!"
h) "Congratulations!"
i) "Good bye!"

Exercise 6.

Traduceţi în limba engleză:

a) Am parcat maşina lângă staţia de metrou.
b) Ai citit la bibliotecă sau acasă?
c) Blocajul rutier nu a fost încă degajat. (to clear of)
d) A mai condus (până acum)?
e) Nu ai comandat încă? (to order)
f) Au înlocuit indicatoarele rutiere în ultimul timp.

Exercise 7.

Cu ajutorul dicţionarului citiţi ştirile de mai jos şi completaţi titlurile articolelor, folosind ***prezentul perfect simplu***. Prima ştire a fost intitulată pentru a vă oferi un model.

a) A TEENAGER HAS FOUND A HIGHLY DANGEROUS EXPLOSIVE

An explosive alert closed Forth Rood Bridge recently. Andrei, a teenager, was walking home about a mile with a stick of gelignite[1)] in his hand. While he was climbing the cliffs, a piece of paper caught his eye. "It was sticking out of a whole", the boy said to the news reporter, "and I pulled it out and found what looked like a spent cartridge. Then I noticed another piece of paper in the same hole and pulled that out, too. It looked like a wet sausage. I had an idea that it could be dynamite, but I didn't think it was dangerous." On his arrival home, Andrei showed it to his father who contacted the police. On examination, they found the gelignite to be "highly dangerous". It was later detonated.

1) gelignite – explosive cu fulmicoton

b)

"One of Scotland's rarest visitors, a white gerfalcon[1)] flew in recently. However, he did not fly in under his own wing power. He traveled to Aberdeen by helicopter. Two days ago, the falcon, whose natural home is in Greenland of the Canadian Artic, landed exhausted on a fisherman[2)] almost 140 miles of Aberdeen. The crew fed him five pounds[3)] of trout[4)] while he was waiting for his flight to the mainland. The manager of the zoo in Aberdeen identified him. "The bird is still exhausted", the manager said, "but we will take him to the zoo and nurse him back to health[5)], then release him."

1) gyrfalcon – şoim irlandez
2) fisherman – vas pescăresc
3) pound – livră, funt; 0,453 kg/pounds
4) trout – păstrăv
5) to nurse back to health – a hrăni (pe cineva) până când îşi revine

c)

"This is a newspaper report of an incident on the M 74 motorway in Scotland. Mercat, a race horse, had been entered for the 3:45 race at Hamilton Race Course. During the warming up, he threw his jockey. He galloped out of the race course breaking every rule in the Highway Code:

- going through traffic lights at red,
- going the wrong way, to the right, on a roundabout,
- proceeding in a dangerous manner.

Mercat, at least, did not exceed the speed limit. A motorway policeman received an SOS on his radio: "Proceed North to Hamilton and look out for a runaway racehorse!"
Driving along the motorway, he passed a line of slow-moving cars. There, at the head of the procession was Mercat! The policeman tried unsuccessfully to catch him. At a moment, a car drew up. Fortunately, the driver was a member of the Glasgow Mounted Police[1)] and he rode Mercat back to the race horse."

1) Mounted Police – poliția călare

d)

"Eight families in Manchester dressed in their night clothes rushed from their flats in the early hours of the morning. A dog, Bruce, had given a fire alarm: he barked when the fire broke out. His howling[1)] awakened 14-year-old Elizabeth. She met a "wall of fire" in the kitchen. She quickly wakened her sister and mother. The other families living in the block of flats were evacuated from their houses when the firemen came."

[1)]to howl – a urla (despre câini)

e)

"A Brazilian seaman was recently taken to a Liverpool hospital. He was in a very weak condition after spending 11 days in the Atlantic Ocean. He and his shipmates made a raft after their fishing boat sank off the coast of Guyana in South America. As day followed day, the survivors became weaker and weaker. One by one the helpless men lost their hold to the raft[1)] and slipped to their deaths[2)]. When Inocencio was too exhausted to hold on the raft, a British ship approached. Only when he woke up in hospital did he realize that he had managed to survive a terrible ordeal."

1) to lose one's hold on something – a scăpa din mână, a pierde controlul situației.
2) they slipped to their deaths – au căzut în mare (unde şi-au găsit moartea); s-au înecat.

Exercise 8.

Scrieți un paragraf de 5-7 rânduri care să înceapă cu prepoziția "I've had one of those days." Menționați activități terminate înainte de momentul vorbirii, fără precizarea timpului.

I've had one of those days. I've left my office keys at home.
I...
....
....
....
....
....
....
....

However, one good thing has happened to me.

I...
....
....
....
....
....
....
....

Exercise 9.

Puneți verbele din paranteză la timpul prezent perfect simplu. Atenție la topică (locul cuvintelor în propoziție.)

a) "Dona, you look tired."
"I (just, finish) a report."
b) Alex is waiting for Dona. (She, come, yet?)
c) "Where are the car keys?"
"I (forget) them upstairs."
d) "Poor him, he (fail, already) another driving test."
e) "Don't worry. He is experienced. He (drive) racing cars before.

Exerise 10.

Completați cu "***so***" sau "***neither***".

a) Alex likes pop music.
.... does Dona.
b) The audiences have danced for hours.
.... have Dona.
c) Alex isn't tired.
.... is Dona.
d) Pop music makes Dona feel young.
.... does dancing.
e) Dona's husband isn't bored.
.... is Alex.

Exercise 11.

Uniți cu o linie cuvântul cu definiția corectă:

1. deafening	a. leads an orchestra, choir, concert
2. roadie	b. successful song
3. hum	c. extremely loud
4. conductor	d. helps bands on tours
5. hit	e. to sing with closed lips

Exercise 12.

Formulați câte un comentariu pe marginea situațiilor date, ***folosind prezent perfect simplu + for.***

Exemplu: Dona got married when she was 23. She is now 32 (marry)
Dona has been married for 9 years.

a) Alex met Dona 3 month ago. (know)
b) The pop concert started at 8 o'clock. It is now 11 o'clock. (last)
c) Dona's husband started playing the guitar at 5 o'clock. It is now 7 o'clock. (practice).
d) The pop band met the new manager last month. They've now still working with him. (work).
e) The singer came in the studio 3 hours ago. (record).

Exercise 13.

Reformulați propozițiile următoare folosind ***prezentul perfect simplu + since***.

Exemplu: The pop singer started singing at 2 o'clock.
The pop singer has sung since 2 o'clock.

a) He last practiced the piano on Sunday.
b) The girls went to the disco last week.
c) The band's last recorded a cassette in December.
d) Dona's husband started listening to rock music last month.
e) Alex met a pop star last year.

Exercise 14.

Completați cu ***FOR*** sau ***SINCE***.

a. He's practiced the violin …………….. noon.
b. Dona has danced ………….. a couple of hours.
c. They've listened to music …………….. one hour.
d. I've tried to tune the piano …………… 2 o'clock.
e. She's had the music box …………… childhood.

Exercise 15.

Răspundeți la întrebări folosind structura ***SINCE + PAST TENSE.*** Cuvintele din paranteză vă ajută să răspundeți.

Exemplu: How long have they danced? (concert, begin)
They've danced since the concert began.

a. How long have they worked together? (meet, new manager)
b. How long has the band recorded? (they, come to the studio)
c. How long haven't you turned your violin? (I, drop it down)
d. How long has the press conference lasted? (the photo session, finish)
e. How long hasn't the orchestra rehearsed. (the conductor, leave)

Exercise 16.

Scrieți câte o propoziție care să exprime rezultatul situației descrise folosind subiectul și verbul sugerate în pranteză.

Exemplu: Many teenagers were in front of the concert hall. (they/enter)
They have entered the concert hall.

a. A new CD by (Tory Amos) is new in the music shops. (the record company/release)
b. The signature of (Laurențiu Cazan) is in my autograph book. (Laurențiu Cazan/sign)
c. The song has new lyrics. (the writer/change)

d. A new walkman is in my room. (we/buy).
e. Adriana looks different (her stylists/design).

Exercise 17.

Scrieţi un paragraf despre cântăreţul/formaţia de muzică pop preferat/preferată, menţionând:

a) locul şi data naşterii,
b) *de cât timp locuieşte la adresa actuală,*
c) *activitatea artistică*: - instrumentele musicale la care cântă, de când;
- melodii, casete, CD înregistrate (nume importante, număr);
- colaborări cu alţi artişti, cântăreţi;
- turnee.
d) *activitatea socială*: - concerte de binefacere, etc.

Exercise 18.

Citiţi şi încercuiţi aspectele despre care discută cei doi tineri:

a. start's life
b. history
c. fans
d. traveling
e. charts

A: What do you think of "Ace of Base?"
B: I like their music, especially "All that she wants." It was a chart topper all over the world.
A: Do you know they produced their songs cheaply? They didn't have any contacts or sponsors.

B: No, I don't, but I know both Marian and Jenny used to sing in a church choir.
A: Isn't it funny? They've never dreamt of their present popularity.
B: Some of their fans are absolutely mad. A German woman has been sent to prison for attacking Jenny.
A: That's awful.
B: And private guards have been hired to protect them such obsessed fans.
A: No wonder Marian is not very keen on having such great success. She likes being popular at home. Besides, she is terrified of flying.
B: That's rather inconvenient for a star.

Exercise 19.

Notaţi T (true) sau F (false) în dreptul următoarelor propoziţii:

	T	F
a) The DJ helps the bands with unloading of the equipment.		
b) A tuneless melody isn't pleasant to listen to.		
c) An award acknowledges the value of a song or band.		
d) A stylist helps artists with their hair and clothes.		
e) Nowadays, a synthesizer is hardly ever used by bands.		

Exercise 20.

Puneţi verbele din paranteză la ***prezentul perfect simplu***.

a) I (not, tune) the piano since the last concert.
b) How long (you, play) the flute?
c) The band (go) on many tours since they began singing together.
d) Their fans (send) them lots of letters for the past months.
e) The orchestra (rehearse) for 2 hours.

Exercise 21.

Traduceţi în limba engleză.

a) Ei cântau împreună de când aveau 18 ani.
b) Mi-au plăcut versurile cântecelor ei.
c) A ascultat aceeaşi muzică asurzitoare de când a venit acasă.
d) În câte turnee aţi fost în ultimul an?
e) Fredonează melodia de câteva minute, dar nu şi-a amintit-o încă.

Exercise 22.

Citiţi lista de activităţi de mai jos. Notaţi □ în dreptul activităţilor pe care le-aţi efectuat şi ◊ în dreptul activităţilor pe care nu le-aţi efectuat. Scrieţi cel puţin 5 propoziţii urmând exemplul de mai jos.

Exemplu: I've never gone on a safari.
I've seldom painted.

go on a safari ◊	playing the piano	mountain climbing
ride bike	acting	ice skating
sail a boat	dancing	playing basketball
go camping	painting □	living
cook pizza	badminton	building a sand castle

Exercise 23.

Răspundeţi la întrebările de mai jos, folosind adverbele de frecvenţă.

Exemplu: Have you ever swim under water?
No, I haven't.
sau Yes, I have. I've sometimes swum under water.

a) Have you ever cooked birthday cakes?
b) Have you ever lost your money?
c) Have you ever met a VIP? (very important person)
d) Have you ever read English books?
e) Have you ever watched English programmer?

Exercise 24.

Alcătuiţi propoziţii după modelul de mai jos!

Exemplu: Dona has never gone fishing.
Alex has often told funny stories.

Activity	Dona					Alex				
	always	often	sometimes	seldom	never	always	often	sometimes	seldom	never
go finishing					□				□	
sing in public	□							□		
make chocolate		□								□
go jogging			□			□				
tell funny stories				□			□			

Exercise 25.

Formulați câte o întrebare pentru situațiile de mai jos, folosind **ever + before:**

Exemplu: A: I'm going to the gym this afternoon.
B: Have you ever gone to the gym before?

a. I'm painting my friend's portrait.
b. I'm going to a rock concert tonight.
c. They're running the Marathon.
d. She is training her dog.
e. Dan is representing our class in the school singing festival.

Exercise 26.

Uniți cu o linie adjectivele din coloana A cu substantivele din coloana B și verbele din coloana C. Alcătuiți propoziții în care prezentul perfect simplu urmează după un adjective la gradul superlativ.

Exemplu: This is the tastiest food I've ever eaten.

A	B	C
interesting	story	wear
expensive	food	meet
strong	newsreel (buletin de știri)	see
amazing	man	watch
boring	film	eat
tasty	dress	hear

Exercise 27.

Traduceți în limba engleză:

a. Este cel mai inteligent elev pe care l-am întâlnit.
b. "Repar radioul astăzi."
"L-ai mai reparat."
c. Ai călătorit vreodată în străinătate?
d. N-am mâncat niciodată melci.
e. Am spus glume rareori.

Exercise 28.

Alcătuiți familia de cuvinte a substantivului "***noise***". Alcătuiți propoziții cu cuvintele obținute.

Exercise 29.

Folosind prezentul perfect simplu, alcătuiți propoziții care să exprime o activitate pe care:

a) nu a-ți efectuat-o niciodată;
b) o efectuați pentru prima dată;
c) ați efectuat-o rareori;
d) o raportați la propria experiență;
e) prietenul/prietena dumneavoastră a efectuat-o deseori.

Exercise 30.

Traduceți în limba română:

a) He has never walked through the woods alone.
b) It's first time I've climbed a tree.
c) She has always told good jokes.
d) She's the kindest person I've ever known.
e) Have you ever gone that far before?

Present Perfect Continuous Tense
(Timpul Prezent Perfect Continuu)

Exercise 1.
Puneți verbele din paranteză la ***Prezentul Perfect Continuu***.

a) She (stick) pictures in her album for an hour.
b) They (talk about) their friends since 3 o'clock.
c) Dana (study) in Toulouse for 3 months.
d) She (experiment) on new materials.
e) She (work) hard for her graduation paper.

Exercise 2.
Transformați propozițiile următoare în enunțuri negative.

a) The professor has been lecturing in their town for a year.
b) The students have been writing their papers since the holidays were over.
c) He has been looking for a 1990 edition of the atlas.
d) Our team has been researching on synthetic materials for years.
e) She has been gathering information for her article for the past weeks.

Exercise 3.
Formulați întrebări pentru propozițiile de mai jos. Cuvintele îngroșate trebuie să fie răspunsul.

a) I've been reading in the library **for 3 hours**.
b) She's been **taking pictures** since she was a child.
c) **They**'re been dating for 3 months.
d) Mr. Ionescu has been giving **lectures** for 10 years.
e) The students have been attending the courses **since the new professor came.**

Exercise 4.
Formulați câte o explicație pe marginea situațiilor de mai jos.

Exemplu: She's tired. **She's been working in the garden.**

a) I cannot find my dictionary.
b) The teacher stopped talking for a moment.
c) We've very wealthy.
d) The dean put the glasses aside.
e) The book are scattered all over the room.

Exercise 5.
Reformulați propozițiile de mai jos folosind Prezentul Perfect Simplu urmat de un numeral.

Exemplu: Dana has been reading in the library since 3 o'clock (5 chapters).
She has read 5 chapters.

a) He has been writing articles for "The Scientist" for 3 years. (scores of articles)

b) Dan has been looking up words in the dictionary for half an hour. (20 words)
c) They've been taking exams for the past month. (4 exams)
d) The committee has been discussing about environment since 2 o'clock. (3 topics)
e) The professor has been examining students for 3 hours. (10 students)

Exercise 6.

Alcătuiţi dialoguri scurte după exemplul următor.

Exemplu: Dana – lab – 3 months – 25 experiments.
A: How long has Dana been working in the lab?
B: She's been working there for 3 months.
A: How many experiments has she made?
B: She's made 25 experiments.

a) Mr. Popovici – University – 10 years – hundreds of lectures.
b) Dona – to take pictures – for years – over 5000.
c) The student – library – 1 hour – almost 50 pages.
d) Mr. David – primary school – 20 years – 5 generations.
e) The teacher – test papers – since 6 o'clock – 15 test papers.

Exercise 7.

Uniţi cuvântul cu definiţia corectă şi apoi formulaţi propoziţii cu verbele la ***Prezentul Perfect Continuu/Simplu***.

1) library	a) discourse before a class on a given topic
2) bibliography	b) head of professors in a University
3) camera	c) room containing books for reading.
4) dean	d) list of books to be read
5) lecture	e) apparatus for taking pictures

Exercise 8.

Răspundeţi la întrebări folosind ***Prezentul Perfect Simplu sau Continuu***.

a) How long have you been here ?
b) What have you been doing?
c) How many letters have you written?
d) Whom have you been writing to?
e) How many letters have you received from them so far?

Exercise 9.

Traduceţi în limba engleză.

a) De când citeşte Alina în camera ei?
b) Scrie lucrarea de diplomă de o jumătate de oră?
c) Caută atlasul acela vechi, din vara trecută.
d) Dona a făcut o mulţime de fotografii până acum.
e) Câte capitole ai scris din noul roman?

Exercise 10.

Înlocuiţi cuvintele scrise cursiv cu verbul **"write"** urmat de **out, down, back, in, up**.

1) The company has *issued* a report on the last year's financial results.
2) I've *corresponded with* the editor-in-chief (redactor-şef).
3) She is *transcribing* the professor's notes.
4) *Put* your name on the paper, please.
5) Haven't you *replied* your aunt's invitation?

Exercise 11.

Completaţi spaţiile libere cu expresiile: at one time, in no time, in time, from time to time, all the time.

a) They visit us ....
b) She's been sitting up ....
c) I can't do both things..................... .
d) The boy came back ....
e) I hope we'll be there ....

Exercise 12.

Răspundeţi la întrebări folosind cuvintele ajutătoare din paranteză.

Exemplu. Why are we running out of space to discharge our garbage in?
Because people have dumped it instead of recycling.

a. Why the vain forests are begin destroyed? (people/cut down/for agriculture)
b. Why are many indigenous people fighting for the rain forests? (they/be/their homes/centuries)
c. Why are governments passing laws for protecting animal species? (many of them/disappeared/Earth)
d. Why is the African elephant an endangered species? (leave/very few specimens)
e. Why is the air polluted? (factories/release/sulfur oxide)
f. Why is the ozone layer becoming thinner? (people/release chemicals/into the atmosphere)
g. Why are the UV rays penetrating to Earth? (ozone layer/become thinner)
h. Why are many fishing zones depleted? (people/catch/to much fish)
i. Why is the dolphin population put at risk (people/catch a lot of tuna)
j. Why is whale hunting forbidden? (people/hunt/near extinction)

Exercise 13.

Citiţi cu atenţie recomandările din această listă. Scrieţi propoziţii pentru a menţiona ce activităţi aţi/nu aţi efectuat până în prezent. Folosiţi ***prezentul perfect continuu***.

Exemplu: I have been using unleaded petrol.
I haven't been using unleaded petrol.

GO GREEN!

So we have convinced you. You want to go green. Here are ten simple things to help you go green.

1. Have your car converted to unleaded petrol.
2. Leave wild flowers alone. - don't dig them up.
3. Take your bottles to the recycling point.
4. Start using recycled products whenever possible.
5. Start checking your sprays; make sure they are ozone – friendly.
6. Start using beauty products than haven't caused cruelty to animals.

7. Visit your health food shop more often – they can be caves Aladdin of chemical free and environment friendly food.
8. Start buying organic foods or grow your own if you can.
9. Start reading labels more carefully.
10. Start protesting and make yourself heard!

Exercise 14.

Alcătuiți propoziții folosind informațiile din tabel. Folosiți prezentul perfect simplu sau continuu. Atenție la topica adverbelor de timp.

Exemplu: 1. People have been assaulting the natural world for years.

No.	Period of time	Subject	Actions
1.	for years	people	assault natural world
2.	since the latter half of the century	radioactive waste	poison the seas and rivers
3.	already	smoke and fumes	pollute the air
4.	up to now	people	destroy many forests and lakes
5.	yet	wildlife	disappear/completely
6.	for centuries	governments	extract the Earth's mineral riches
7.	often	scientific community	warn against the danger
8.	since the'80s	the public opinion	challenge the forces of destruction
9.	always	environment organizations	protest against abuses to environment
10.	lately	their actions	shocked governments

Exercise 15.

Completați propozițiile cu cuvintele întâlnite în această lecție.

a. Greenpeace sent small ……………………… boats to protest against whale hunting.
b. …………….. are the largest marine mammals.
c. The ……………… on whale killing hasn't been lifted yet.
d. Environment organizations aim at making people ………. of the danger they are facing.
e. Some ocean areas have become ………………….. with excessive fishing.
f. Japan ………….. 95% of its bottles and 50% of its aluminum.
g. Garbage …………… areas around cities can damage the land quality.
h. Scientists haven't solved yet the problem of nuclear ……………… which are radioactive.

Exercise 16.

Reformulați propozițiile folosind ***FOR+present perfect continuous.***

Exemplu: I started to work on this case three months ago.
I have been working on this case for three months.
sau
I have been working on this case for the last three months.

a. I started to look for reliable evidence last year.

b. I began to cross-examine a great number of witnesses two weeks ago.
c. Last month I began to talk to more detectives involved in the case.
d. I started to train my own team six months ago.
e. I started to read the witnesses statements three days ago.

Exercise 17.

Folosiţi cuvintele ajutătoare şi alcătuiţi scurte dialoguri conform modelului.

Exemplu: C. Auguste Dupin – lose most of his fortune – collect rare books.
What has C. Auguste Dupin been doing since he lost most of his fortune?
He has been collecting rare books.

a. Dupin ____ make the writer's acquaintance – live in reclusion (izolare).
b. Dupin ____ down – read or write
c. Dupin ____ start walking – talk about horses.
d. Dupin ____ arrive in the Rue Morgue – examine the scene carefully.
e. The sailor – come – give an account of the events.

Exercise 18.

Completaţi propoziţiile cu ***SINCE*** sau ***FOR***:

a. The police inspector has been reading the reports _______ he came.
b. The police have been looking for him ________ over a year now.
c. The witness has been writing his statement ________ half an hour.
d. The expert has been talking to the accused ________ 3 o'clock.
e. He has been watching his victim _______ the last three months.

Exercise 19.

Scrieţi întrebările pentru un interogatoriu folosind ***prezentul perfect continuu*** şi cuvintele date.

Model: work together
How long have you been working together?

a. wear a beard
b. send threatening letters
c. plan the murder
d. train yourself
e. hide in the country

Exercise 20.

Răspundeţi la întrebări argumentând o stare prezentă de lucruri.

Model: Why have you got mud on your shoes?
Because I have been working in the garden.

a. Why are you hands dirty?
b. Why are you panting (a respira cu greutate)?
c. Why are you wearing this black overall?
d. Why are you burning these letters?
e. Why are you got stains on your shirt?

Future Continuous and Future Perfect
(Timpul Viitor Continuu si Viitorul Perfect)

Exercise 1.

Citiţi agenda unui cosmonaut pentru ziua următoare şi alcătuiţi propoziţii conform modelului. Agenda cuprinde notiţe în forma prescurtată.

Model: Fax NASA with details of conference.
At 8:30 he will be faxing NASA with the details of the conference.

AM		PM	
8:30	fax NASA with details of conference	**12:30**	read and interpret results
9:00	go to see dietician	**13:00**	lunch with crew
9:30	training	**14:30**	speech at junior school
10:00	training	**17:00**	meet Professor Smith from Physics Department discuss results
10:30	training	**18:00**	medical check-up at the health centre
11:00	training	**19:00**	jog with Mike
11:30	experiments gravitational field	**20:00**	talk to Sally (school)

Exercise 2.

Ce vor realiza oamenii până în 2100? Citiţi lista de mai jos şi bifaţi realizările ce vor fi fost înfăptuite până atunci. Alcătuiţi propoziţii conform modelului.

Model: By the year 2100 people ***will have built a lab on the Moon.***
By the year 2100 people ***won't have contacted other life forms***.

1. build a lab on Moon
2. contact other life forms
3. reach the edges of the known universe
4. discover stars that might host planetary systems
5. design more powerful telescopes
6. study the Asteroid Belt
7. produce new materials
8. use microchips for storing any information
9. understand the reaction of plants to microgravity
10. build space stations around Mars.

Exercise 3.

Pentru accentuarea unei idei, topica obişnuită nu mai este respectată şi auxiliarul ocupă locul dinaintea subiectului.

adv. **aux.1** **S.** **aux.2** **V.**

When the solar wind can **no longer** be detected will Pionner 10 have truly reached the interstellar space.

Accentuaţi adverbele sau locuţiunile subliniate, aşezându-l la începutul propoziţiei. Efectuaţi orice alte schimbări necesare.

a. Space shuttle missions were postponed ***indefinitely*** while NASA set out to design a space shuttle for safety.
b. Apollo 11 ***dramatically*** achieved America's goal to walk on the Moon.
c. A human being had ***never*** traveled in space around the Earth before Juri Gagarin did it in 1961.
d. A space station will serve ***permanently*** as an orbiting scientific laboratory.
e. The outer planets have changed ***little*** since they were formed.

Exercise 4.

Completați forma de viitor corespunzătoate (*continuu sau perfect*) a verbelor din paranteză.

a. By the middle of the 21th century we ____________ (build) space stations orbiting the Earth.
b. These space stations ___________ (circle) the Moon, too.
c. We ___________ (establish) sky labs on planets likeMars.
d. Lots of radars _____________ (watch) nearly 8,000 objects in space.
e. The objects flying around the Earth ____________ (increase) in number by the year 2050.

Exercise 5.

Uniți propozițiile cu explicațiile corespunzătoare.

1. I'm exhausted. I think I'***ll take*** a couple of days off.
2. New means of transport ***will be implemented*** in the near future.
3. She's going to buy train tickets.
4. The back-up system has failed. The two trains ***are going*** to crash.
5. We'***re visiting*** the tower tomorrow afternoon.
6. The train leaves the station at 8:00 and ***reaches*** London an hour later.
7. I'***ll be touring*** London this time next month.
8. Don't worry! The budget for the new railway ***will have been approved*** by the time the commission arrives.
9. Mr. Smith **will have been working** as a test pilot for 25 years by the time he retires.

a. an interdiction to do something
b. personal arrangements for the future
c. a prediction about the future
d. information about a fixed timetable
e. an action in progress at a certain moment in the future
f. a decision made on spot
g. there is evidence that something will happen
h. the duration of an action up to a certain time in the future
i. an action completed within a time period related to a moment in the future

Exercise 6.

Răspundeți la întrebări folosind forma de viitor corespunzătoare.

a. What are you plans for the weekend?
b. What will you have done by the end of this year?
c. What will you are doing this time next week?

d. What is your prediction about your career?
e. What do you intend to do to improve your lifestyle?

Exercise 7.

Puneți verbele din paranteză la ***timpul viitor*** cerut de context.

1. Before you ______ (go) on a trip, there are a few things you should bear in mind.
2. I'm sure ___________ (agree) to explain to us how this new engine works.
3. He's sure his parents __________ (buy) him a car by the time he graduates.
4. They __________ (travel) around the world for 60 days by the end of this month.
5. I can't join you because I _________ (drive) my aunt to the station this afternoon.
6. How ___________ (travel) people in a hundred year's time?
7. What time __________ (take off) the plane?
8. "I'm sorry I can't stay longer. I'm in a hurry."
   "I __________ (give) you a lift."

Exercise 8.

Translate into English.

a. O să-i vorbesc despre proiect când îl văd.
b. Mâine duc eu copiii la școală cu mașina.
c. Rețeaua de drumuri va fi substanțial îmbunătățită.
d. Delegația sosește la aeroport la ora unu.
e. Mâine la ora asta mă voi întâlni cu noul director de program.
f. E târziu și mașina e stricată. Voi lua un taxi.
g. Până la sfârșitul anului drumurile rurale vor fi modernizate.
h. Micșorează viteza. Mașina va derapa pe drumul alunecos.

Exercise 9.

Uniți propozițiile din coloana A cu funcțiile enumerate în coloana B. Primul răspuns a fost completat ca model.

1. The weather forecast says we'll have a thunderstorm tomorrow.	personal arrangement
2. I'll send you a present.	making a promise
3. The office opens at 9:00 a.m.	making a prediction
4. I'm visiting my relatives this Sunday.	expressing intention
5. They're going to move into a flat.	unalterable timetable

Exercise 10.

Formulați întrebări pentru răspunsurile de mai jos.

Model: On September 1st.
When will the conference take place?

a. Yes, you'll meet some of your friends.
b. In the garden.
c. Yes there'll be a barbeque.
d. Elena will (help me).
e. Yes, you'll be able to dance.

Exercise 11.

Formulaţi propoziţii care să exprime acţiuni viitoare pornind de la cauze existente în prezent.

Model: The sky is cloudy.
It's going to rain.

a. Dana is shutting the computer down.
b. Ionut buying more food and drink than usual.
c. They are covering the furniture.
d. I'm very tired.
e. He is ringing up his girl-friend.

Exercise 12.

Puneţi verbele din paranteză la forma de viitor corespunzătoare pentru a exprima o acţiune viitoare (*future simple*) sau o intenţie ("*going to*" future).

a. "Why are you carrying those books?" "I (study) for my exams.
b. "I (call) you if I need any help."
c. "Are you sure she (come)?"
d. "If you (smoke), please, open the window."
e. "They (visit) us next weeks."

Exercise 13.

Folosiţi informaţiile din tabel şi alcătuiţi propoziţii conform modelului.

Model: Jim is giving a house – warming party next weekend.
He is going to invite a lot of people.
They'll dance in the garden if the weather is fine.

1. ARRANGEMENTS	2. INTENTIONS	3 a) If he weather is fine
-give a house-warming party -re-arrange the furniture; -meet a chef for advice; -send invitation letters.	-invite a lot of friends; -entertain his guests; -play his new CD; -ask each guest to tell a joke.	-dance in the garden; -have a barbecue in the garden **3. b) As soon as the guests arrive.** -serve cold drinks; -introduce them to one another.

Exercise 14.

Traduceţi în limba engleză.

a. Când îţi vei reamenaja locuinţa?
b. Voi vorbi cu ea de îndată ce va deschide scrisoarea.
c. Rămâneţi multă vreme la noi?
d. Am de gând să invit toţi prietenii mei.
e. Prima sesiune de examene începe în ianuarie.
f. Dacă vei folosi culori deschise, casa va fi mai luminoasă.
g. Familia Smith pleacă în excursie sâmbătă.

Exercise 15.

Intenţionaţi să daţi o petrecere pentru a sărbători un eveniment fericit. Scrieţi o scrisoare în care să menţionaţi clar folosind forma de viitor corespunzătoare, planurile Dvs. referitoare la:

- locul şi timpul petrecerii;
- felul acesteia;
- mâncare/băutură ce urmează să fie servite;
- organizare.

***Language notes*:**	your arrangements	- I'm giving a party ....
	your plans	- I'm going to invite/spend ....
		- I've arranged to ....
		- I'm planning to ....
		- I'm thinking of ....
	timetable	- The workday finishes at ....
		- Taxis arrive ....
		- Shop open at ....
	hopes and desires	- I hope we will ....
		- I'd like to / I want to ....
		- One thing I'd like to arrange is to ....

Exercise 16.

Puneţi verbele din paranteză la forma de ***viitor corespunzătoare***.

a. Florin (graduate) from university next year.
b. I (phone) you as soon as I (get) to Paris.
c. I'm not feeling too well so I (spend) the evening indoors.
d. The next elections (take place) in the year 2000.
e. We (come back) from holiday next Sunday.

Exercise 17.

Completaţi propoziţiile cu verbele corespunzătoare la ***prezentul simplu*** sau ***continuu*** pentru exprimarea unor acţiuni viitoare.

a. The plane _______________ off at 16:45.
b. I _________________ an exam in English next week.
c. Examinations __________________ place at the end of July.
d. He _____________ abroad this month.
e. A new training programme ________________ every other month.
f. They _____________ a training programme this month.

Simple Past vs. Perfect Present
(Trecutul Simplu Vs. Prezent Perfect)

Exercise 1.

Puneţi verbele din paranteză la *timpul trecut* sau *prezent perfect*.

Exemplu: Dona and Alex .... the report (finish)
They .... the report yesterday.
Dona and Alex **have finished** the report.
They **finished** the report yesterday.

a) Florin ....them the tables. (give)
He ....the tables two days ago.
b) Tina .... further information (add).
She .... further information last week.
c) They ....about the report (talk).
They ....about it with the manger two hours ago.
d) The manger ....a meeting to discuss the report (hold).
He ....the meeting early in the morning.
e) Everybody...........the meeting.(attend)
They ....the meeting at 8 o'clock.

Exercise 2.

Completaţi dialogul după exemplu:

Exemplu: Have they seen the manger?
Yes, they have.
When did they see him?
They saw him at 8 o'clock.

a) Have you had the coffee break yet?
....
When did you have it?
....

b) Have they repaired the photocopier?
....
Who repaired it?
....

c) Has Diana drawn the graphs?
....
When did she draw them?
....

d) Have you managed by yourself?
....
What did you do?
....

e) Have you seen Florin?

....

How long ago did you see him?

....

Exercise 3.

Încercuiţi răspunsul corect.

a) Alex had a meeting with the new client *so far / yesterday.*
b) The market has enlarged *for the past months / last year.*
c) The manager has read the report *by now / two hours ago.*
d) The manger has promoted Dona and Alex *recently / last month.*
e) Their colleagues congratulated them *when they heard the news / recently.*

Exercise 4.

Citiţi CV-ul (curriculum vitae) lui Alex. Alcătuiţi propoziţii folosind:

a) **trecutul simplu** pentru exprimarea acţiunilor effectuate într-o perioadă de timp specificată
b) **prezentul perfect** pentru exprimarea acţiunilor care descriu experienţa lui Alex până în prezent.

Age	: 33
1985-1989	: graduation from the University in Leeds, studies in Economics;
1989-1994	: job with A & B Ltd:
1995	: teaching evening classes in a state school;
1996	: contributor to "The Economist"
1996.1998	: director of a local youth club;
Jan 1998	: Romanian branch of A & B Ltd; Manager Assistant.

Exemplu: a) He was born in 1965. He graduated the University in 1985. He studied .... from .... to .... After that, he ....

b) He has studied Economy. He has ....

Exercise 5.

Puneţi verbele din paranteză la ***prezent perfect simplu / continuu*** sau ***trecut simplu***.

a) Alex (make) a lot of friends since he (come) in Romania.
b) He (learn) several Romanian words so far.
c) He (take) Romanian lessons with Dona.
d) That (help) him a lot.
e) He (buy) an English-Romanian dictionary some time ago.

Exercise 6.

Traduceţi în limba engleză:

a) Cât timp aţi lucrat împreună?
b) Scrie raportul de când a venit la birou.
c) În tinereţe a lucrat în străinătate timp de doi ani.

d) A lucrat aici doi ani.
e) Nu am primit răspunsul la scrisoare.

Exercise 7.

Tăiaţi cu o linie cuvântul care nu se potriveşte cu celelalte.

a) write, spell, type, read;
b) timetable, action, agenda, programme;
c) typewrite, computer, letter, photocopier;
d) ago, recently, lately, so far;
e) repair, break, fix, mend.

Exercise 8.

Uniţi cuvintele cu definiţiile din dreapta. Formulaţi propoziţii cu cuvintele din stânga, făcând orice alte schimbări necesare.

1. sport	a. playful
2. challenge	b. a small sign against an item in a list
3. sportful	c. housework
4. chore	d. amusement / fun
5. tickmark	e. invite to a contest / game

Exercise 9.

Înlocuiţi cuvintele subliniate cu sinonimele lor: *made sport of, was in for, takes exercise, sayings, healthy.*

a) The old *proverbs* are a treasure of wisdom.
b) My grannie is 80, but she is in a *perfect condition.*
c) The football team *trains* daily.
d) He was too short and the others *made fun* of him
e) When he was younger, he *participated* in the Marathon race.

Modal Verbs
(Verbele Modale)

A. Can - expressing ability

Exercise 1.

Scrieţi o propoziţie pentru fiecare situaţie de mai jos conform exemplului:

Exemplu: Dona has studied English.
She can speak English.

a) Alex is on the football ground.
b) My radio set is working again.
c) Mirela is attending the art school.
d) The boy is on horseback.
e) We are going to the skating rink.

Exercise 2.

Procedaţi la fel ca în exerciţiul 1, dar de data aceasta scrieţi comentarii negative. Folosiţi **forma negativă contrasă** (scurtă).

Exemplu: There are a lot of spelling mistakes in her composition.
She can't write English.

a) Paul has been trying to solve that problem for two hours.
b) You have no ear for music.
c) They don't practice their English enough.
d) Her soup tastes bad.
e) These pictures don't show anything.

Exercise 3.

Formulaţi întrebări folosind cuvintele de mai jos.

Exemplu: You/change a fuse (siguranţă).
Can you change a fuse?

a) Your son/dive/in deep water.
b) You/draw/portraits.
c) They/play/chess.
d) Mirela/make/pancakes.
e) Dona/knit/a pullover.

Exercise 4.

Alcătuiţi cinci propoziţii completând tabelul de mai jos. Prima propoziţie a fost scrisă ca model.

Nr.	Who (subiect)	can	do (verb)	what (complement direct)	how (compelemnt de mod)
1.	I	can	speak	English	quite well.
2.					
3.					
4.					
5.					
6.					

Exercise 5.

Scrieţi propoziţii cu "**can/could**" despre persoanele menţionate mai jos. Folosiţi verbele următoare, la care adăugaţi complementele corespunzătoare (folosiţi topica de la exerciţiul anterior).

dance, play (an instrument), dance, sing, play (sports), paint, act, rule a people, discover, write, suppose.

Exemplu: k) Adrian could discover new physical lows.
e) Florin can rule a people powerfully.

can	**could**
a) Robert	f) Cristi
b) Florin	g) George
c) Dan	h) Nicu
d) Dana	i) Marian
e) Petre	j) Robert

Exercise 6.

Dona ştie limbile străine menţionate în tabelul de mai jos. Citiţi cu atenţie şi interpretaţi conform grilei alăturate. Completaţi propoziţiile. Prima propoziţie constituie model:

	English	**French**	**Italian**
Reading	4	3	3
Writing	3	2	1
Listening	4	4	2
Speaking	3	3	3

1 = hardly at all
2 = not very well
3 = well
4 = very well

a) She **can** read English very well, but she **can** speak it well.
b) She …… writes French very well, but she …….. understand it very well.
c) She …… understand English and French very well, but she ……. understand Italian very well.
d) She …… speaks French and Italian as well as she …….. speak English.
e) She …… can read French as well as she ….. speak it.
f) She …… writes English better than she ……. write French and Italian.

Exercise 7.

Formulaţi propoziţii cu cuvintele ajutătoare. Folosiţi "**could**" pentru exprimarea abilitaţii de durată în trecut şi "**was**"/"**were able to**" pentru exprimarea unei realizări trecute de scurtă durată.

Exemplu: speak English / ask for her way.
She **could** speak English, so she *was able to* ask for her way.

a) climb trees / rescue the little boy;
b) use a computer / edit the text;
c) understand difficult problems / pass the examination;
d) remember people's name / identify the baby-sitter;
e) play the piano / give a charity concert.

Exercise 8.

Scrieţi propoziţii cu "**shall**" / "**will be able to**" pentru a exprima o realizare viitoare.

Exemplu: I am attending a computer course this month.
I shall be able to use a computer.

a) I am taking French lesson this year.
b) Alex is going to Italy for holidays.
c) Dona is helping her children with their Maths problems.
d) Grannie is showing me how to knit.
e) The coach is training his team harder than before.

Exercise 9.

Pentru accentuarea ideii de efort sau reuşită, înlocuiţi "**be able to**" cu "**manage to**" sau "**succeed in + -ing**" la timpul şi persoana menţionate în propoziţie.

Exemplu: Sorin was able to climb to that mountain peak (vârf muntos).
1. Sorin managed to climb to that mountain peak.
2. Sorin succeed in climbing to that mountain peak.

a) Dona was able to persuade (a convinge) Alex.
b) How were you able to survive?
c) Mihai was able to decipher the code.
d) Alex wasn't able to finish the race.
e) The students were able to solve the equation.

Exercise 10.

Traduceţi în limba engleză. Folosiţi "**can**" / "**could**" / "**be able to**" / "**manage**" / "**succeede in**":

a) Marius ştie să joace şah foarte bine.
b) Pentru că înota bine, el a putut să salveze un băieţel de la înec. (to rescue from drowning)
c) Florin a reuşit să îmblânzească acel cal sălbatic. (to tame)
d) Ea ia lecţii de patinaj, deci va putea patina.
e) Ştii să cânţi la pian?
f) Au trecut două săptămâni. Aţi reuşit să găsiţi o soluţie?

Exercise 11.

Citiţiţi situaţiile şi scrieţi comentarii folosind CAN pentru exprimarea abilităţii de durată.

Exemplu: a) Mihai has been studying English for five years. (speak)
He can speak English.
b) You have no talent for poetry. (write)
You can't write poems.

a. My students find the theory of relativity difficult (understand).
b. Andrei has written an interesting essay on Romantic poetry. (comment)
c. Professor Brown has extensive knowledge about post-war economics. (lecture)
d. Miss Alice knows how to use the electronic analyzer. (demonstrate).
e. Freshers sometimes have difficulties in adjusting themselves to university life. (adapt)

Exercise 12.

Alcătuiţiţi propoziţii pentru a exprima o încercare reuşită în trecut, prezent şi viitor.

Exemplu: speak English fluently – explain the situation
a) He speaks English fluently so he will be able to explain the situation.
b) He speaks English fluently so he is able to explain the situation.
c) He spoke English fluently so he was able to explain the situation.

a. solve difficult algebraic exercises – teach me
b. manage critical situations – advice me
c. explain abstract notions simply – help me understand philosophy
d. read a score (partitură) – play the musical piece
e. draw accurately – win the first prize

Exercise 13.

Reformulaţi propoziţiile folosind MANAGE TO, care este mai puţin formal decât BE ABLE TO. Atenţie la forma verbală!

Exemplu: The chemistry problem was too difficult. (Florin/solve)
Florin didn't manage to solve the chemistry problem.

a. The conference in held in English. (Irina/translate)
b. You need a little French to ask your way. (they/get to Louvre)
c. The traffic was heavy. (Professor Brown/arrive in time)
d. This theory is too complicated. (I/understand)
e. He has finished the experiments for a new cure. (He/discover)

Exercise 14.

Solicitaţi permisiunea formal sau informal. Primele două exemple au fost rezolvate ca model.

1. You want to borrow your colleague's notes: *Can I borrow your notes?*
2. You want to work under professor Smart's guidance: *Would you mind if I worked with you?*
3. You want to leave the literature course earlier: ....
4. You want to use the laboratory of the university for your research: ....
5. You need a word processor and your friend has got one: ....
6. You want to quote (a cita) your professor in a paper on history: ....

7. You want your parent's car for a drive in the country: ………………………………

Exercise 15.

Completați particula potrivită pentru a obține propoziții logice.

a. Film critics wrote ………..…. the performance of the leading actors.
b. The computer was completely written ………… .
c. I would write her ………… as a hypocrite.
d. She is now writing ………..…. a detailed article on academic assessment.
e. Later, he wrote the story outline …………… in a three-act play.
f. Do you mind writing …..…….. your educational background?
g. Finally she admitted to write ……………... the years spent abroad.

Exercise 16.

Completați propozițiile astfel încât să exprime abilitatea (de durată sau temporară) și permisiunea.

a. He ………..… read Japanese so he …..……… to translate this haiku for you.
b. Father says you ………….…… bring your friends here.
c. The questions were too difficult. I ………….. to answer only half of them.
d. ………….. you ……………. joining our team for the project?
e. The children were so frightened that she …….. say a word.
f. ………….. he …………….. if I wrote an article about his activity?

B. May - expressing permission

Exercise 17.

Reformulați propozițiile următoare folosind "***may***" urmat de verbul din propoziție.

Exemplu: I sometimes ride my brother's bike.
I may ride my brother's bike.

a) She watches late TV programs.
b) He drives his father's car.
c) I buy whatever I want.
d) They sometimes come home at 11 p.m.
e) She often listens to loud music.
f) Your daughter is wearing a mini skirt.

Exercise 18.

Citiți situațiile descrise mai jos. Formulați întrebări pentru solicitarea permisiunii în mod formal.

Exemplu: You want to borrow your friend's car.
May I borrow your car?

a) Your colleague is reading the newspaper. You want to have a look at the headlines.
b) You want to use your sister's calculator.
c) Your aunt has cooked some delicious cakes. You want one more.
d) You have been standing and want to have a sit.
e) You are at your friend's place and want to make a phone call.

f) You want to watch TV, but the TV set is off.

Exercise 19.

Completați propozițiile de mai jos folosind **"might / might not"** după un verb la trecut.

Exemplu. It was late, so Dona's daughter might not watch TV.

a) The camera wasn't too expensive, so her mother said she ....
b) When I was 10, I ....
c) Grandma felt better, so the children ....
d) The manager was busy, so Dona ....
e) She passed a difficult examination, so she ....

Exercise 20.

Fetița Donei are 7 ani și nu are voie să facă o mulțime de lucruri. Ce va putea face când va avea 18 ani? Scrieți propoziții cu **"to be allowed to"** la viitor folosind sugestiile de mai jos.

Exemplu: She'll be allowed to vote

When people come of age[1] they:

- vote;
- get a driving license;
- get married without their parent's consent[2] ;
- drink alcohol in public places;
- get a full-time job;
- have a say[3] in family matters;
- join a party[4];
- adopt children;
- make use of an inheritance[5].

[1] – a deveni majori, a împlini vârsta de 18 ani.
[2] – acord, consimțământ
[3] – a avea un cuvânt de spus
[4] – partid
[5] - moștenire

Exercise 21.

Aveți ocazia să plecați la mare în mod neașteptat. Pentru că nu sunteți pregătit, rugați pe unul din prieteni să vă împrumute unele lucruri de care aveți nevoie:

- sunglasses	- sun lotion
- sun hat	- T-short
- suitcase	-money

a) ....
b) ....
c) ....
d) ....
e) ....

Exercise 22.

Completați particula corespunzătoare.

after, on, away, off, up to, out, at, for, in

a) Father is …….. now. Can you call later?
b) I can hear voices. Is the TV………. ?
c) Will you be ……… foot the whole summer?
d) We've done everything possible. Now, it is ……….. you.
e) Is Mr. Ionescu ………..? I have an appointment with him.
f) I can't see anything. The light is ………
g) The manager isn't ………….. her promotion.
h) "He doesn't love you." "What is he ……… then?"

Exercise 23.

Uniți cuvântul cu sinonimul corespunzător, conform modelului. Alcătuiți propoziții cu cuvintele din dreapta.

1. straight	a. notice
2. hasty	b. next to
3. irritation	c. directly
4. perceive	d. being annoyed
5. pushy	e. hurried
6. by	f. insistent

Exercise 24.

Citiți cu atenție situațiile de mai jos. Ce se poate întâmpla? Folosiți ***MAY*** pentru a exprima posibilitatea.

Exemplu: You're standing in a drafty place.
You may catch a cold.

1. The handle of the pot is hot.
2. The floor is too wet to walk on.
3. Your friend is working overtime again.
4. Your arms and legs itch.
5. Don't eat that fast!
6. Fix the ladder first!
7. Don't carry heavy boxes!

C. Must - expressing obligation, necessity, interdiction.

Exercise 25.

Alcătuiți propoziții cu "***must***"/"***must not***" pentru exprimarea obligației/interdicției. Folosiți verbele de mai jos:

turn round	stop	put up campfires	drink/eat
go straight	take photos	keep dry	go faster than
overtake	turn left	slow down	turn right

Exercise 26.

Scrieți comentarii folosind " **needn't**" pentru a exprima un fapt a cărui realizare nu este necesară.

Exemplu. "I'll wait for you, too"
"You needn't. I'll be back by 11 o'clock."

a) Can you tell me what disco you're going to?
b) My husband will come to take you from the disco.
c) I don't want to argue with you.
d) I'm worried about you.
e) I'll ring up your parents.

Exercise 27.

Formulați întrebări folosind "**need I / you**" și verble din paranteză. Dați răspunsuri scurte.

Exemplu. I'm 18. (show my ID*)
Need I show you my ID?

a) I can't find my bag.	(look for)
b) The show finishes late.	(come to take)
c) Our secretary is on holidays.	(type the letter)
d) I have a lot to work tomorrow morning.	(get up earlier)
e) I'm afraid of dark.	(come with)

* ID – identification card – buletin de identitate

Exercise 28.

Citiți agenda Alinei pentru săptămâna în curs. Formulați propoziții cu "**have to**" pentru a exprima obligația internă.

Exemplu:	exam	I have to study for the exam.

a) visit my aunt in hospital	....
b) meet the English teacher	....
c) clean my room.	....
d) arrange the books in the bookcase	....
e) buy train tickets	....

Exercise 29.

Scrieți comentarii folosind "***will have to***" și verbele din paranteză.

Exemplu. The baby is sleepy. (take to bed)
I'll have to take him to bed.

a) The exam is next week. (finish studying)
b) Your English is not fluent. (practice talking)
c) It's dangerous to go to discos alone. (go with you)
d) There's no more coffee. (buy)
e) Grannie isn't feeling well. (call a doctor)

Exercise 30.

Completați propozițiile cu *"**must**"/"**need**"/"**have to**"* și verbele din paranteză pentru a exprima ideea menționată în paranteză.

Exemplu: After the test,………. (write down your names – future obligation)

After the test, you'll have to write down your names.

a) She didn't watch the film because ………… (study – past obligation)
b) She isn't 18, so ………… (accompany – necessity)
c) The rules are clear: you ……… (leave the manual here – internal obligation)
d) It's too far, so ………… (take a taxi – future necessity)

Exercise 31.

Înlocuiți spațiile libere cu următoarele cuvinte: ***pushy, irritation, straight, hasty, perceived.***

a) There was ……… in her voice.
b) Dona …………… a difference in colour.
c) You get what you want if you are …………… enough.
d) Alina must come ………… home.
e) Young people are generally …………….. .

Exercise 32.

Completați "***must***"/"***need***"/"***have to***" la timpul și forma potrivită.

a) Children …………….. obey their parents.
b) …………….. I always do as you like?
c) …………… she ………….. buy some more sugar.
d) She …………… walk to the disco. Florin is driving her there.
e) Alina ……………… baby-sit because Dona was in.
f) Hurry up or else we ……………… take a taxi.
g) Water is too deep. You …………….. swim here.

Exercise 33.

Traduceți în limba engleză:

a) Trebuie să fiu la școală la ora 8 în fiecare dimineață.
b) A trebuit să îl ajut pentru că nu știa răspunsul.
c) Am luat eu pâine. Nu va trebui să cumperi și tu.
d) – E nevoie să-ți suni părinții de fiecare dată când întârzii?
– Nu, nu e nevoie.
e) Nu e nevoie să traduceți. Vorbesc engleza.
f) Nimeni nu trebuie să intre în laborator.

Exercise 34.

Citiți cu atenție sfaturile pe care le dă un antrenor în cazul efortului excesiv. Reformulați aceste sfaturi folosind ***MUST*** pentru a exprima obligația impusă din exterior. Prima propoziție a fost formulată ca model.

Always ***do*** a series of gentle stretching exercise before and after an intensive workout.	*You must do a series of gentle stretching exercises.*
If you ***rest*** between exercises, make it more than 30 seconds.	
Always ***exercise*** with a definite workout plan in mind.	

Don't exercise at maximum intensity all the time.	
Be careful with recent injuries: exercise can easily aggravate them.	
Allow the injured part to rest each day.	
Don't set yourself unrealistic targets; work up to what you want to do gradually.	
Don't do advanced workouts before you are physically ready.	

Exercise 35.

Comentaţi pe marginea chestionarului de autoevaluare a capacităţii fizice folosind modelul ***HAVE TO*** pentru a exprima obligaţia care decurge dintr-o situaţie particulară. Primul comentariu a fost scris ca model.

SELF-ASSESSMENT

1. Do you take regular exercise?	I have to take more regular exercise.
2. Do you spend some of your time doing physical activity?	
3. Do you avoid unhealthy food?	
4. Are you overweight?	
5. Have you got a good posture?	
6. Are you deskbound (ţintuit de birou) at work?	
7. Are you armchair bound at home?	

Exercise 36.

Alcătuiţi scurte dialoguri conform exemplului.

Exemplu: lose weight
Do I have to lose weight?
A) No, you don't have to, but you would look better.
B) Yes, you have to because you are rather fat.

a. invest in gym equipment;
b. train for an extended period;
c. take dance lesson;
d. hire a personal trainer;
e. learn relaxation techniques;
f. do muscle-stretching exercises.

Exercise 37.

Motivaţi enunţurile.

a. You must go to the gym because ....
b. I have to lose weight. That's the reason why ....
c. You mustn't start with a strenuous programme because ....
d. Take regular exercise as ....
e. She doesn't have to work out that much because ....

Exercise 38.

Completaţi propoziţiile cu cuvintele învăţate în această lecţie.

a. She has got the medical .... in my radio programme.
b. People must go to the doctor's for a regular ....
c. Please, ... the card with the information required.
d. The .... operation lasted for about three hours.
e. Attending fitness classes regularly .... motivation.
f. Her trainer created a moderate .... for her own needs.
g. Straighten your back! that's not the right ....

Exercise 39.

Completaţi propoziţiile cu cuvintele care lipsesc. Alegeţi dintre: ***hand, brains, guts, heels, fist, foot, skeleton, shoulders, arm.***

a. You put your .... in it when you said she was growing old.
b. His books is based on first .... experience.
c. Tell him not to come back. I hate his ....
d. Why are you this sensitive. Have you got any .... in the closet.
e. They have fallen in love head over ....

Exercise 40.

Completaţi particula adverbială corespunzătoare: after, ***for, in, off, out, over, to, up.***

a. Who is taking .... the business when you retire?
b. In the beginning I took it .... a bear.
c. I think the boy takes .... his father.
d. It's too difficult for me. I have to read it again and again to take the information ....
e. Young man, take .... your hat when you're talking to a woman.

D. Exerciţii recapitulative

Exercise 41.

Citiţi propoziţiile de mai jos. Care ar putea fi problema? Folosiţi ***MIGHT/COULD*** pentru a exprima o posibilitate mai redusă.

Exemplu: Dona's burn doesn't look good.
The pain might/could increase.

1. You look very weak.
2. She look as though she's going to faint.
3. The doctor appears confident of the new medicine.
4. She looks as if she's going to cry.
5. Her parents seem very worried.

Exercise 42.

Formulaţi propoziţii folosind cuvintele ajutătoare şi verbul *might* pentru a exprima o posibilitate redusă cu referire la viitor.

Exemplu: ointment – I – use my hand again
Without that ointment I might not use my hand again.

1. syrup – my cough – relieve;
2. gargle – the soprano – sing;
3. health insurance – grannies – pay for the cure;
4. antidote – the venom – damage his brain;
5. the family's help – the patient – overcome this critical moment.

Exercise 43.

Scrieţi comentarii conform modelului pentru a exprima imposibilitatea cu referire la prezent.

Exemplu: I talked to him an hour ago.
He *cannot be in hospital.*

1. I've seen the surgeon at work. He ....
2. You're not coughing and your throat is O.K. You ....
3. Let's take the baby to the nearest hospital. It ....
4. The first aid kit is on your left hand. You ....
5. He hasn't studied medicine. He ....

Exercise 44.

Ce se poate întâmpla dacă sfaturile de mai jos nu sunt urmate?

Exemplu: Don't eat that much ice-cream. *You can have a sore throat.*

1. Don't hold the book that close to your eyes!
2. Put on warmer clothes!
3. Wear protection gloves!
4. Don't climb too many steps at one time!
5. Go on a diet!

Exercise 45.

Răspudeţi la întrebări exprimând nesiguranţa în legătură cu acţiunile respective.

Exemplu: Where's Dona?
She could be at the doctor's.

1. Where have you put the first aid kit?
2. Why does is still hurt?
3. What time does the chemist's close?
4. How does the new therapy help?
5. When does the pain stop?

Exercise 46.

Citiţi simptomele de mai jos şi scrieţi ce probleme au pacienţii respectivi. Folosiţi unele din următoarele cuvinte: flu, indigestion, food poisoning, rheumatism, insomnia, cough, nervous breakdown, overworking. Puteţi folosi şi dicţionarul.

Exemplu: temperature, sore throat, running nose – It must be flu.

1. sadness, tiredness, quietness ....
2. backache, cannot lift weights, cannot bend ....
3. headaches, dizziness ....
4. throw up, stomach ache ....
5. cannot sleep at night ....

Exercise 47.

Aşezaţi replicile dialogului în ordine, astfel încât să obţineţi un schimb de replica coerent.

a) A: No, it wasn't. The redness has become more and more intense. And so has the pain.
b) A: I've burn myself and there is a large red spot on my hand.
c) A: What do you advice?
d) B: It appears to be a serious burn.
e) B: Was the spot that large from the beginning.
f) B: Take this prescription to the chemist's and follows it strictly.

Exercise 48.

Ce exprimă enunţurile de mai jos? Notaţi C (certainty), P(possibility), I(impossibility).

a. You must have flu. ....
b. She can't be that ill. ....
c. "Don't wait for me. I might drop by the hospital to see her." ....
d. The wrist could be sprained. ....
e. Be more cautious. You may catch a virus. ....

Exercise 49.

Completaţi MAY/MIGHT, CAN/COULD, MUST la afirmativ sau negaativ.

a. The lights are off. They .... be at home.
b. Eat more carefully! You .... make an indigestion.
c. Look into the kit. It .... be there.
d. She .... never do this. She's too honest.
e. "Are you sure it was her voice?"
"It ...."
f. Put on one more sweater. It .... be cold in April.

Exercise 50.

Menţionaţi ce exprimă verbele modale din fiecare dintre propoziţiile date. Primul exerciţiu a fost rezolvat ca exemplu.

a. Her fiancé **can** speak three foreign languages fluently. ability
b. We **may** go to the seaside on our honeymoon. ....
c. Look at her! You **must** be very proud of you daughter . ...
d. **Need I** come with you to the hairdresser's? ....
e. I **have to** go to the tailor's for the final fitting of my wedding dress. ....
f. **May I** have one more piece of your wedding cake? It's delicious. ....
g. Your stomach **can** hurt if you eat too much. ....
h. You s**houldn't** be so hard her. ....
i. Children grow up and leave us. Parents **must** come to terms with it. ....
j. **Can I** have a look at your photos? ....

Exercise 51.

Completaţi textul cu verbele modale corespunzătoare.

I heard a knock at the door. I opened and saw a young woman smiling at me. “Hello, Dan!” she cried. “(1) ___________ I come in?” “How do you know my name?” I asked. “We met three years ago on a cruise ship and you gave me your address.” You (2) _________ be wrong” I said. “I’ve never gone on a cruise.” “No, I (3) _________ be wrong” she said and showed me a card with my address and name on. “I’m sorry, but I (4) ____________ remember giving you my card.” “Come on Dan. I’m wondering why you (5) __________ say that. Oh! Don’t tell me you got married. In that case it (6) __________ be very embarrassing for you.” “No, it’s not that.” I added trying to be relaxed. “My fiancée (7) __________ come and she (8) __________ be very jealous.” “Of course, you (9) __________ tell her anything about this” she went on. “There’s nothing I (10) _________ tell her about” I insisted. She finally gave up and went away. I (11) _________ be more attentive where I leave my business cards.

Exercise 52.

Traduceţi în limba engleză.

1. Ştii să faci cremă de zahăr ars (custard)?
2. Nu pot să folosesc computerul. Poţi să mă ajuţi?
3. Nu te pot auzi din cauza zgomotului.
4. Vei putea relua (resume) antrenamentul când ţi se va îmbunătăţi starea.
5. Ieri s-au certat din nou aşa că poate Maria nu vine.
6. “Poţi să săruţi mireasa acum.”
7. Poate că el este perechea (match) potrivită pentru tine.
8. Nu e nevoie să te căsătoreşti cu el dacă nu-l iubeşti.
9. Ieri a trebuit să comand alte invitaţii (invitation cards). Cele vechi nu mi-au plăcut.
10. “Trebuie să-ţi iubeşti şi să-ţi respecţi soţia.”
11. “Ar trebui să discutăm cu soţul tău despre asta.”
12. Trebuie să fii foarte îndrăgostită de el dacă nu vezi ceea ce e limpede ca lumina zilei (as plain as daylight).

Exercise 53.

Ce aţi spune în următoarele situaţii.

a. you can hardly believe your best friend is cheating on you;
b. you are likely to go to Monaco for your honeymoon;
c. you are absolutely sure your friend knows what she’s doing;
d. you doubt the truth of your parent’s words;
e. a person you don’t get along well is unlikely to attend your wedding.

Exercise 54.

Completaţi textul cu cuvinte din sfera semantică a noţiunii “***marriage***”.

RERLATIONSHIP

(1) __________, money, sex and children have little to do with marital (2) __________. According to research in the field, the prospects for you (3) ___________ lasting depends simply on how you argue. In the view of these studies, (4) __________ can be predicted in couples with a 60% accuracy rate. That only by watching how the (5) _________ people can handle their difficulties. (6) ___________ who can talk about their differences without sparking a full-scale row are the ones who will make it.

It can be very frustrating not to tell your (7) ____________ what you really think and feel. The moment either the wife or the (8) ____________ thinks seriously about what it would be like to (9) ____________ someone else is a serious warning signal. But it is never too late to stop and learn ways to improve a (10) ____________ .

Exercise 55.

Completați verbele modale sau echivalentele modale ale acestora.

It (1) ____________ be a man's world now, but tomorrow belongs to women. With their graduate certificates and mothering instincts, women (2) ____________ to do even more of the world's work. Does that matter? Biologists (3) ____________ answer: not much. To them, men (4) ____________ supply genetic material. Also from a biologist's point of view a lot of aggressive male behavior (5) ____________ be a kind of genetic advertising. As men compete against each other, that (6) ____________ to enable women, in a mysterious way, to pick the best genes to pass on.
At this point we (7) ____________ go back to the real life. Men still have more jobs than women and, on average, earn higher salaries. However, down at the bottom of the ladder, there (8) ____________ be problems of an entirely different nature. Most of the previous man's jobs have declined and so have the marital prospects. The reason is simple: what woman (9) ____________ want to marry an unemployed man? For men, work and family are linked. When the link is broken, some men, in some places (10) ____________ to become loose molecules: uneducated, unskilled, unmarried and unemployed. (11) ____________ this will change.

Exercise 56.

Încercuiți verbul modal potrivit în context pentru a completa previziunile de mai jos.

GEMENI – Next week you (1) may/must see someone you (2) shouldn't/haven't been able to find for a long time. That person (3) can/should have a bad influence on you so you (4) need/should keep away from him or her.

CANCER – This (5) must/could easily be the week hen you finally meet Mr. Smith! However, he is a person who (6) may/need have no intention to get married. He (7) may/must be a very young person who (8) shouldn't/is not allowed by his family. So you (9) may/must be careful.

LEO - You feel dissatisfied with yourself and therefore (10) shouldn't/couldn't go on as you are now. Besides, there are some things you (11) can't/needn't do as well as you'd like and other things you (12) mustn't/may not do very well.

VIRGO – Don't think you (13) can/need be lonely because friends (14) have to/may appear just around the corner. You (15) should/may take this opportunity and make up for the time you lost.

Have to/Should

Exercise 1.

Citiţi cu atenţie situaţiile de mai jos. În spaţiile libere scrieţi ce sfaturi aţi da persoanelor implicate.

a) You have noticed a colleague cheating in a test. That's not unusual with students, but you've studied hard for the test and, besides, you are against cheating.

....

b) your girlfriend/boyfriend refused your invitation to the cinema under the pretence of having to study. You've just seen her/him walking hand in hand with another boy/girl on the other side of the road.

....

c)You got drunk at a party some time ago and a classmate saw you. He is threatening you to tell your parents but you know they'll get angry as you are under age.

....

d) It so happened that you've come late to work recently and a friend covered you by telling lies to the supervisor. You are confused because you haven't asked him to.

....

e) Your best friend is taking driving lessons. Although she hasn't got her driving license yet, she has invited you on a drive to the country.

....

Exercise 2.

Citiţi cu atenţie relatarea de mai jos. În dreptul fiecărei secvenţe scrieţi comentarii folosind have to / don't have to, should / shouldn't. Primele comentarii au fost scrise ca model.

a) The Ionescu are having breakfast. Mirela, the teenager daughter, is in a hurry, grabs a sandwich and leaves for school slamming the door behind her.	She should sit at the table. She has to greet her parents. She shouldn't slam[1] the door.
b) During the break she meets her friends, Alina şi Diana. She is eager to show them her new outfit[2] made of back and white leather. She squeezed it into[3] her schoolbag before leaving the school.	
c) She goes to the ladiest toilet to change her uniform with the disco clothes. She also took her make-up kit[4] and some hair mousse. Half an hour later she has a totally different look.	
d) Mihai, who is 19, has been waiting for her at the bar round the corner. He knows she is playing truant[5] again but,	

when he sees her, all he can do is to compliment her on her gorgeous look.

e)Next minute they kiss each other passionately.

f) Alas[6]! Mirela's father enters to buy a packet of cigarettes and is astonished with the scene. He can hardly believe his eyes.

g)"That puts the lid on it[7], young lady!" "Come home this moment! We'll have to put a stop to this." Mihai tries to smooth things over. "Mr. Ionescu, remember you were our ages once!" "Don't you dare say one more word!" replies Mr. Ionescu angrily.

[1]slam	a trânti, a închide cu zgomot
[2]outfit	costum de baie
[3]squeeze in	a strecura
[4]kit	trusă
[5]play truant	a chiuli (de la ore)
[6]alas	vai!
[7]it puts the lid on it	asta pune capac la toate
[8]smooth	a linişti, a domoli

Exercise 3.

Ce soluţii există pentru a rezolva conflictul descris în exerciţiul anterior? Răspundeţi la întrebările de mai jos.

a. What should Mirela do?
b. What shouldn't she do?
c. What does she have to say?
d. What doesn't her father have to do?
e. Should Mihai call and explain it to Mirela's father?
f. Does Mirela have to stop keeping in touch with Mihai?
g. How should Mirela improve her behavior?

Exercise 4.

Fragmentul de mai jos a fost extras din scrisoarea unei adolescente către redactorul unei emisiuni pentru tineret. Ce sfat i-aţi da?

Useful language:

a) sympathizes with the sender / I'm sorry to hear that…

b) warm against a course of action.

It isn't a good idea to ...
You have to be aware that…
Don't…
Have you thought about…
Whatever you do, don't ...

c) suggest a course of action:

you should...
From my own experience I know...
I really think you shouldn't …
You should also consider…
Why not…
My advice is to…

"I have a problem. I'm seventeen years old and I often have rows with my parents on different matters. They seem to forget I'm growing. They keep telling me I have to be in by 10 o'clock every evening, including weekend. They don't even want to hear I have a boyfriend and refuse to meet him. I'm not allowed to have my own key on the pretext I'm under age. I feel frustrated and all my friends are allowed to stay out until midnight. What's worse they don't like my clothes, my hair, everything! What should I do? Please can you suggest some kind of solutions?"

Exercise 5.

Completați dialogul.

A: Are you going to the disco tonight?
B: (1)……………………………….
A: Why not?
B: (2)……………………………….
A: Why don't you have to meet boys?
B: (3)……………………………….
A: What happened?
B: (4)……………………………….
A: You should try to make your parents understand.
B: (5)……………………………….
A: Well. I'm sure you'll have to be more convincing.

Exercise 6.

Grupați adjectivele de mai jos în perechi de antonime.

tolerant, rude, reckless, obedient, polite, sensible, lenient, severe, prankish, authoritarian.

a. …………… …………… **d.** …………… ……………
b. …………… …………… **e.** …………… ……………
c. …………… ……………

Exercise 7.

Pentru fiecare dintre problemele de mai jos scrieți câte două propoziții: una explicând obligația și cealaltă un sfat.

1. How can I make my parents listen to my problems?

a) …………………………………………………….
b) …………………………………………………….

2. I simply can't understand why I am not allowed to go to the disco.

a) …………………………………………………….
b) …………………………………………………….

3. My parents don't even want to hear about all-night parties.
a) ....
b)..

4. Is then any way I can convince my parents that rock concerts are not dangerous?
a) ....
b) ....

Exercise 8.

Completați dialogul cu unele din expresiile de mai sus astfel încât să obținem un text coerent.

A: Have you heard of "Deadly Games?"

B: Sort of. I know a shoemaker invented them to entertain his son. It is a role-playing. It must be interesting.

A: Yes, it is about real life role playing and I didn't think it's interesting at all. (1).................. they are extremely dangerous as some of the players can end up in carrying out the deed which sometimes implies killing.

B: I suppose that's an extreme case. With some precautions, casualties may be avoided.

A: (2) .... the precautions, they can still be harmful.

B: (3) .... psychiatrist sees it as a useful outlet for the stress of everyday life.

A: (4) .... living temporarily into fantasy may be a necessary skill to cope with the modern world.

B: (5) .... other people criticize these games for their improper influence on young people because they encourage violence. Teenagers waste their time and energy.

A: (6) .... really wonderful adventure books lay on library shelves.

B: (7) .... I think computers won't do any moral damage if they are used sensibly and decent.

A: You've crossed your t.

Used to / Would

Exercise 1.

Citiţi biografia de mai jos şi alcătuiţi propoziţii conform exemplului.

a. be a clerk in an office — <u>She used to be a clerk in an office.</u>
b. not enjoy her boring life ....
c. escape into fantasy world of film or theatre ....
d. have a boyfriend in her home town ....
e. not like the people in the neighborhood ....
f. do some gardening at weekends ....
h. not rich ....
i. attend evening classes in drama ....

Exercise 2.

Formulaţi propoziţii negative despre statutul social al femeii în urmă cu 100 de ani.

Exemplu: go to university
100 years ago women didn't use / usedn't go to university.

a. vote ....
b. earn less than men ....
c. be plenty work for them ....
d. wear short skirts ....
e. have their hair cut ....
f. socialize much ....
g. have a say on family issues ....
h. choose a husband by themselves. ....

Exercise 3.

Înlocuiţi cuvintele subliniate cu "***would + infinitive***" pentru a exprima obiceiuri trecute.

a. <u>She complained</u> about her job <u>all the time</u>. – She would complain about her job.(exemplu).
b. When she had a problem she <u>always asked for advice</u>.
c. She <u>was in the habit of arriving</u> home by 10 o'clock.
d. They <u>went</u> picnicking <u>each time</u> the weather was fine.
e. He <u>played</u> team sports <u>repeatedly</u>.
f. Mihai <u>didn't go</u> to work <u>regularly</u>.

Exercise 4.

Completaţi ***used to*** sau past continuous pentru verbele din paranteză. Folosiţi forma afirmativă, negativă sau interogativă.

a. He .... her to work, but he doesn't any longer. (drive)
b. She .... part-time when I last saw her. (work)
c. Florin .... her bunches of roses. (offer)
d. Sorina .... an employee before she started her own business. (be)
e. We .... Sundays, but we do now. (enjoy)
f. .... you .... her the sights yesterday? (show)

Exercise 5.

Traduceţi propoziţiile de mai jos acordând atenţie diferenţei dintre "used to" şi trecutul continuu.

a. Femeile sărace lucrau ca servitoare (maid) pentru a-şi ajuta familia numeroasă.
b. Când au trecut pe la el (call on) lucra la noul roman.
c. Era una dintre cele mai bune studente ale mele.
d. Unde erai când te-am sunat?
e. Nu se plângea de munca grea pentru că era puternică.
f. Citea toate anunţurile din ziar cu speranţa unui loc de muncă.
g. Citeam ultimul capitol al romanului când cineva a bătut la uşă.

Exercise 6.

Completaţi particula corectă: down, into, off, on, out, over, to, up.

a. They have turned .... his project.
b. A friend of his turned ....
c. She will turn .... on excellent singer.
d. Would you turn .... the cassette for me, please?
e. Things will turn ...... well soon.
f. Turn .... the tap immediately!
g. He knew there was someone to turn .... her in trouble.
h. I turn .... the light? It's dark in here.

Exercise 7.

Reformulaţi propoziţii folosind used to / would.

a. Poor women often worked as servants in rich people's houses.

....

b. Men always earned more than women.

....

c. She seldom read the newspaper in the morning.

....

d. They were accustomed to having their own tutor.

....

e. As a child she almost always looked often her younger brothers.

Exercise 8.

În ce situaţii puteţi afirma următoarele:

a. "It's a matter of decency to right the wrong you've done to her."
....
b. "She's cunning enough to err on the right side."
....
c. "I have no doubt he'll be on the right side of the edge this time as always."
....
d. "Don't listen to him. He's not in his right mind."
....
e. "The moment I heard her, I stood right on the spot." / *stunning surprise* (ca model)
f. "One cannot possibly make any adjustment. The device he has designed is as right as rain."

……………………………………………………

g. "It's reckless to take the job off from her. She's the right woman/person in the right place."

……………………………………………………

h. "The Indian community has finally been set to rights."

……………………………………………………

i. "She was fed up with him and sent him to the right about."

……………………………………………………

j. "Don't worry! I feel we're on the right scent."

……………………………………………………

Conditional Sentence – type 1
(Propoziția subordonată condițională de tipul 1)

Exercise 1.

Din ce în ce mai multă şi mai variată informaţie este imprimată pe CD-ROM-uri. Propoziţiile de mai jos constituie comentarii pe margine avantajelor prezentate de acestea. Puneţi verbele din paranteză la timpul potrivit.

Exemplu: If you (use) "Encarta" you (never look at) conventional Encyclopedia again.
If you use "Encarta" you'll never look at a conventional Encyclopedia again.

a. You (keep) yourself up-to-date if you (use) a database.
b. You (learn) better, faster and easier if you (buy) a multimedia CD-ROM.
c. Imaginary life (develop) if computer companies (produce) electronic novels.
d. If you (buy) an extra floppy disc, you (find) information on the author's life.
e. Interactive fiction (emerge) as a new genre if more and more educational institutions (be receptive) to it.

Exercise 2.

Uniţi "condiţiile" şi "rezultatele" pentru a obţine fraze care conţin subordonate condiţionale:

Exemplu: If you play interactive games you'll – change the way you think about high-technology.

Conditions	Results
a. see "the largest future active indoor park" b. play "Seaworld" c. use virtual reality d. want to have a complete interactive experience e. enjoy flying	a. believe it can be possible b. ride through the ocean's depths c. truly feel like you are chasing a monster d. spends days in a row. e. takes part in a virtual aerial combat.

Exercise 3.

Folosiţi cuvintele ajutătoare şi scrieţi fraze care conţin subordonate temporale.
Exemplu: Robert will do the chores when I am 64.

Facts	Connectors	Time
a. robots – do chores	when	be 64.
b. teaching machines – replace teachers	before	25 years – elapse
c. computers – translate instantly	while	people – attend a conference
d. people take active part in TV programmes	as soon as	have computer terminals – in homes
e. you see who you are talking to	when	video-phones – be widespread

Exercise 4.

Traduceți în limba engleză ținând cont de modurile și timpurile folosite în subordonatele condiționale și temporale.

a. **Dacă** nu va fi suficient spațiu, oamenii vor construi orașe sub mări.
b. Telepatia (telepathy) va deveni un mijloc obișnuit de comunicare **când** oamenii de știință vor dovedi că fiecare om are asemenea calități.
c. Oamenii vor controla vremea **când** sateliți staționari (stationary sattelites) vor gravita (revolve) în jurul Pământului.
d. Oamenii vor consuma (eat) mâncare sintetică (synthetic food) **dacă** se va amplifica (increase) criza alimentară (food shortage).
e. **Dacă** oamenii vor contacta ființe inteligente, teama de extratereștri (aliens) va dispărea.

Exercise 5.

Scrieți o scrisoare unui redactor oferind argumente și contraargumente pentru substituirea profesorilor cu mașini de învățat. Scrisoarea trebuie să aibă următoarea structură:

general statement of the issue / current situation ⟶ Advantages ⟶ Disadvantages ⟶ Conclusion / coming to some decision.

Exercise 6.

Citiți și marcați propozițiile de mai jos cu T(true) sau F(false).

	T	F
a. The ideal age for starting using computers is a debatable issue.		
b. Multimedia computers are a real fascination for children.		
c. CD-Rom is bad substitutes for cartoons.		
d. Computer culture is sure to change into a social challenge,		
e. Computer courses for under tens are pre-school educational activity.		
f. Using computers too long a time cause nightmares.		
g. People share different opinions on using computers in school.		
h. Parents will have to stop children for using computers.		

Exercise 7.

Puneți verbele din paranteză la timpul corect.

a. If you (not use) a screen filter, it (damage) your eyes.
b. Supposing you (already, use) office devices, you (not, here) any problems.
c. He (be allowed) to play on computer, unless he (work) harder at school.
d. I (wait for) an answer as soon as you (receive) my fax.
e. There (be) no health concern when scientists (discover) a new universal cure.

Exercise 8.

Traduceți în limba engleză.

a. Nu-și va dezvolta gândirea dacă folosește tot timpul calculatorul.
b. Poți să citești în bibliotecă dacă nu-ți plac jocurile pe computer.
c. Îți voi cumpăra un nou joc video cu condiția să nu fie mai scump.

d. Vom folosi noul medicament când vom fi siguri că nu vor fi efecte secundare.
e. De îndată ce voi primi mesajul, te voi anunța.

Exercise 9.

Scrieți comentarii despre situațiile descrise folosind ***subordonata condițională de tip 1***. Primul comentariu a fost scris ca model.

a. Your friend wants to buy a house and you advise him to ask for a loan.
If you ask for a loan, you'll be able to buy a house.

b. se prices are rather high and your estate agency hasn't sold many.
…………………………………………………………………………

c. Your sister wants to rent a flat but she doesn't like being alone.
…………………………………………………………………………

d. Your granny likes grass which isn't too much around your house.
…………………………………………………………………………

e. There is too much furniture in the room and you don't feel comfortable.
…………………………………………………………………………

Exercise 10.

Completați propozițiile folosind ***subordonata condițională de tip 1***.

a. If Andreea and Maria .... prepare the salad, Marius .... the house.
b. If Sue .... the onions for the salad, Camelia .... the mushrooms.
c. Florin .... he sitting room if Alin and Tom .... the furniture.
d. If Adrian .... up the kitchen, Adriana .... the toilet.
e. Elena .... the drinks if somebody .... her carry the bottles.
f. If Andrei and Ramona .... the food, Maria and Cristi .... the sandwiches.
g. If Bogdan .... after the barbecue, Sandra .... the guests in.
h. Francesca .... the DJ if the others .... along their CDs.
i. Alin .... the drinks if Ioana .... him some of her cocktail recipes.
j. If they all .... their best, the party .... great.

Conditional Sentence – type 2
(Propoziția subordonată condițională de tipul 2)

Exercise 1.

Transformaţi propoziţiile într-o frază care conţine o subordonată condiţională de tip 2.

Exemplu: They don't understand the problem. They won't find a solution.
If they understood the problem, they would find a solution.
(They would find a solution if they understood the problem.)

a. He watches TV too much. He doesn't study at all.
b. "I can't hear you." "Turn down the radio and you will".
c. You don't buy economic reviews. You are not interested in Economics.
d. Dona doesn't like the interviewer's questions. She can ask more interesting questions.
e. Mihai is a good photographer. He hasn't had the chance to see exotic places.
f. Traian is a gifted writer, but unambitious. In your opinion, he is a potential Pulitzer Prize winner.
g. There's too much violence in the media. The young people aren't protected.
h. The more they know, the better. They will learn how to take care of themselves.

Exercise 2.

Comentaţi pe marginea propoziţiilor exclamative.

Exemplu: It's too expensive!
I'd buy it if it weren't so expensive.

a. It's too violent!
b. The language is too aggressive!
c. It's too difficult to understand!
d. It's too melodramatic!
e. This series is too long!
f. The announcer speaks too quickly!
g. The questions are too difficult!
h. It's too immoral!

Exercise 3.

Reformulaţi propoziţiile folosind ***whish + subjonctiv prezent***.

Exemplu: I regret they don't share my opinion.
I whish they shared my opinion.

a. It's a pity they don't change the programme.
b. I'm sorry I won't be here for your show.
c. I regret the interview doesn't turn out to be a good one. / ***if only + subjunctive present***.
d. I'm sorry our newspaper doesn't sell well.
e. I regret I will miss another opportunity.

Exercise 4.

Reformulați propozițiile folosind verbul modal ***may***.

Exemplu: Maybe Mr. Ionescu will make a good editor
Mr. Ionescu may make a good editor.

a. Perhaps the script is not a good one.
b. Maybe our audience will become larger.
c. New ideas are likely to help.
d. Maybe younger characters will appeal to our public.
e. A happy ending is a possible solution.

Exercise 5.

Formulați propoziții folosind cuvintele ajutătoare.

Exemplu: Mass media – people – so well informed.
If mass media didn't exist, people might not be so well informed.

a. a good management – the newspaper – so successful
b. television – news – so quickly
c. good TV reporters – programmes – so interesting
d. a solid documentation – articles – so reliable
e. talent – a journalist – so famous

Exercise 6.

Citiți cu atenție situația de mai jos. Scrieți o scrisoare scurtă cuprinzând sfaturile pe care le-ați da persoanei respective. Folosiți cât mai multe dintre expresiile sugerate.

You have been offered a well-paid job by the editor-in-chief of a successful newspaper. You badly need the money, but people have told you that blackmail (șantaj) is a common practice there.

paragraph 1 – express your regret for the situation:
- I'm sorry to hear that
- It's a pity (+the indicative)
- I wish (+present subjunctive/V2)

paragraph 2 – give several pieces of advice:
- My best idea would be to …
- If I were you, I'd …
- I really think you should
- You might consider
- It might be a good idea to …
- You should/could/might
- My advice would be to

Exercise 7.

Traduceți în limba română.

a. If you had a large sum of money, what would you spend it on?
b. Your articles would be better if you worked harder.
c. If he didn't go on this documentation trip, he wouldn't be able to write the book.

d. If only we got the subsidy!
e. Your conclusion may be wrong.
f. The sales might increase if you changed the layout.
g. I wish the newspaper sold better.

Exercise 8.

Citiţi articolul şi potriviţi ideile (topic sentences) cu paragraful corespunzător.

a. Since its first issue, "The Good News Newspaper" has attracted plenty of media attention.
b. The newspaper was founded in 1994.
c. It is said that "no news is good news", but the readers of "The Good News Newspaper" will disagree.
d. There may be a strong spiritual element to "The Good News Newspaper" which people talk about.
e. He thus noticed that most of the news was conveying negative feelings.

The Good News Newspaper

1. That newspaper prints only "good news" or articles of a positive nature and sets itself apart from the rest of the media.
2. At the time, the founder, a former actor, was himself coming out of a serious depression caused by the failure of a prior business. During a two-year period of inactivity, he had time to read a lot and watch TV.
3. He made some research and found out that every day hundreds of "positive stories" were rejected by editors-in-chief. That fact determined him to found a newspaper to report positive stories from all over the world.
4. Besides, the number of its readers amounts to scores of thousands. The business has proved to be so successful that the owner of this newspaper will sign a contract with MGM to develop a nightly TV show based on good news.
5. It has already been labeled as a "New Age Newspaper". The founder himself has objections to this expression although he admits he is a spiritually aware person. He even confesses he believes in the power of angels.

Exercise 9.

Incercuiţi raspunsul corect care completează enunţurile de mai jos.

1. Playing the lottery is a .... issue.
   a) thorny b) common c) debatable
2. Dona has already .... how to spend the big prize.
   a) decided b) intended c) supposed
3. She will open two .... for her children.
   a) checkb) accounts c) counts
4. Sociologists consider playing the lottery a .... for social disaster.
   a) recipe b) way c) means
5. She can't tell if she might .... winning a lot of money.
   a) stand b) hand c) handle

Conditional Sentence – type 3
(Propoziţia subordonată condiţională de tipul 3)

Exercise 1.

Citiţi propoziţiile şi identificaţi explicaţia potrivită. Menţionaţi ce moduri şi timpuri sunt întrebuinţate pentru fiecare propoziţie condiţională.

1. If you come across some job ads, let me know.
2. If I hear about vacant positions, I'll send you a word.
3. If I were you, I'd look for a more interesting job.
4. If you had had a credit option, you could have started your own business.

a. action likely to happen in the future;
b. imaginary situation contrary to the facts in the past;
c. untrue condition in the past;
d. giving advice.

Exercise 2.

Răspundeţi la întrebări folosind ***condiţionala de tip III***.

What would you have done if:

a. you had been rejected after a job interview?
b. there hadn't been any vacancies in your field?
c. family commitments had interfered with your career?
d. You had been assigned the manager of a distant branch of a company?
e. You had identified a business opportunity overseas?

Exercise 3.

Completaţi ***subordonatele condiţionale de tip III***.

a. The bank wouldn't have approved the loan if ....
b. I wouldn't have joined the venture if ....
c. The organization wouldn't have commissioned the poll if ....
d. The staff would have supported her if ....
e. She would have failed in business if ....

Exercise 4.

Traduceţi în limba engleză acordând atenţie modurilor şi timpurilor folosite în propoziţia condiţională.

a. Dacă ar fi avut ocazia, ar fi studiat comerţul internaţional.
b. Eşecul afacerii ar fi fost împiedicat dacă ai fi apelat la un serviciu de consultanţă.
c. Dacă ar fi ştiut să profite de ocazie, acum ar fi condus biroul din străinătate al firmei.
d. Dacă se întâmplă să ai nevoie de ajutor, nu ezita să mă suni.
e. M-aţi ajuta foarte mult dacă aţi vrea să-mi aprobaţi concediul.

Exercise 5.

Puneţi verbele din paranteză la modul şi timpul potrivit.

a. If you (want) to buy a house, it is very rate to deal directly with the person selling.
b. If you go to an estate agency, they (help) you find a house for your needs.
c. If you (choose) a house "on their books", they will take a commission.
d. If you are interested in a house, they (arrange) a "viewing"?
e. If you (want) to rent a house from a private landlord, you would read the local newspaper.
f. If the owner wanted to get you out, he/she (have to) get an evacuation order.
g. If you (cause) damages when moving in, you would break the law.

Exercise 6.

Completați *subordonatatele condiționale de timp III*.

a. Their motivation .... if they .... a goal during the first half.
b. If the goalie .... up, he .... the ball.
c. If the midfielders .... the ball more exactly, out team .... more chances to attack.
d. The fullbacks .... one or the other if they .... their opponents.
e. If the forwards .... faster, they .... more goals.
f. If our team .... the match, they .... up in the league.
g. If the referee .... the foul, he .... a penalty kick to our team.
h. Our team .... in better from if they .... harder the weeks before.
i. If it .... a home game, our team .... the match.
j. The game .... better if the trainer .... a substitute in during the second half.

Exercise 7.

Completați *subordonatele condiționale de tip III*, punând verbele la forma corectă.

1. If you (study)............ for the test, you (pass) .... it.
2. If you (ask) .... me, I (help) .... you.
3. If we (go) .... to the cinema, we (see) .... my friend Jacob.
4. If you (speak) .... English, she (understand) ....
5. If they (listen) .... to me, we (be) .... home earlier.
6. If I (write) .... you a postcard if I (have) .... your address.
7. If I (not / break) .... my leg, I (take part) .... in the contest.
8. If it (not/ start) .... to rain, we (walk) .... to the museum.
9. We (swim) .... in the sea if there (not / be) .... so many sharks there.
10. If she (take) .... the bus, she (not / arrive) ....on time.

Exercise 8.

Completați *subordonatele condiționale de tip III.*

1. If we .... the town map, we .... lost.
2. If it ...., the children .... outside.

3. If Fred ………………………… at the test, his teacher ……………………… his father.
4. If Tom …………………… more salad, he …………………………… a cold.
5. If you …………………… the car, it ……………………… down in the middle of the desert.
6. If they …………………… for another 10 minutes, they …………………….. the pop star.
7. If he ………………….. slower, Peggy …………………….. him.
8. If we ……………… to a good restaurant, we …………………….. a better dinner.
9. If you ……………………. fresh green vegetable, your salad ……………………. better.
10. If the weather ……………….. nice, they ………………………….. football.

Exercise 9.

Completați *subordonatele condiționale de tip III*.

1. If the teacher ………………………..the homework, I ……………………… it.
2. If his older brother ……………………. so fast, he …………………… into the other car.
3. If my parents ……………………… so tired, they ………………………….. the film on TV.
4. If the boys ……………………… the bus to school, they ………………………… on time.
5. If Alex ………………….. me, I ………………………the documents.
6. If I …………………….. the radio, I ………………… about the second goal.
7. If the police ……………….. earlier, they ………………………. the burglar.
8. If we ………………….. the town map, we ……………………… lost.
9. If John …………………… more words, he …………………… a good report.
10. If the police …………………… me, I …………………… you in time.

The Passive Voice
(Diateza Pasivă)

Exercise 1.

Imaginaţi-vă că sunteţi într-un restaurant. Scrieţi propoziţii care descriu ce se întâmplă în momentul respectiv folosind cuvintele ajutătoare, diateza pasivă şi timpul prezent continuu.

Exemplu: champagne-por
Champagne is being poured into glasses (by the waiter).

1. glasses – raise
2. waiter – call
3. orders – take
4. wine list – bring
5. food – smell
6. cutlery – use
7. Dan – pay for
8. voices – hear
9. voices – hear
10. tables – clear out

Exercise 2.

Folosiţi cuvintele ajutătoare şi diateza pasivă la timpul prezent perfect pentru a exprima rezultatele prezente ale unor acţiuni efectuate în trecut.

Exemplu: flowers – water (v.)
The flowers have been watered.

1. banisters – polish
2. stair step – sweep
3. glasses – wash up
4. chair and tables – dust (v.)
5. menus – lay
6. pictures – hang
7. walls – white wash
8. parquet – wax (v.)
9. bottles and galsses – arrange
10. light bulbs – fit up

Exercise 3.

Dacă nu vă plac băuturile alcoolice puteţi încerca un milkshake (o băutură pe bază de lapte cu difereite fructe şi arome). Ingredientele şi ustensilele sunt menţionate în tabelul de mai jos. Scrieţi reţeta pentru ”banana milkshake” folosind verbele din a treia coloană la diateza pasivă, prezent simplu. Enunţaţi etapele preparării folosind adverbele din coloana ”Sequencing” (ordonare)

Ingredients	Ustensils	Actions	Sequencing
banana (1) yoghurt (2-3 spoonfuls) honey (e spoon) milk (liter)	a knife a spoon glasses a blender	slice add pour put mix (10 secunde) make portions (4)	First Next/Then After that When it is... Finally

First the banana is sliced. Next the banana pieces ....
....
....

Exercise 4.

Completați dialogul scriind întrebările corespunzătoare fiecărui răspuns.

A: (1) .... ?
B: I'd like a pint of beer please.
A: (2) ....?
B: No, I'm not fond of strong drinks.
A: There's always a first time. (3) .... ?
B: Because I get drunk easily and I can't stand that.
A: I have always enjoyed a glass of nice drink. What about you? Apart from beer, (4) .... ?
B: Oh, I particularly like tonic, you know, its bitter taste.
A: In that case, (5) ....?
B: That's nice of you, but as far as I can remember it's my turn.
A: That's all right. I don't mind it.

Exercise 5.

Încercuiți răspunsul corect pentru a completa propozițiile de mai jos.

1. Will you pay the ………….. for me, please. I left my credit card at home.
   a. price b. bill c. money
2. I couldn't understand a word. He was as drunk as a ………….. .
   a. lord b. price c. lawyer
3. ………….. products are used as adjuncts to improve the taste.
   a. wheat b. hop c. maize
4. His ……….. behavior appalled everyone present.
   a. drunk b. drunken c. drunkard
5. It's a pity he is drinking ………………… his youth.
   a. away b. in c. up

Exercise 6.

Transformați propozițiile de mai jos în enunțuri cu verbul la diateza pasivă.

1. Fill a kettle with water ………………………….. .
2. Boil the water ………………………….
3. Put a teaspoon of tea in the teapot ……………………….. .
4. Pour boiling water into the teapot …………………………. .
5. Leave the tea to brew for three minutes ……………………….. .
6. Take a cup, saucer, teaspoon and sugar …………………………. .

The Infinitive Mod
(Modul Infinitiv)

Exercise 1.

Completați propozițiile cu complemente directe exprimate printr-un verb la ***modul infinitive.***

Exemplu: The British government promised ....
The British government promised to send more ships.

a. They have decided ....
b. Why did they refuse ....?
c. Cunningly, he pretended ....
d. One more time they attempted............................
e. They didn't want ....

Exercise 2.

Răspundeți la întrebările de mai jos.

Exemplu: Did the crew intend to kill the captain to take over the commandant?
The crew intends to take over the command.

a. Did he try to fix the compass or the helm (cârma)?
b. Did the ship owner decide to finance a new scientific expedition or a commercial one?
c. Did the boy want to serve before the mast or join the army?
d. Did the captain promise to give them land or gold?
e. Did she sailors refuse to surrender or obey the orders?

Exercise 3.

Scrieți comentarii folosind verblele ***make / let*** urmate de infinitivul scurt.

Exemplu: Ordinary people wanted to settle in Australia. The government agreed (let).
The government let ordinary people settle in Australia.

a. The merchant's ship was loaded with merchandise. The crew unloaded it. (make)
b. The storehouses were 300 meters away. The supervisor asked them to carry the boxes there. (make).
c. The captain didn't agree. The crew was paid to sail, not to carry the merchandise.
d. The merchant offered to raise the pay. The sailors had a suggestion. (let)
e. Spices were in high demand and expensive. The merchant said the sailor could have small amounts. (let)

Exercise 4.

Completați particulele potrivite.

a. As the weather was fine, the boat made .... the open sea.
b. HMS Belfast has been made .... into a museum.
c. The crew was made .... of twenty members.
d. Man Friday couldn't make .... what Robinson Crusoe meant.

e. The captain tried to make …… all the members of the crew.
f. Did he think a bag of gold would make ……….. the loss?

Exercise 5.

Completați propozițiile astfel încât să obțineți o construcție infinitivală.

a. He has decided ……………………………….
b. The ship owner wanted ………………………..
c. The passengers hoped ………………………..
d. They pretended ………………………………
e. He swears ……………………………………..

Exercise 6.

Traduceți în limba engleză.

a. James Cook a promis să descopere noi teritorii pentru Coroana britanică.
b. Guvernul a hotărât să trimită condamnații în Botany Bay.
c. Uneori condamnații amenințau să se răzvrătească.
d. Oamenii de rând sperau să înceapă o nouă viață.

Exercise 7.

Propozițiile de mai jos reprezintă relatarea succintă a momentului in care Robin Crusoe l-a salvat pe cel pe care-l va numi Man Friday. Citiți cu atenție și ordonați propozițiile pentru a obține o relatare coerentă.

a) Then I noticed thirty people dancing around the fire; I was horrified when I realized they were cannibals.

b) One of them was unconscious while the other was left unattended for the moment.

c) One morning, I was surprised to see no less than five canoes on the shore.

d) However, I kept my temper when I saw that the fugitive swam across the stream around my hiding place.

e) Hardly knowing what to do, I lay in my hiding place.

f) In no time, I grabbed my two guns.

g) On my way to the sea I knocked down one of the pursuers and shot the other one who had a bow and arrow and was ready to use them.

h) That very moment the poor wretch ran with incredible swiftness towards where I was hiding.

i) I was terrified when I saw other two people were following him.

j) After waiting for a good while, I climbed up to the top of the hill.

k) Several steps further, I could see two wretches.

l) The poor man was finally out of danger.

Exercise 8.

Completați propozițiile folosind ***modul infinitiv***. Folosiți verbele enumerate și alte cuvinte pe care le considerați corespunzătoare.

attend, help, print, finish, be able to use, erase, get advice.

Model: Did he offer ………………………….. ?
Did he offer to help with the project?

b) I expect ....
c) Of course I hope ....
d) Mark refused ....
e) Now you are learning how ....
f) I'd like ....
g) Did you try ....

Exercise 9.

Răspundeți la întrebări folosind ***modul infinitiv***.

Model: Where did you decide to place the PC?
I decide to buy a separate piece of furniture for it.

a. What are you trying to do now?
b. What CD-Rom do you want to buy?
c. When do you hope to install the new programme?
d. Who do you intend to invite to the presentation?
e. Where did you agree to meet him?
f. How would you like to help your colleagues?

Exercise 10.

Combinați propozițiile de mai jos conform modelului.

Model: Will you print the document for me? I'd like that.
I'd like you to print the document for me.

a. Can't you connect me to the local network? I'd love that.
b. Paul will scan the pictures tomorrow instead of today, I'd prefer that.
c. You won't change the password. I don't want that.
d. Can Maria access my e-mail box? I'd like that.
e. Did you buy the new accounting programme? I wish that.

Exercise 11.

Dați cât mai multe răspunsuri la următoarele întrebări folosind structura ***verb+complement direct+infinitiv***.

	want your friends to understand?
	prefer your life to be?
What do you	expect your manager to be?
	allow your children to do?
	warn your colleagues not to do?
	like a PC to do?

Exercise 12.

Reformulați propozițiile conform modelului.

Model: When Paul found the document he was surprised.
Peter was surprised to find the document.

k. Marius was glad when he received her message.
l. Traian was afraid that he might lose important information.

m. Petre was upset when he didn't find the disk.
n. Andrei was excited when he got a PC as a birthday present.
o. Traian was proud when he won the competition.

Exercise 13.

Completați propozițiile folosind ***modul infinitiv*** al verbelor din paranteză după cuvintele interogative. Adăugați alte cuvinte necesare.

Model: I didn't know what ....
I didn't know what to do

a. Can you tell me how .... ? (get there)
b. Show me where ....? (put)
c. Do you know where ....? (buy)
d. I didn't know where ....? (come)
e. She explained clearly what ....? (do)
f. He wondered whether .... or ....? (go/stay)

Exercise 14.

Reformulați propozițiile astfel încât să folosiți o ***construcție infinitivală*** fără a schimba sensul.

a. I regret that I have to say it.
b. They're promised that they'll come still I have my doubts.
c. She's explaining to me how I should use this device.
d. Bogdan was pleased when he found her among the guests.
e. I don't want that you meet him any more.
f. It's advisable that you see a doctor.

Exercise 15.

Puneți verbele din paranteză la ***infinitivul continuu*** pentru a exprima posibilitatea referitoare la o acțiune în curs de desfășurare în momentul vorbirii/într-o perioadă dată.

Exemplu. I can hear voices. Maria might (talk) over the phone.
Maria might be talking over the phone.

a. Their things are scattered all over the place. They might (go) on holidays.
b. The professor is in the lab. He could (test) the new material.
c. What could I (do) in such a boring town?
d. I may (work) on my project over the weekend so don't call me.
e. The man may not (wave) to us. He doesn't know us.

Exercise 16.

Răspundeți la întrebări folosind ***COULD*** pentru exprimarea posibilității.

Exemplu: Who could she be talking to this time?
It could be her new boyfriend.

a. What could you be doing if you were not involved?
b. Why could they be moving the house again?

c. Where could he be hiding this time?
d. Who could she be using for her new scheme?
e. Who could they be coming with at the party?

Exercise 17.

Folosiţi cuvintele ajutătoare pentru a formula propoziţii care exprimă ***imposibilitatea*** cu referire la o acţiune în curs de desfăşurare în prezent.

Exemplu: go out/dressed like that
You can't be going out dressed like that.

a. sell/the orchard
b. think of/going on an expedition in the Alps
c. tell/the truth
d. go to the disco/by herself
e. show/the secret passage

Exercise 18.

John Brown conduce grupul "Friends of the Earth". Citiţi activităţile în care este implicat şi formulaţi propoziţii folosind ***MAY/MIGHT + infinitiv continuu***.

Exemplu: gives interviews
John Brown may/might be giving interview now.

a. convinces people of the importance of a clean environment
b. holds press conferences
c. has talks with government representatives
d. visits building sites
e. participates in charity activities

Exercise 19.

Reformulaţi propoziţiile folosind ***MAY + infinitv continuu***

Exemplu: Perhaps they're talking to the prime minister.
They may be talking to the prime minister.

a. They are likely to examine the critical environmental problems at the moment.
b. Perhaps they are looking for a solution to garbage dumping.
c. Nowadays, pollution is likely to threaten the survival of the human race.
d. Perhaps ordinary people are unconsciously contributing to the disaster.
e. Today, garbage dumping is likely to degrade larger areas of soil than ever.

Exercise 20.

Traduceţi în limba engleză.

a. Am putea aplica (implement) noua metodă zilele acestea.
b. Nu puteţi face un lucru atât de nesăbuit. (reckless)
c. Poate că acum ţine conferinţa de presă.
d. Cui aş putea să-i vorbesc ca să găsesc înţelegere?
e. S-ar putea să plec într-o scurtă vacanţă.

The Infinitive and the Present Participle
(Construcţii cu infinitivul şi participiul prezent)

Exercise 1.

Folosiţi cuvintele ajutătoare şi alcătuiţi propoziţii cu acuzativul cu infinitiv. Atenţie la regimul fiecărei categorii de verbe!

Model: Mrs. Smith / **want** / husband / check the door.
Mr. Smith wanted her husband to check the door.

a. they / **see** / strange things / happen
b. they / **believe** / it / a practical joke
c. they / **allow** / son / leave the house
d. they / **expect** / neighbors / laugh at them
e. it / **not make** / they / appear insane

Exercise 2.

Transformaţi frazele în propoziţii în care să folosiţi construcţia acuzativ cu infinitiv.

Model: Scientists declared that the phenomenon was unusual.
Scientists declared the phenomenon to be unusual.

a. They believe that it had a connection with young people's personality.
b. They know that teenager's life is more hectic.
c. They reckon that poltergeists are young playful spirits.
d. They suppose that energetic entities come and visit kindred spirits.
e. They think that the visible and the invisible communicate.

Exercise 3.

Reformulaţi la diateza pasivă propoziţiile de la exerciţiul anterior, în care aţi folosit acuzativul cu infinitivul.

Model: Scientists declared the phenomenon to be unusual.
The phenomenon was declared to be unusual.

Exercise 4.

Completaţi propoziţiile folosind construcţia acuzativ cu participiu şi verbele din paranteză.

Model: Pots and plates were flying through the air. (see)
He saw pots and plates flying through the air.

a. A noise of footsteps was coming from the attic. (hear)
b. The floor was quaking (a se cutremura) under their feet. (feel)
c. They felt a danger was approaching. (sense)
d. The furniture was moving all over the place. (watch)
e. The water was bursting from the tap. (see)

Exercise 5.

Traduceți în limba engleză folosind construcții cu infinitivul sau participiul prezent, după caz.

a. Ştiu că e inteligentă.
b. Aş vrea să vii cu noi.
c. Presupun că se sperie uşor.
d. Nu-l lăsa să te păcălească.
e. Am auzit două persoane vorbind.
f. Se crede că fenomenul este mai extins.
g. A fost văzut că intră în pivniță.
h. Simțea inima bătându-i tare (throb).
i. În timp ce conduceam, am văzut o lumină venind din față.
j. A fost observat un obiect plat îndepărtându-se cu o viteză inimaginabilă.

Exercise 6.

Traduceți în limba română folosind construcții cu infinitivul sau participiul prezent, după caz.

a. I heard him speak.
b. I'd like you to stay.
c. She considers him to be her best friend.
d. They declared him to be fit for that job.
e. Poltergeist haunting is believed to take place ....
f. The boy was seen to come.
g. She was expected to win.
h. They saw objects fling around.
i. They heard someone pattering.

Past Simple Tense and Present Perfect Simple Tense
(Timpul Trecut Simplu şi Timpul Prezent Perfect Simplu)

Exercise 1.

Citiţi cu atenţie propoziţiile şi identificaţi reprezentarea grafică adecvată. Scrieţi răspunsurile în grilă. Primul răspuns a fost completat ca model.

1. Alice has been a bay watcher since she was a teenager.
2. She trained at six in the morning.
3. She rescued an old woman when she was 19.
4. She has rescued an old woman so far.
5. She was a bay watcher for seven years.
6. She has been a bay watcher for seven years.

A.
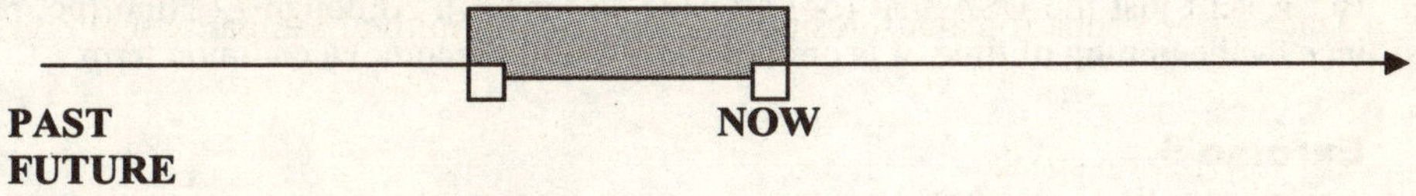

B.
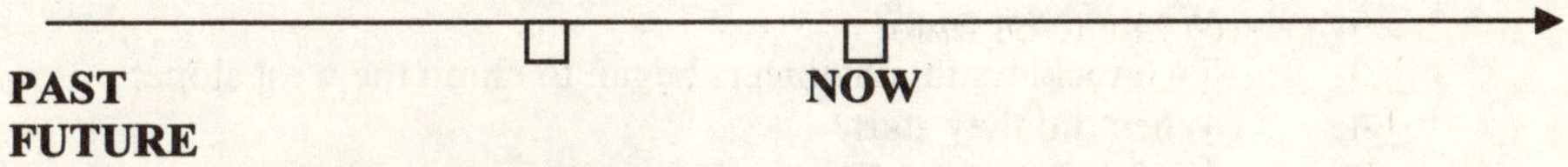

C.
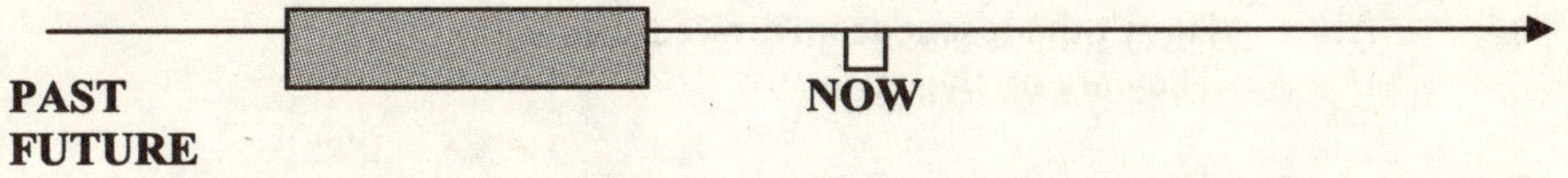

A	B	C
1, _, _	_, _	_

Exercise 2.

Completaţi corespunzător adverbele şi locuţiunile adverbiale de timp: *since she was 19, is her teens, so far, as a high school student, for seven years*.

a. Alice started working at a pool …………………………… .
b. ……………………………………………… she trained hard.
c. She has worked at the same swimming pool…………….. .
d. She has been a full-time bay watcher …………………… .
e. She has rescued more people ……………………… .

Exercise 3.

Scrieţi dialoguri scurte conform modelului pentru a exersa diferenţa dintre ***trecutul simplu*** şi ***prezentul perfect***.

Exemplu: rescue a person/last month
A: Have you ever rescued a person?
B: Yes, I have.

A: When did it happen?
B: I rescued a boy last month.

a. attract people's attention/at Palm Beach
b. two years ago/win a swimming competition
c. train at night/in my teens
d. obtain your certificate/last year
e. work at this pool for a long time/start six month ago

Exercise 4.

Puneți verbele din paranteză la timpul ***trecut simplu*** sau ***prezent perfect***.

Nine people in California and thirty-nine in Florida (die) last year in storms produced by El Nino. [...] Over a year ago oceanographers (detect) a rise in ocean temperatures off Peru – the first sign of El Nino. Their predictions ever since then (be) accurate. Los Angeles (get) more rain in February than in any other February since records (begin) in 1877.

But it isn't just the USA that (be) affected so far [...]. Although El Nino (be, probably) around since the beginning of time, it is only recently that it (become) a common term.

Exrcise 5.

Traduceți în limba română.

A: What's happened?
B: Two reckless mountaineers began to climb the west slope.
A: When did they start?
B: Half an hour ago. The communication was cut off.
A: Hasn't the rescue team arrived yet?
B: They are on their way.

Exercise 6.

Completați dialogul în mod corespunzător.

A: (1) .... about lifeguards.
B: Well, (2) .... they are a nuisance.
A: Why (3) .... ?
B: Because (4) ....

Exercise 7.

Completați cuvântul corect

a. Life guarding is not as .... as they show it in TV series.
b. Fortunately, bay watchers don't have to make many .... a day.
c. Bay watchers' main activity is to .... accidents.
d. They are not only .... but also fit.
e. All of them spend hours with hard ....

Exercise 8.

Înlocuiți cuvintele subliniate cu: A) verbul ***wash*** urmat de ***particulă adverbială***; B) ***expresii idiomatice*** învățate în această lecție.

A) a. Continuous storms ***have removed*** the base of the cliffs.
b. The tide (fluxul) ***carried*** the remainders of the raft ***to the shore***.
c. The paint spots ***haven't go out by washing***.

B) a. Let's drop the subject! It is ***over now and I can't help it.***
b. He has a particular skill to ***manage in difficult situation.***
c. If I were you, I wouldn't to that. You might ***get into trouble.***

Exercise 9.

Puneți verbele din paranteză la timpul trecut simplu sau prezent perfect.

a. I (be) at the beach today.
b. She (work) at this pool since she (graduate) school.
c. When she (be) a teenager, she (train) for hours in a row.
d. El Nino (already, make) lots of casualties and damages.
e. "How many lives – you – (rescue) so far?"
"Three".
"When – you – (make) the latest rescue?"
"It (be) about three months ago."

Exercise 10.

Folosiți informațiile și alcătuiți propoziții folosind ***trecutul simplu*** sau ***prezentul perfect***. Folosiți verbul corespunzător.

Model:

a) Dr. Kari Stephenson, a scientist, - license to exclusively exploit the genetic information of the 270.000 Icelanders.
Dr. Kari Stephenson, a scientist has obtained the license to exclusively exploit the genetic information of the 270.000 Icelanders.
b) Dr. Stephenson – private company, DeCode genetics Inc., several years ago.
Dr. Stephenson – private company, DeCode genetics Inc., several years ago.

a. The people of Iceland – isolated for a long time; it means it is genetically homogenous.
b. Dr. Kari Stephenson – twenty years at Harvard Medical School.
c. From the very beginning he – to chase the "bad" genes from his native country.
d. The geneticists from DeCode – the DNA of all the members of this unusually large family.
e. On its commencement, Prime Minister David Oddsson - the project ardently.
f. He – an unexpected opportunity to attract scientists and create jobs.
g. So far, the scientists - a gene responsible for uncontrollable trembling of the limbs.
h. Opponent voices – when confidentiality of some medical records was breached.
i. A commission of informational ethics – the case at that moment.
j. Then Dr. Stephenson – a bill to the Parliament to ser the legal framework for his research.
k. The Parliament – the law with 37 cotes to 20.
l. Dr. Kari Stephenson – the exclusive right to use all medical information available in his country.

Past Perfect Simple and Continuous Tense
(Timul Trecutul Perfect Simplu şi Continuu)

Exercise 1.

Completaţi spaţiile libere cu ***THAN*** sau ***WHEN***. Prima propoziţie a fost completată ca exemplu.

a. No sooner had the curtain raised **than** the chorus entered the stage.
b. Hardly had the clown gone out with the guest list ……… Romeo took it from him.
c. Barely had he read through it ……… he saw Rosaline's name on it.
d. No sooner had he read her name ………….. he decided to go to the ball.
e. Scarcely had Romeo entered the ball room ………….. he put on a mask.
f. No sooner had he made several steps ………….. he saw Juliet.
g. Barely had he seen Juliet ………….. he spoke to her.
h. Hardly had he finished speaking ……… he kissed her.
i. Hardly had Juliet answered Romeo's words …..... her nurse called her.
j. No sooner had Juliet left him, ……… Romeo asked the nurse about her family.
k. Scarcely had Juliet found out about Romeo, ….…. she felt sorrow.

Exercise 2.

Scrieţi o scrisoare unui prieten pentru a-l invita la teatru. Folosiţi expresiile următoare.

a) Expressions of invitation.
- I was wondering if you can join us
- Could you come for … on … ?
- What about coming …
- I'd like you to …
- I'd like to invite you to …/for …

b) Persuasion (convingere)
- I do hope that you'll be able to come.
- I do hope you'll join me.
- Do try to be there
- I'm really looking forward to seeing you.

Exercise 3.

Ce aţi spune în situaţiile următoare?

a. When something reminds you of a similar story.

………………………………………………………………

b. When you want to make sure you told someone about your first boy friend/girl friend.

………………………………………………………………

c. When you want to finish a digression within a story about your first night out.

………………………………………………………………

d. When you want to put an end to a story about your attempt to elope.

………………………………………………………………

Exercise 4.

Completaţi cuvintele care lipsesc. Atenţie la forma gramaticală.

a. The Capulets and the Montagues were two noble ....
b. Juliet .... to being Romeo's wife although he was her family's foe (duşman).
c. .... Lawrence accepted to marry them hoping that the .... would change into love.
d. Romeo .... Tybalt to death and Prince Escalus .... him.
e. Juliet drank a .... and everybody thought her dead.
f. Romeo entered the burial .... and .... himself next to Juliet's.
g. In her turn, Juliet killed herself with Romeo's ....

Exercise 5.

Înlocuiţi cuvintele evidenţiate cu verbul ***act + particulă adverbială.***

a. She was overwhelmed and didn't know how to ***react*** at his behavior.
b. While the director was on holidays, his deputy (adjunct) ***represented*** him.
c. The tourist didn't speak the language and he tried to ***illustrate*** the words ***by gestures***.
d. It is easier to state principles rather than ***behave accordingly***.
e. The actor's subtlety of voice ***affected*** the audience.

Exercise 6.

Puneţi verbele din paranteză la timpul corespunzător pentru a exprima raportul de anterioritate.

a. Before Romeo met Juliet, he (be) in love with Rosaline.
b. After Romeo and his friends (put) on masks, they went to the ball.
c. When Romeo (take) Juliet's hand, he started to talk to her.
d. Juliet, too, fell in love with him as soon as she (see) him.
e. She wanted to know the young man's name after he (leave) the ball room.

Exercise 7.

Uniţi cele două propoziţii folosind structurile ***hardly ... when*** şi no ***sooner ... then***.

a. Juliet appeared at the window. Romeo was enthralled (captivat).
b. Juliet said the first words. Romeo didn't know what to do: to listen more or to speak.
c. Romeo swore by the moon. Juliet stopped him.
d. Romeo and Juliet confessed their love to each other. The nurse called her.
e. Juliet went inside. She returned to the window.

Exercise 8.

Formulaţi întrebări ale căror răspunsuri sunt cuvintele evidenţiate. Prima întrebare a fost formulată ca model.

James Burbage, who built the first theatre in London in 1576, died in 1597 while he was in the middle of business discussions with the landlord. Because Burbage's theatre had already made **much money**[(a)], the landlord wanted to increase the rent of the land where the **theatre**[(b)] had been built. After the landlord had failed **to come to an agreement**[(c)] with Burbage's family, he decided to pull the theatre down and sell the wood. By the night of the 28th December 1598, **the two sons of James Burbage**[(d)] had secretly arranged for some workmen to take down the theatre and transport it across the River Thames. The new theatre was called The Globe. The whole operation cost money and they formed a new company to raise the necessary capital. Shakespeare was already wealthy because he had bought **a share**(e) in the previous company. That way he didn't have to rely on the **small amount of money**(f) he had earned from **writing and acting**(g) in plays.

(a) What had Burbage's theatre made? (Much money.)
(b) What .... ?
(c) What ....?
(d) Who ....?
(e) What ....?
(f) How much ....?
(g) Where .... from?

Exercise 9.

Anliza viselor poate oferi indicii pentru identificarea problemelor psihice. Citiţi notiţele unui psihiatru despre visele unui pacient şi alcătuiţi propoziţii pentru a reconstrui visul conform relatării pacientului. Procedaţi conform modelului.

Model: drives a car – wheel comes off
I was driving a car when a wheel came off.

a. walks across a bridge – meets tiger
b. climbs stairs – sees a ghost
c. rows a boat – Indians attack him
d. lies on beach – lion comes out of the sea
e. digs garden – finds a treasure

Exercise 10.

Folosiţi cuvintele ajutătoare pentru a descrie experienţa unui pacient. Procedaţi conform modelului.

Model: I hadn't known anything about psychoanalysis before met Dr. Zen.
After I had been following Dr. Zen's treatment, I felt more relaxed.

A) _________ before I met Dr. Zen.
a. not write down dreams
b. not have reasonable explanations for fears
c. not be familiar with relaxation techniques
d. discover the healing power of conversations

B) After ________, I felt more relaxed.
a. talk to someone about fears
b. meet people with similar problems
c. be on a short holiday
d. start a diary

Exercise 11.

Reconstruiţi visul completând verbele la ***timpul trecut*** potrivit. Efectuaţi alte schimbări necesare.

I – dream – try to climb – steep hill. Hill – be – covered – in brambles – I – keep getting caught and scratched – thorns. I – begin to cry – want – reach the top. Suddenly – I – find – I – fly – up in the sky – over the top of the hill. Sun – shine – I feel – light and happy. I – land – other side of the hill – huge orchard – many trees. There – be – ladder reaching up into one of the trees. I – climb – ladder – tree – find – I – be surrounded – ripe yellow lemons. I – begin to pick and eat – lemons. They – taste – sweet.

Exercise 12.

Puneți verbele din paranteză la ***timpul trecut*** corespunzător.

I (1-read) a newspaper by the light of a candle. The article I (2-read) (3-be) about a tiger that (4-escape) from the Zoo. Suddenly I (5-not be) in the house any longer. I (6-ride) on the back of the tiger as it (7-run) away from the Zoo. The tiger (8-carry) me deep into the mountains where it (9-begin) to snow heavily. Then the tiger (10-disapper) and I (11-be) alone in the snowstorm. I (12-try) to struggle to the top of the mountain. That moment a big brown bear (13-appear) from behind an enormous rock. I (14-turn) to run but too late. The bear (15-attack) me and we (16-begin) to fight. I (17-bleed) badly but just as I (18-give up) hope, the snow (19-stop), the clouds (10-clear up) and the bear (11-run off). I found that I (22-stop) bleeding and my wounds (23-disappear). I (24-stand up) and (25-look) around. Somehow I (26-get) to the top of the mountain. A rainbow (27-stretch) across the valley.

Reported Speech. Statements.
(Stilul/Vorbirea indirectă. Propoziții enunțiative)

Exercise 1.

Leul din fabulă este foarte bolnav. Maimuța nu înțelege ce spune acesta și vulpea repetă cuvintele lui.

Exemplu: "I'm not feeling well!"
He's saying/telling that he is not feeling well.

a. "I'm feeling very weak."
b. "I can't walk at all."
c. "I am too faint to hunt."
d. "I'm going to stay in my den today."
e. "I'm sue I'll feel better tomorrow."

Exercise 2.

Rescrieți propozițiile în stilul indirect folosind verbul din regentă la ***timpul trecut***.

Exemplu: He's saying that he is not feeling well.
He said he was not feeling well.

a. He's telling that he is feeling very weak.
b. He's saying that he can't walk at all.
c. He's saying that he is too faint to go hunting.
d. He's telling that he is going to stay in his den today.
e. He's saying that he is sure he will feel better tomorrow.

Exercise 3.

Transformați următoarele enunțuri în stilul indirect folosind verbul din regentă la timpul trecut.

Exemplu: "I can resist everything except temptation." (Oscar Wilde)
Oscar Wilde admitted he could resist everything except temptation.

a. "England is a nation of shopkeepers." (Napoleon)
Napoleon remarked that …………………………………………………. .
b. "The report of my death was an exaggeration." (Mark Twain)
Mark Twain stated that ……………………………………………………. .
c. "I think, therefore I am." (Descartes)
Descartes reflected that …………………………………………………. .
d. "That's one small step for a man, one giant leap for mankind." (Neil Armstrong)
Neil Armstrong thought ……………………………………………….. .
e. "I came, I saw, I conquered." (Julius Caesar)
Julius Caesar stated that ………………………………………………... .

Exercise 4.

Citiți enunțurile din "Bottle Hill", o legendă irlandeză, și rescrieți-le folosind stilul indirect.

Exemplu: "I have a poor farm in Ireland." (Mick Mulligan)
Mick Mulligan said he had a poor farm in Ireland.

a. "I'll give you this bottle in exchange." (the stranger)
b. "This bottle is worth all the cows in Ireland." (he)
c. "Your cow may die before you get to Cork." (the stranger)
d. "I hope Molly won't be angry with me." (Mick)
e. "She'll surprise at what this bottle can do." (the stranger)

Exercise 5.

Citiți situațiile descrise din basmul "***The Princess and the Pea***" și transformați vorbirea indirectă în vorbire directă.

a. The Queen thought she would soon see about that(1). She told the king she was going to lay three small peas on the bedstead(2). She added she would put twenty mattresses on top(3).

b. Next morning the princess said she had had a horrid night(4). She had hardly been able to close her eyes the whole night(5). Heaven knew what had been in her bed, but there had been something hard under her and her whole body was black and blue with bruises (6). She couldn't tell the Queen what she had suffered(7).

Exercise 6.

Citiți cu atenție expresiile de mai jos și scrieți un paragraf de zece rânduri despre o experiență personală a cărei morală poate fi exprimată prin proverbul "*A friend in need is a friend in deed.*" (Prietenul la nevoie se cunoaște.)

- As far as I can remember ..
- I remember quite clearly that …
- After that …
- Before that…
- While that was happening…
- The next thing I did was to …
- I'm not sure I can remember all the details, but …
- I'll never forget…

Exercise 7.

Uniți cuvintele din coloana A cu explicațiile din coloana B. Alcătuiți propoziții.

1. tale	**a.** a story with a moral message, especially with animal characters which represent people's behavior;
2. legend	**b.** short amusing story that happened to you or someone else;
3. fable	**c.** a story about interesting or exciting imaginary events involving magic and adventure;
4. anecdote	**d.** old story about gods or the origin of the world which is partially believed to be true;
5. myth	**e.** a very old story about strange or magical events or persons who lived long ago and were very brave or had magical powers.

Exercise 8.

Completaţi particula corectă: ***by, down, in, into, off, out, up***.

a. The laid ………………. a good supply of fuel.
b. The board laid ……………… the new regulations.
c. Grannies lay ……………..... a good supply of preserves when autumn started.
d. The architect lay ….......... a new project for the exhibition.
e. I couldn't stand his cheekiness and laid ……………….. him.
f. The man told them to lay ………………… teasing the girl.
g. She is laying ……………… small amounts of money weekly for a trip to London.

Exercise 9.

Transformaţi: A) ***vorbirea directă în vorbire indirectă***;
B) ***vorbirea indirectă în vorbire directă***.

Folosiţi *timpul trecut* în propoziţia regentă.

A.
a. "I cannot allow you to live." (the genie)
b. "I must ask you something first." (the fisherman)
c. "I can hardly believe you fitted in this vase." (the fisherman)
d. "I'll swear it." (the genie)
e. "The Sultan will give you more money than you have ever had in your life." (the genie)

B.
a. The third fairy said she would give the princess common sense.
b. King Ludwig didn't think much of that gift. He said that all she needed was charm.
c. The dragon threatened that he must have a princess to devour or he would breathe out his fiery breath and destroy the kingdom.
d. One of the counselors was thinking of advertising for a knight to slay the dragon. That was generally done in those cases.
e. The king answered that they didn't have time. The dragon had only given them until the following morning.

Exercise 10.

Transformaţi ***enunţurile directe în vorbire indirectă***. Verbul din propoziţia principală este la timpul trecut; folosiţi tot un timp trecut în propoziţia subordonată.

Exemplu: "Look! How impressive it is!" (wonder/the girl)
The girl wondered at how impressive it was.

a. "Happy Easter!" (wish/the boy)
b. „Good morning, Mrs. Ionescu." (greet/Maria)
c. "You never listen!" (complain/his mother)
d. "Thank you very much for your help." (thank/the student)
e. "I'm afraid I won't do what you want." (disagree/his sister)
f. "Sorry for being late." (apologize/the clerk)
g. "That's nice of you, but I have to work late today." (refuse/Dana)
h. "I wouldn't join him, if I were you." (advise/Traian)
i. "Would you like to come with me to the disco?" (invite/Andrei)
j. "Don't do that again!" (tell/mother).

Exercise 11.

Transformați dialogul în ***vorbire indir**ectă* completând textul cu lacune. Prima propoziție a fost completată ca model.

Maria:	Mum, look! The light up in the sky! Is that a flash of lightning?
Mrs. Brown:	No, Maria. It's fireworks.
Maria:	They are so colorful and bright!
Mrs. Brown:	Let's go upstairs to see better.
Maria:	That's a great idea!
	(Later on)
Maria:	Can I sit on the window sill?
Mrs. Brown:	You might fall over. You should stand next to me.
	(A voice in the neighborhood)
Mr. Marinescu:	Good evening, Mrs. Brown.
Mrs. Brown:	Good evening Mr. Marinescu.
Mr. Marinescu:	Are you enjoying the fireworks? I'm going to the square. Will you and your daughter join me?
Mrs. Brown:	We'd love to. Thanks for inviting us.
Mr. Marinescu:	I'm waiting for you downstairs.
	(Ten minutes later)
Mrs. Brown:	Sorry for keeping you waiting. We've put on warmer clothes.
Mr. Marinescu.	That's all right. Maria, will you have an apple?
Maria:	Thank you, Mr. Marinescu.
Mr. Marinescu:	Not at all. Let's get started or we are missing the show.

Maria pointed at the sky and (1) *asked her mother if the light in the sky was a flash of lightning.* Her mother answered that (2) …………………… . Maria said admiringly that (3)………………………… . Then her mother suggested (4) ………………….. and Maria agreed gladly saying that (5) …………………… . Later on, Maria asked for permission to (6) ……………………… , but her mother objected that (7) …………………… . She advised Maria to (8) ………………… . Mr. Marinescu greeted from next door and Mrs. Brown answered. He wanted to know if they (9) ………………… . He also added that he (10) ……………… and invited them (11) ……………….. . Mrs. Brown accepted (12) …………………… and thanked (13) ……………… . Mr. Marinescu said he (14) …………………… Ten minutes later, Mrs. Brown apologized for (15) ……………… . She explained that (16) ……………… . Mr. Marinescu (17) ……………… and offered (18) …………………… which she (19) ……………… . Mr. Marinescu suggested (20) …………………… .

Exercise 12.

Transformați în vorbire directă.

Mihai, said hello to Tom. Mihai wanted to know if Tom's Halloween costume was ready. Tom answered it was and added that he would be a witch. He went on saying that he hadn't done his jack o'lantern. Mihai suggested helping him saying that it was easy. He advised Tom to take a smaller pumpkin because it was easier to cut out the eyes and the mouth. When it was ready, Mihai exclaimed that it was scary and Tom agreed. Tom also asked Mihai whom he was going treat-or-tricking with. Mihai answered he hadn't found anyone up to that moment. Tom invited him to go together. Mihai accepted gladly and offered Tom a piece of pumpkin pie. He thanked adding that it was his favorite. Mihai told him not to eat too much because the costume might not fit him any more.

Exercise 13.

Completaţi textul cu cuvintele pe care le consideraţi potrivite. Nu scrieţi mai mult de un cuvânt în fiecare spaţiu.

Initially, Easter was a (1) .... holiday. People in England go to church on Good (2) .... and Easter (3) .... On this occasion, they eat hot (4) .... with spices in them and with a (5) .... marked on top. Easter is a day for (6) .... Nowadays, children receive them, but they are chocolate ones. If the children are (7) .... , Easter Bunny brings them (8) .... He hides them different (9) .... of the house and in the morning the children must (10) .... for them. Easter Monday is a (11) .... and people go out and enjoy themselves. If the weather is (12) ...., they drive into the country and stop for a (13) .... Easter is a very (14) .... holiday because most people get four (15) .... off from work. In England it is the first holiday after (16) .... and it is the (17) .... of winter and the beginning of (18) ....

Exercise 14.

Citiţi explicaţiile şi identificaţi cuvântul corespunzător.

a. lack of success = ____________________
b. conspiracy or secret plans = ____________________
c. a model of a person = ________________
d. natural color, texture and appearance of the skin of the face = ________________
e. a person who is disloyal especially to his/her country = _____________

Exercise 15.

Completaţi particula potrivită.

a. She was once let .... by her boyfriend and now she trusts nobody.
b. "John, let the guests .... , will you?"
c. "I know I am letting myself .... a lot of unpaid work."
d. He accidentally let .... his rifle and injured one of his companions.
e. "Did you talk to her?" "Yes, I did. Unfortunately she didn't let .... too much."

Exercise 16.

Transformaţi dialogul în vorbire indirectă.

Florina: Hello, Mirela. I'm glad we've met.
Mirela: Hello, Florina. Can I be of any help?
Florina: No, it's not that. I'm giving a small Mother's Day party. I'd be delighted if you could come.
Mirela: I'd love to. Thanks for inviting me.
Florina: My pleasure. Oh! Put on something casual. There'll be only our closest friends.
Mirela: Have you finished the preparations? I can come earlier to help.
Florina: That's kind of you, but everything's already arranged.

Exercise 17.

Winston Churchil, care a fost primul-ministru al Marii Britanii în timpul celui de-al doilea război mondial, este renumit nu numai pentru discursurile sale politice, dar şi pentru remarcile sale pline de umor. Transformaţi mini-dialogurile în vorbire indirectă folosind verbul de declaraţie la timpul trecut.

a. George Bernard Shaw invited Churchill to the first night of his play, enclosing two tickets. ”One for yourself and one for a friend – if you have one.” Churchill answered: ”Unfortunately I can't make it. Can I have tickets for the second night – if there is one?”
b. A young man who photographed Churchill on his 80th anniversary: ”I hope to do the same on your hundredth”. ”You look reasonably fit to me.”
c. When he was very old and went to the House of Commons, an MP remarked: ”After all, they say he is potty (ţicnit, nebun de legat).” ”They say he can't hear either” muttered (a murmura) Churchill.
d. A Female MP: ”You're intoxicated (în stare de ebrietate), Sit.” Churchill retorted (a replica, a răspunde): ”And you, madam, are ugly. But I shall be sober (trezit din beţie) tomorrow.”

Exercise 18.

Citiţi fragmentul de interviu cu un MP. Rescrieţi interviul folosind stilul indirect şi verbul din propoziţia principală la timpul trecut.

Interviewer: When did you first become interested in politics?

D.A.: I've always been interested in politics, as far back as I can remember. I used to listen to Radio 4 every morning. I listened to it avidly and formed views on the world and what I would do if I were Prime Minister. I remember one of my ambitions was to be Secretary General of the United Nations.

Interviewer: You've been an MP for two years now. Is it as you expected it to be?

D.A.: I like an idea of what being an MP was like. I had been on a local authority for several years and as a journalist I'd visited the House of Commons. It is more or less what I expected.

Interviewer: What do you like about the job?

D.A.: I like the opportunity to put my political principles into practice. I also meeting people and I'm pleased to be able to fulfill the hopes of so many people.

Interviewer: What do you think about your fellow MPs?

D.A.: Well, it's the most male-dominated place I've ever worked in. It's a strange place because I'm 34 and anywhere else I'm middle aged, but in the House of Commons I'm a sort of bright young thing. Most of the people here are in their fifties or sixties.

Exercise 19.

Traduceţi în limba engleză.

a. A replicat că nu ştie nimic despre planurile consiliului local.
b. A recunoscut că face aşa întotdeauna.
c. Ministrul a declarat că va lua măsuri severe împotriva angajaţilor săi.
d. Omul nu ştia cui trebuia să se adreseze pentru problema sa.
e. A vrut să ştie unde se află biroul de informaţii.
f. L-au întrebat dacă mai luase legătura cu altcineva.

g. Purtătorul de cuvînt (spokesperson) a răspuns că ministrul va organiza o conferință de presă.
h. Mi-au spus să nu fac nicio declarație.
i. Ziaristul a remarcat că parlamentarul a evitat să dea un răspuns clar.
j. A zis că au trimis deja o echipă de experți să ancheteze cazul.

Exercise 20.

Transformați în ***stilul indirect*** următoarele afirmații ale unui politician.

a. "In the last decade, our country has changed for the better."
   He said that ....
b. "Every election is a time of decision."
   He remarked ....
c. "This election will decide whether we put our resources to good use."
   He added ....
d. "What are our main goals ?"
   He asked ....
e. "Do you really want to make a destiny of your own?"
   He wanted to know ....

Let/Make/Have/Get

Exercise 1.

Transformaţi propoziţiile conform modelului.

Model: The director **had** him **edit** the scene.
The director **had** the scene **edited.**

They are going to have the casting director change the leading actress.
The director is having his assistant shooting the most difficult scenes.
We should have the screenwriter shorten the lines.
They plan to have a famous play the score.
He always has people do dangerous stunts in his film.

Exercise 2.

În vorbirea familiară, construcţia ***get + participial trecut*** poate exprima un ordin ce trebuie îndeplinit de persoana căreia i se dă ordinul. Lucraţi confom modelului.

Model: Do this job!
Get this job **done**!

a. Turn on the spotlights!
b. Check light intensity!
c. Add some filters!
d. Shoot the scene again!
e. Change the ending!
f. Refresh your make-up!
g. Record some background noise!
h. Fix the setting!

Exercise 3.

Scrieţi scurte comentarii folosind verbele din paranteză.

Model: This scene is too violent. (change)
I'll have/get it changed.

a. The plot is too intricate. (revise)
b. The leading actor can't do the stunt. (do)
c. The costumes are too heavy. (alter)
d. The supporting actor is too dramatic. (replace)
e. My hair is too long. (do)
f. The film is too expensive. (cut down.)

Exercise 4.

Citiţi activităţile incluse în agenda unei devete de film şi alcătuiţi propoziţii folosind **have/get acuzativ.**

<u>**today**</u>	<u>**tomorrow**</u>
best dress/clean	eyes/test

car/service — a film/develop
audition/postpone — hair/done
fitting/reschedule — speech/write
the new script/deliver — stand-in/replace

Exercise 5.

Utilizaţi verbele următoare si puneţi-le la timpul potrivit in spaţiile libere.

let, make, have, get

Sam really wanted a dog, but his parents wouldn't ____________ him have a pet.

2. Professor Smith ______________ each of her students write an essay describing their future goals in life.
3. Professor Smith ______________ her students use a dictionary while they were taking the test.
4. Sally ____________________ me take off my shoes before I went into her house.
5. Susie __________________ her son take out the trash before he went to the park to play soccer.
6. How did you ___________________ the doctor to make a house call? I haven't heard of a doctor actually going to a patient's house in years.
7. Tommy didn't want to go to his cousin's birthday party, but his mom ________________ him go.
8. Cheryl didn't want to wash her car, so with a little smooth talk she _________________ her boyfriend to wash it for her.
9. If you ask me nicely, I'll ____________________ you lick the bowl after I make the cookies.
10. Jack found a fly floating in his coffee, so he _______________ the waiter bring him a new cup.

Exercise 6.

Scrieţi comentarii folosind verbele ***make/let*** urmate de infinitivul scurt.

Model: Ordinary people wanted to settle in Australia. The government agreed. (let)
The government let ordinary people settle in Australia.

a. The merchant's ship was loaded with merchandise. The crew unloaded it. (make)
b. The storehouses were 300 meters away. The supervisor asked them to carry the boxes there. (make)
c. The captain didn't agree. The crew was paid to sail, not to carry the merchandise. (let)
d. The merchant offered to raise the pay. The sailors had a suggestion. (let.)
e. Spices were in high demnad and expensive. The merchant said the sailors could have small amounts. (let)

Exercise 7.

Completaţi propoziţiile următoare cu ***HAVE*** sau ***GET***. Prima propoziţie a fost completată ca model.

1. Carl had food poisoning and had to ***have*** his stomach pumped.
2. I won't ………………… Richard criticised like that when he's not here to defend himself.

3. When they .... it explained to them again, the students could understand the point of the experiment.
4. I won't .... my valuable time taken up with useless meetings!
5. We always .... the car cleaned by the children who live next door.
6. We .... the painting valued by an expert at over 20,000 dollars.
7. She left the lights on overnight and in the morning couldn't .... the car started.
8. When he tried to tidy up his desk, he .... all his papers mixed up.

Exercise 8.

Completați cu ***let - make - have - get*** următoarele propoziții.

a. Rebecca Smith requested a copy of that expense report, so I _______________ the courier take one over to her last week.

b. I can't believe she _______________ you look at her vacation pictures again last night. We have to look at those stupid pictures every time we go to her house.

c. Diane thinks television is a waste of time, so she won't _______________ her children watch TV.

d. I don't know how you convince your children to clean up their rooms. I couldn't _______________ my children to clean up their rooms if my life depended on it.

e. I can't believe the zoo keeper _______________ you feed the snake. That was so cool!

f. Debbie's husband hates the opera. But after days of nagging, she finally _______________ him to go see the new production of La Boheme.

g. Sam really wanted a dog, but his parents wouldn't _______________ him have a pet.

h. My boss _______________ me get him coffee, pick up his dry cleaning and buy presents for his wife. He can't do anything by himself!

i. Rebecca Smith requested a copy of that expense report, so I _______________ the courier take one over to her last week.

j. If you ask me nicely, I'll _______________ you lick the bowl after I make the cookies.

k. Professor Bates _______________ each of her students write an essay describing their future goals in life.

l. Sally _______________ me take off my shoes before I went into her house. She said she wanted to keep the carpet clean.

m. Professor Young _______________ her students use a dictionary while they were taking the test.

Exercise 9.

Alegeți varianta corectă.

1. She ________ that he wouldn't tell anyone.
   a. made him promise
   b. made him promised
   c. promised to make
2. Does your tooth still hurt? Yes, I have to get a dentist ________ soon.
   a. look at it
   b. to look at it
   c. to get it looked at
3. I ________ a couple of days ago.
   a. had my bike to be fixed
   b. had my bike fix
   c. had my bike fixed

4. I will not ________ with this!
a. allow you get away
b. let you get away
c. to let you get away

5. Don't ________ these things about you!
a. let him say
b. let him to say
c. let him said

6. The movie ________ sad.
a. made to feel
b. made him feel
c. made him to feel

7. I ________ from my other address.
a. get my mail forward
b. get my mail to forward
c. get my mail forwarded

8. Have your assistant ________ these letters immediately!
a. to send
b. send
c. to be sent

9. He ________ yesterday.
a. had his hair cut
b. had his hair to be cut
c. had hair to be cut

10. The professor ________ early.
a. to let the students leave
b. let the student leave
c. let the student to leave

The ing form and the gerund
(Forma in –ing şi gerundivul)

Exercise 1.

Folosiţi verbele ***prefer, enjoy, love, adore, detest, not mind,*** şi expresiile ***can't bear/stand*** pentru a formula propoziţii despre preferinţele dumneavoastră.

Model: I prefer ***swimming*** to ***skating***.
I don't mind ***getting*** up early.
I detest ***watching*** day dramas (telenovele).
I can't stand ***filling*** in forms.

sports	housework	pastime	Office work
Swim Skate Job Ride a bike hike	Tidy up Go to the marketplace Cook Wash dishes Lay/clean the table	Watch TV Read novels Visit friends Go to the cinema Write letters	Answer the phone Type letters Attend staff meetings Sort the mail Use a computer

Exercise 2.

Descrieţi personalitatea celui mai bun prieten al dumneavoastră folosind tabelul de mai jos.

Model: She/He's brilliant at Maths.
She/He's sick of working over the weekend.

<table>
<tr><td rowspan="7">She/
He's</td><td>brilliant
excellent
expert
very good
poor</td><td>no good
very slow
useless
hopeless
terrible</td><td>at</td><td rowspan="7">(doing) Maths.
(learning) foreign languages
meeting new people.
going to discos.
bringing up children
buying new clothes.
doing puzzles.
watching old films.
mountain climbing.
hurting people's feelings.
counseling people.
telling jokes.
singing in public.
hitch-hiking.
competing with others.
playing chess.</td></tr>
<tr><td colspan="2">interested/successful/experienced</td><td>in</td></tr>
<tr><td colspan="2">keen</td><td>on</td></tr>
<tr><td>fond
sick
afraid</td><td>tired
incapable
scared
proud</td><td>of</td></tr>
<tr><td>mad
crazy</td><td>enthusiastic</td><td>about</td></tr>
<tr><td>used
accustomed</td><td>opposed</td><td>to</td></tr>
<tr><td>fed up
bored</td><td>annoyed
preoccupied</td><td>with</td></tr>
</table>

Exercise 3.

Transformaţi perechile de propoziţii conform modelului.

Model: He told lies. He admitted it. He admitted telling lies.

a. Please, close the door. Do you ***mind***?
b. "Let's go out." He ***suggested***.
c. He was writing a report. Has he ***finished***?
d. Living in the country side! Just ***imagine*** that!
e. I've visited Paris. I'll never ***forget***!
f. I used to smoke. I ***stopped*** two months ago.
g. I feel that this is wrong. I ***can't help*** it.
h. She moved all the furniture. Her husband ***helped*** her.
i. These papers have to be sorted out. They ***need*** it.
j. "Are you going to the party?" I ***don't feel like*** it.

Exercise 4.

Completaţi spaţiile libere cu prepoziţia corectă şi cu forma ***-ing*** a verbului din paranteză.

Model: I'm looking forward ...... (hear) from you.
I'm looking forward to hearing from you.

a. The police accused him ______________(steal) £ 500 from the shop.
b. I must apologize ______________ (do) such a stupid thing.
c. They all praised her _____________ (be) very brave.
d. The children were punished ______________ (come) home very late.
e. Thank you __________ (give) me all their information.
f. They blamed the woman ____________ (cause) the accident.
g. Her parents don't approve _____________ (study) late at night.
h. She has always dreamt _____________ (go) on a cruise on the Mediterranean.
i. His teachers congratulated him ________________ (get) the best score in the exam.
j. Mr. Smith insisted ________________ (hold) the meeting in their office.

Exercise 5.

Traduceţi în limba engleză următoarele propoziţii folosing forma în ***–ing*** şi ***gerundivul***.

a. După ce am plecat de la hotel, m-am dus la gară.
b. Ea este foarte bună la desen.
c. Îmi place să stau în hoteluri.
d. Aştept cu nerăbdare să-l cunosc.
e. Este obişnuită să meargă distanţe mari.
f. Peisajul e magnific. Merită să mergi acolo.
g. Nu are rost să te prefaci că îl iubeşti.

Present tenses in the passive voice
(Timpurile prezentului la diateza pasivă)

Exercise 1.

Puneţi verbele din paranteză la ***diateza pasivă***.

a. Great emotional and intellectual resources (demand) in quarrels.
b. No one (bear) a good quarreler.
c. The elementary principle is that anything may (say).
d. When you (love) by someone for some time and that relationship changes suddenly, it is more painful.
e. With a quarrel, the original cause must (forget).
f. Stop repeating that! I (drive) up the wall by all that nonsense you are saying.

Exercise 2.

Alcătuiţi scurte dialoguri conform modelului pentru a exersa întrebuinţarea ***diatezei pasive la prezentul continuu***.

Model: in the garden/tea/serve
What's happening in the garden?
The tea is being served.

a. in the nurse/baby/feed
b. in the bedroom/grandpa/see by the doctor
c. in Mary's room/music/play loud
d. in the kitchen/snacks/prepare
e. in the back yard/the fence/mend

Exercise 3.

Alcătuiţi propoziţii pentru a exersa întrebuinţarea ***diatezei pasive la timpul prezent simplu***. Prima propoziţie a fost completată ca model.

a) in a home	- by mother	Food is prepared by mother
	- by father	…………………………………………..
	- by children	…………………………………………..
b) on holiday's	- by mother	The luggage is carried by father.
	- by father	…………………………………………..
	- by children	…………………………………………..
c) at weekends	- by mother	The pet is taken out by the children.
	- by father	…………………………………………..
	- by children	…………………………………………..

Exercise 4.

Folosiţi-vă imaginaţia şi definiţi obiectele de mai jos folosind verbul modal urmat de ***infinitiv pasiv***. Primul obiect a fost definit ca model.

a) an egg — It can be eaten. / It must be eaten fresh. / It can be broken.
b) an apple — ....
c) a car — ....
d) a carpet — ....
e) a book — ....

Exercise 5.

Traduceți în limba engleză folosind ***diateza pasivă***.

a) Relația părinți-copii a fost schimbată de condițiile sociale în ultimul timp.
b) Apa din piscină este schimbată săptămânal.
c) Acum se schimbă aranjamentul (placement) mobilei.
d) Cursul evenimentelor nu poate fi schimbat.
e) Vreau să mi se spună adevărul.

Exercise 6.

Puneți verbele din paranteză la ***diateza pasivă*** și la ***timpul verbal*** potrivit.

a. Her parents (persuade) by the English teacher to send her abroad to study.
b. The basic moral rules (not change) overnight.
c. The 10-year-old child (hear) by the judge at the moment.
d. Can this stuff (eat) without getting ill?
e. She seems to (carry) away by her feelings towards him.

Exercise 7.

Traduceți în limba engleză.

a. Copii sunt tratați în mod egal de către părinții lor.
b. În prezent, oamenii se mută din orașul natal ca să lucreze, deci familia se împrăștie.
c. Unele dintre aceste schimbări au fost determinate de legi noi.
d. Vreau ca totul să fie aranjat înainte să vină mama.
e. Aproximativ 750,000 de bătrâni trebuie să fie îngrijiți.

The suffixes
(Sufixele)

Exercise 1.

Adăugați *sufixele* potrivite pentru a forma noi cuvinte care să completeze propozițiile. Alegeți dintre sufixele: ***-able, -age, -al, -er, -ful, -ic,-ing, -in, -ly, - y.***

PAPER a. When the old lady touched me, I felt her dry ___________ skin.
RECYCLE b. Plastic and paper bags are __________.
SAVE c. The new device we acquired is a time-and money ________.
WASTE d. It's ___________ to throw these away. We could use them one day.
GLASS e. She pierced me with her _____________ eyes.
USE f. Damaging environment serves no ____________ purpose.
POLLUTE g. The men are clearing all the ___________ off the beach.
CARRY h. The British call a ____________ a strong bag with handles to take goods away in.
METAL i. Its color was bright ___________ blue.
PACK j. He sent a large ____________ of books.

Exercise 2.

Adăugați *sufixul* corect pentru a forma cuvinte cu care să completați propozițiile date. Alegeți dintre sufixele: ***-al, -age, -ed, -ing, -ment.***

WED a. Hurry up! The ___________ service has just started.
MARRY b. How could she possibly do it? She is a __________ woman.
BETROTH c. We're celebrating our __________. We would like you to come.
MARRY d. unfortunately, their __________ didn't last long. They were too different.
WED e. "Will you have this man as you __________ husband?"
BETROTH f. Let me introduce the newly ___________ couple to you.
ENGAGE g. Have you heard that Maria has broken off her __________ to Mihai?

Exercise 3.

Completați propozițiile de mai jos cu cuvintele din stânga la forma pozitivă. Adăugați *sufixele*: ***-ish, -less, -able, -ic, -ing, -ive, -ate, -y.***

SELF 1. Don't be ……………. . Sharing things is a job.
RELY 2. One can count on her as she is a ……………. person.
SENSE 3. It is …………… asking her for help. She won't lift a finger.
SYMPATHY 4. She is so ………….. and understanding. Try to talk to her.
WIT 5. The girl's ………… remarks amazed the people present.
PASSION 6. It was a pity he didn't share her …………… love.
CARE 7. She was fortunate to have a …………….. and loving mother.
IMPULSE 8. Boys are said to be more ……………….. than girls.
ASSERT 9. Be more ……………… and people will surely trust you.
DECIDE 10. Her final argument was …………….. and she won the law suit.

Exercise 4.

Completați *sufixul* corect: **-ism, -ly, -ness, -word, -less, en, -eons**, astfel încât propozițiile să aibă sens.

a. "If you consider right …….. of the matter.
Caesar has had great wrong." (Shakespeare – "Julius Caesar")
b. He is known for his moral righteous …..…. .
c. The right ………. of the Tower of Pisa has changed in time.
d. The road goes right …….. for half a mile and then it comes to a closed end.
e. No lawyer will take your case as your claim is right……. .
f. His fellows didn't share his right ……….. .
g. It will be wise of you to right…. things up.
h. Both men end women deserve a right……. treatment, socially speaking.
i. They were grateful to him judging the case rightful…..… .

Exercise 5.

Substantivul ***"lion"*** poate primi următoarele *sufixe*:

lion + ***esque*** [laiə'nesk] leonin
lion + ***ess*** ['laiənis] leoaică
lion + ***et*** ['latənit] pui de leu
lion + ***ize*** ['laiənaiz] a trata ca pe o celebritate
adjectiv compus: lion-***hearted*** neînfricat

Completați propozițiile cu unul din cuvintele de deasupra.

a. The chief distinguished himself by his …………………… power.
b. In front of the den, the …………….. played joyfully with her cubs.
c. As he was one of the nominees (candidați) for the award, his friends ……………. him.
d. The king was confident in his soldiers because they all were …………………… .
e. While she was on a safari, she found a ………………… in a bush.

Exercise 6.

La fiecare dintre verbele din cele 2 liste adăugați *sufixele* corespunzătoare ***er*** sau ***or*** pentru a obține substantive care denumesc agentul.

-er		-or	
write	writer	instruct	instructor
learn		supervise	
read		inspect	
train		comment	
examine		assess	
lecture		process	
compute		calculate	
research			
compose			
analyse			

Exercise 7.

Adăugați ***prefixe*** (super-, un-) și ***sufixe*** (-al, -ation, -ed, -ism, -istic, -ist, -iye, -ly, -ness) pentru a obține paradigma lexicală a cuvântului nature. Completați apoi propozițiile cu unele dintre cuvintele obținute.

a. Try to look ____________ for your photograph.

b. He became ____________ after living in France for ten years.
c. ______________ implies showing world and people exactly as they are with the deficiencies of the social environment and the shortcomings of human beings.
d. Skating comes ______________ to the Scandinavian people.
e. Alexander von Humbold was a famous German ___________.

Exercise 8.

Formulaţi noi cuvinte pentru completarea propoziţiilor. Folosiţi *sufixul* corespunzător:-al, -ar, ary, -or/er, -dom, -ic, -ion, -y. Atenţie că uneori cuvântul dat se modifică înaintea adăugării sufixului.

STAR	a. The ___________ is infinite.
EMANATE	b. The probe is detecting a powerful __________ of helium.
GALAXY	c. The crew is exploring the ___________ space.
SUN	d. Pioneer 10 will go beyond the boundary of the ______ system.
PLANET	e. His team has written studies on the ___________ motion.
SPACE	f. This programme will provide information on ____ relationships.
NAVIGATE	g. Christopher Columb was a famous ____________.
STAR	h. The __________ winter sky was a real marvel.
ASTRONOMY	i. Carl Sagan was an outstanding American.
ORBIT	j. The satellite will enter its ________ trajectory in about ten hours.

Exercise 9.

Folosiţi cuvintele din coloana stângă pentru a forma cuvintele care lipsesc din fiecare propoziţie. Alegeţi sufixul corespunzător formelor verbale cerute: -aritz; -ate; -en; -ence; -ful; -ize; -ous.

AGONY	a. How long will _________ like this?
GRIEF	b. Your _________ mistake could affect the rest of your life.
CONFIDE	c. They failed to win public __________ and lost the elections.
FEAR	d. He was ________ of this mother's anger.
THREAT	e. The incident might _________ to ruin his reputation.
DESPAIR	f. The management resorted to __________ measures to save the company.
SOLID	g. We should appeal to people's __________.

Exercise 10.

Completaţi spaţiile libere cu cuvintele obţinute prin sufixarea celor din paranteză.

The Internet has changed (1) _________ (communicate) as we know it. From education to (2) ___________ (advertise) this new (3) ____________ (technology) advance has affected (4) ____________ (practical) every aspect of our lives. Magazines, newspapers and even books are on-line and can be read on the computer. You can find (5) __________ (inform) on any topic – the (6) _____________ (possible) are (7) ___________ (end). The Internet can (8) _______ (instant) connect you to other computers, allowing you to chat with people all over the world. It's actually very easy to learn how to use the system, and once you are on-line, you'll never want tot turn the computer off! The (9) ___________ (develop) of such technology has come a long way. These (10) ____________ (amaze) electronic devices have changed many people's lives forever.

Idioms and Idiomatic Expressions
(Expresiile idiomatice)

Exercise 1.

Uniți cu o linie ***expresiile idiomatice*** cu explicația corectă.

1. at your fingertips	a. have something else to do
2. read between the lines	b. begin a new course of improved behavior
3. have other fish to fry	c. delay talking about the main part of the topic.
4. play it by ear	d. complete and ready knowledge of something
5. at arm's length	e. give an opinion in a commanding way
6. turn over a new leaf	f. guess that something wrong is happening
7. in the same boat	g. find hidden meanings
8. beat about the bush	h. in the same unpleasant situation
9. smell a rat	i. act according to changing conditions
10. lay down the law	j. avoid being friendly with someone

Exercise 2.

Completați definițiile cu expresiile idiomatice corespunzătoare. Alegeți dintre expresiile date.

- learn by heart	- as right as rain
- nip in the bud	- a storm is brewing
- keep an iron rod over somebody	- get on like a house on fire
- err on the right side	- before the mast
- learn one's lesson	- as fit as a fiddle

a. If you are on a sailing ship as an ordinary seaman, not as an officer, you sail ……………... .
b. You ………………… when you have suffered so much from doing something bad that you will not do it again.
c. A person who is very healthy is …………………… .
d. When you are very strict with someone you ……………….. that person.
e. Learning a poem ………………. means learning it by memory.
f. When people have a very friendly relationship or start one very easily they ……….. .
g. A person who has recovered from an illness and feels OK is …………………… .
h. To stop something before it has properly started is ……………………. .
i. Something bad is in preparation or ready to happen. It means …………………. .
j. It's better to ……………………; that is to be too careful rather than not careful enough.

Exercise 3.

Citiți și rețineți sensurile câtorva ***expresii idiomatice*** care conțin cuvântul "right" cu diferite valori morfologice (substantive, adjective, verb, adverb).

- to send someone to the right about	= to get rid of someone (a da papucii, a trimite la plimbare)
- as right as rain	= perfect, without flaws
- to right a wrong	= to make up for an unjust deed
- right on the spot	= that very place, immediately
- the right men in the right place	= to fulfill one's destiny
- to err on the right side	= to make the best choose of two evils
- to be on the right path	= to follow a good (safe way)

- to be on the right side of the fence = to stand a good/just position on an issue.
- to set to rights = to put things in order
- to be in one's right mind = perfectly sane/reasonable

Exercise 4.

Completați expresiile idiomatice cu substantivele care lipsesc.

a. The essay doesn't worth the ______ it is written on.
b. I am burning the midnight ______ again tonight.
c. Be careful! You might open a ______ of worms.
d. Don't say any more words! You're wasting your ______.
e. As for going abroad this summer, through a ______ darkly.
f. They buried the ______ and now are good friends.
g. Large sums of money have gone down the ______.
h. How can you read this ______?

Exercise 5.

Completați expresiile idiomatice cu substantivele care lipsesc.

a. At that time it was convenient for them for them to sweep it under the ______.
b. I hate it when people wash their dirty ______ in public.
c. It wasn't me who let the cat out of the ______.
d. He is known for his righteousness; he's certain to blow the ______ on the commission's affairs.
e. You'll feel better if you get it off you.

Exercise 6.

Uniți expresiile idiomatice cu explicația corectă.

1. to mince one's words	a. To speak plainly
2. to lay one's cards on the table	b. Not to come to one's point
3. to call a spade	c. To speak in an affected way
4. to beat about the bush	d. To be open-hearted
5. to pull one's punches	e. To speak carefully when not necessary

Exercise 7.

Completați propozițiile cu expresia idiomatică corespunzătoare. Atenței la forma verbală!

to beat about the bush = to delay talking about the most important pasrt of a subject;
to lay one's cards on the table = to be compltely open and honest about one's position or plans
above board = without any attempt to deceive
to mince one's words = to speak of something unpleasant without using plain, direct words
to call a spade a spade = to speak the plain truth without being delicate or sensitive
to come clean = to admit to guilt or mistake
to pull one's punches = to express one's bad opinion more gently than is deserved.

a. He's one of the most brutally honest men I've ever met. He ______ whoever you are.
b. If you refer to a business as ______, you mean that it is honest and legal.
c. He says things more directly than other writers sometimes do. He doesn't ______.

d. If I were you, I wouldn't trust him. He doesn't always _________.
e. I've always thought that's better to _________; otherwise people may understand you.
f. " Did you watch the talk show last night?" "Yes, I did, I really liked it because they didn't _________ about unemployment.
g. This time the board _________ saying that the situation is due to mismanagement.

Exercise 8.

Completați expresiile idiomatice cu substantivul care lipsește, conform indicației din paranteză.

1. During the first years, he **served before the** ______________ (to be on a sailing ship as an ordinary seaman).
2. If you lose you job, I'll lose mine, so we're both **in the same** _________ (facing the same dangers).
3. It's too late now. He's **gone on** ______________ (to embark).
4. He passed his exams **with flying** ____________ (very successfully).
5. Mary's been **walking on** ______________ since he proposed to her (extremely happy).
6. It didn't even **cross my** ___________ that he would be upset (to come into one's thought).
7. This is our business. Would you like him **to have his** _______ **in our boat**? (to interfere with someone else's business).

Exercise 9.

Înlocuiți expresiile idiomatice cu unul din verbele ***say*** sau ***tell***. Efectuați orice alte schimbări necesare.

1. The Chief Inspector **sent world** to his deputy that he wished to see him.
The Chief Inspector told his deputy that he wished to see him.
2. If you're going to be late, you should **let me known**.
....
3. Just **give it to me** straight. I'm going to find it out any way.
....
4. She stared at the letter, clearly **at a loss for words.**
....
5. We'd better get her on our side before she has a chance to **blow the whistle on us**.
....
6. She denies ever **making the statement** attributed to her the pres.
....
7. I'm not afraid to **speak my mind**.
....
8. I feel so much better now that **I've got that off my chest.**
....
9. Look at this. It's ...... **Words fail me!**
....
10. You never know what he'**ll** come out with next.
....
11. Jim knows about it. I'm afraid I ***let the cat out of the bag.***
....

LIST OF IRREGULAR VERBS (Lista verbelor neregulate)

A. One form

to bet [bet]	**bet** [bet]	**bet** [bet] a paria
to broadcast ['br□:dka:st]	**broadcast** ['br□:dka:st]	**broadcast** ['br□:dka:st]
		a transmite (prin radio)
to burst [bə:st]	**burst** [bə:st]	**burst** [bə:st] a crăpa
to cast [ka:st]	**cast** [ka:st]	**cast** [ka:st] a arunca
to cost [k□st]	**cost** [k□st]	**cost** [k□st] a costa
to cut [kΛt]	**cut** [kΛt]	**cut** [kΛt] a tăia
to forecast ['f□:ka:st]	**forecast** ['f□:ka:st]	**forecast** ['f□:ka:st]
		a prevedea
to hit [hit]	**hit** [hit]	**hit** [hit]a lovi
to hurt [hə:t]	**hurt** [hə:t]	**hurt** [hə:t]a răni
to knit [nit]	**knit** [nit]	**knit** [nit]a tricota
	knitted ['nitid]	**knitted** ['nitid]
to let [let]	**let** [let]	**let** [let] a permite
to put [put]	**put** [put]	**put** [put] a pune
to rid [rid]	**rid** [rid]	**rid** [rid] a libera
	ridded ['ridid]	**ridded** ['ridid]
to set [set]	**set** [set]	**set** [set] a aşeza, a pune
to shed [ʃed]	**shed** [ʃed]	**shed** [ʃed] a lăsa să cadă,
		a vărsa (lacrimi)
to shut [ʃΛt]	**shut** [ʃΛt]	**shut** [ʃΛt] a închide
to slit [slit]	**slit** [slit]	**slit** [slit] a crăpa
to split [split]	**split** [split]	**split** [split] a despica
to spread [spred]	**spread** [spred]	**spread** [spred] a întinde
to thrust [θrΛst]	**thrust** [θrΛst]	**thrust** [θrΛst] a îmbrânci
to upset [Λp'set]	**upset** [Λp'set]	**upset** [Λp'set] a răsturna
to wet [wet]	**wet** [wet]	**wet** [wet] a uda

B. Two form

to abide [ə'baid]	**abode** [ə'bəud]	**abode** [ə'bəud] a locui
to awake [ə'weik]	**awoke** [ə'wəuk]	**awoke** [ə'wəuk] a se trezi
	awaked [ə'weikt]	**awaked** [ə'weikt]
to beat [bi:t]	**beat** [bi:t]	**beaten** ['bi:tn] a bate
to become [bi'kΛm]	**became** [bi'keim]	**become** [bi'kΛm] a deveni
to behold [bi'həuld]	**beheld** [bi'held]	**beheld** [bi'held] a zări
to bind [baind]	**bound** [baund]	**bound** [baund] a lega
to bleed [bli:d]	**bled** [bled]	**bled** [bled] a sângera
to bless [bles]	**blest** [blest]	**blest** [blest] a binecuvânta
	blessed [blest]	**blessed** [blest]
to bring [briŋ]	**brought** [br□:t]	**brought** [br□:t] a aduce
to build [bild]	**built** [bilt]	**built** [bilt] a clădi
to burn [bə:n]	**burnt** [bə:nt]	**burnt** [bə:nt] a arde
to buy [bai]	**bought** [b□:t]	**bought** [b□:t] a cumpăra
to catch [kætʃ]	**caught** [k□:t]	**caught** [k□:t] a prinde
to cleave [kli:v]	**cleft** [kleft]	**cleft** [kleft] a despica

	clove [kləuv]	**cleaved** [kli:vd]
to cling [kliŋ]	**clung** [klΛŋ]	**clung** [klΛŋ] a se agăța
to come [kΛm]	**came** [keim]	**come** [kΛm] a veni
to creep [kri:p]	**crept** [krept]	**crept** [krept] a se târî
to dare [dεə]	**dared** [dεəd]	**dared** [dεəd] a îndrăzni
	durst [də:st]	**durst** [də:st]
to deal [di:l]	**dealt** [delt]	**dealt** [delt] a se ocupa
to dig [dig]	**dug** [dΛg]	**dug** [dΛg] a săpa
	digged [digd]	**digged** [digd]
to dream [dri:m]	**dreamt** [dremt]	**dreamt** [dremt] a visa
to dwell [dwel]	**dwelt** [dwelt]	**dwelt** [dwelt] a locui
to feed [fi:d]	**fed** [fed]	**fed** [fed] a hrăni
to feel [fi:l]	**felt** [felt]	**felt** [felt] a simți
to fight [fait]	**fought** [f□:t]	**fought** [f□:t] a lupta
to find [faind]	**found** [faund]	**found** [faund] a găsi
to flee [fli:]	**fled** [fled]	**fled** [fled] a fugi
to fling [fliŋ]	**flung** [flΛŋ]	**flung** [flΛŋ] a azvârli
to foretell [f□:'tel]	**foretold** [f□:'təuld]	**foretold** [f□:'təuld] a prezice
to get [get]	**got** [g□t]	**got** [g□t] a primi
to grind [graind]	**ground** [graund]	**ground** [graund] a măcina
to hang [hæŋ]	**hung** [hΛŋ]	**hung** [hΛŋ] a atârna
	hanged [hæŋd]	**hanged** [hæŋd]
to have [hæv]	**had** [hæd]	**had** [hæd] a avea
to hear [hiə]	**heard** [hə:d]	**heard** [hə:d] a auzi
to hold [həuld]	**held** [held]	**held** [held] a ține
to keep [ki:p]	**kept** [kept]	**kept** [kept] a ține, a păstra
to kneel [ni:l]	**knelt** [nelt]	**knelt** [nelt] a îngenunchea
to lay [lei]	**laid** [leid]	**laid** [leid] a aşeza
to lead [li:d]	**led** [led]	**led** [led] a conduce
to lean [li:n]	**leant** [lent]	**leant** [lent] a se înclina
	leaned [li:nd]	**leaned** [li:nd]
to leap [li:p]	**leapt** [lept]	**leapt** [lept] a sări
	leaped [li:pt]	**leaped** [li:pt]
to learn [lə:n]	**learnt** [lə:nt]	**learnt** [lə:nt] a învăța
	learned [lə:nd]	**learned** [lə:nd]
to leave [li:v]	**left** [left]	**left** [left] a lăsa, a părăsi
to lend [lend]	**lent** [lent]	**lent** [lent] a împrumuta
to light [lait]	**lit** [lit]	**lit** [lit] a aprinde
to lose [lu:z]	**lost** [l□st]	**lost** [l□st] a pierde
to make [meik]	**made** [meid]	**made** [meid] a face
to mean [mi:n]	**meant** [ment]	**meant** [ment] a însemna
to meet [mi:t]	**met** [met]	**met** [met] a întâlni
to mislead [mis'lu:d]	**misled** [mis'led]	**misled** [mis'led] a induce în eroare
to misunderstand ['misΛndə'stænd]	**misunderstood** ['misΛndə'stud]	**misunderstood** ['misΛndə'stud] a înțelege greşit
to overcome [,əuvə'kΛm]	**overcame** [,əuvə'keim]	**overcome** [,əuvə'kΛm] a învinge
to pay [pei]	**paid** [peid]	**paid** [peid] a plăti
to read [ri:d]	**read** [red]	**read** [red] a citi
to rebuid ['ri:bild]	**rebuilt** ['ri:'bilt]	**rebuilt** ['ri:'bilt] a reconstrui
to rend [rend]	**rent** [rent]	**rent** [rent] a sfâşia
to run [rΛn]	**ran** [ræn]	**run** [rΛn] a alerga

to say [sei]	**said** [sed]	**said** [sed] a spune
to seek [si:k]	**sought** [s□:t]	**sought** [s□:t] a căuta
to sell [sel]	**sold** [səuld]	**sold** [səuld] a vinde
to send [send]	**sent** [sent]	**sent** [sent] a trimite
to shine [ʃain]	**shone** [ʃ□n]	**shone** [ʃ□n] a străluci
to sit [sit]	**sat** [sæt]	**sat** [sæt] a şedea
to sleep [sli:p]	**slept** [slept]	**slept** [slept] a dormi
to slide [slaid]	**slid** [slid]	**slid** [slid] a luneca
to sling [sliŋ]	**slung** [slΛŋ]	**slung** [slΛŋ] a azvârli
to smell [smel]	**smelt** [smelt]	**smelt** [smelt] a mirosi
to speed [spi:d]	**sped** [sped]	**sped** [sped] a goni, a accelera
to spell [spel]	**spelt** [spelt]	**spelt** [spelt] a scrie/pronunţa literă cu literă
	spelled [spelt]	**spelled** [spelt]
to spend [spend]	**spent** [spent]	**spent** [spent] a petrece, a cheltui
to spill [spil]	**spilt** [spilt]	**spilt** [spilt] a vărsa
	spilled [spild]	**spilled** [spild]
to spin [spin]	**spun** [spΛn]	**spun** [spΛn] a toarce
to spit [spit]	**spat** [spæt]	**spat** [spæt] a scuipa
to spoil [sp□il]	**spoilt** [sp□ilt]	**spoilt** [sp□ilt] a strica
to stand [stænd]	**stood** [stud]	**stood** [stud] a sta în picioare
to stick [stik]	**stuck** [stΛk]	**stuck** [stΛk] a înfige
to sting [stiŋ]	**stung** [stΛŋ]	**stung** [stΛŋ] a înţepa
to strike [straik]	**struck** [strΛk]	**struck** [strΛk] a lovi
		stricken [’strikn]
to string [striŋ]	**strung** [strΛŋ]	**strung** [strΛŋ] a înşira, a încorda
to sweep [swi:p]	**swept** [swept]	**swept** [swept] a mătura
to swing [swiŋ]	**swung** [swΛŋ]	**swung** [swΛŋ] a legăna
to teach [ti:tʃ]	**taught** [t□:t]	**taught** [t□:t] a învăţa, a preda
to tell [tel]	**told** [təuld]	**told** [təuld] a zice
to think [θiŋk]	**thought** [θ□:t]	**thought** [θ□:t] a gândi, a crede
to tread [tred]	**trod** [tr□d]	**trod** [tr□d] a călca
		trodden [’tr□dn]
to understand [,Λndə’stænd]	**understood** [,Λndə’stud]	**understood** [,Λndə’stud] a înţelege
to weep [wi:p]	**wept** [wept]	**wept** [wept] a plânge
to win [win]	**won** [wΛn]	**won** [wΛn] a câştiga
to wind [waind]	**wound** [waund]	**wound** [waund] a se răsuci, a şerpui
to work [wə:k]	**worked** [wə:kt]	**worked** [wə:kt] a lucra
	wrought [r□:t]	**wrought** [r□:t]
to wring [riŋ]	**wrung** [rΛŋ]	**wrung** [rΛŋ] a frânge, a stoarce

C. Three form

to arise [ə’raiz]	**arose** [ə’rəuz]	**arisen** [ə’rizn] a se ridica
to be [bi:]	**was** [w□z]	**been** [bi:n] a fi
to bear [bεə]	**bore** [b□:]	**borne** [b□:n] a purta
to begin [bi:’gin]	**began** [bi:’gæn]	**begun** [bi’gΛn] a începe

to bid [bid]	**bade** [beid] [bæd]	**bidden** [’bidn] a oferi, a licita
to bite [bait]	**bit** [bit]	**bitten** [’bitn] a muşca
to blow [bləu]	**blew** [blu:]	**blown** [bləun] a sufla
to break [breik]	**broke** [brəuk]	**broken** [’brəukn] a sparge
to choose [tʃu:z]	**chose** [tʃəuz]	**chosen** [’tʃəuzn] a alege
to do [du:]	**did** [did]	**done** [dΛn] a face
to draw [dr□:]	**drew** [dru:]	**drawn** [dr□:n] a trage
to drink [driŋk]	**drank** [dræŋk]	**drunk** [drΛŋk] a bea
to drive [draiv]	**drove** [drəuv]	**driven** [’drivn] a mâna
to eat [i:t]	**ate** [et, eit]	**eaten** [’i:tn] a mânca
to fall [f□:l]	**fell** [fel]	**fallen** [’f□:ln] a cădea
to fly [flai]	**flew** [flu:]	**flown** [fləun] a zbura
to forbid [fə’bid]	**forbade** [fə’bæd]	**forbidden** [fə’bidn] a interzice
to foresee [f□:’si:]	**foresaw** [f□:’s□:]	**foreseen** [f□:’si:n] a preda
to forget [f□’get]	**forgot** [fə’g□t]	**forgotten** [fə’g□tn] a uita
to forgive [fə’giv]	**forgave** [fə’geiv]	**forgiven** [fə’givn] a ierta
to forsake [fə’seik]	**forsook** [fə’suk]	**forsaken** [fə’seikn] a părăsi
to freeze [fri:z]	**froze** [frəuz]	**frozen** [’frəuzn] a îngheța
to give [giv]	**gave** [geiv]	**given** [’givn] a da
to go [gəu]	**went** [went]	**gone** [g□n] a merge
to grow [grəu]	**grew** [gru:]	**grown** [grəun] a creşte
to hide [haid]	**hid** [hid]	**hidden** [’hidn] a ascunde
to know [nəu]	**knew** [nju:]	**known** [nəun] a şti
to lie [lai]	**lay** [lei]	**lain** [lein] a fi culcat
to misgive [mis’giv]	**misgave** [mis’geiv]	**misgiven** [’mis’givn] a inspira neîncredere
to mistake [mis’teik]	**mistook** [mis’tuk]	**mistaken** [mis’teik] a înțelege greşit
to outdo [aut’du:]	**outdid** [aut’did]	**outdone** [aut’dΛn] a întrece
to overdo [,əuvə’du:]	**overdid** [,əuvə’did]	**overdone** [,əuvə’dΛn] a face exces
to ride [raid]	**rode** [rəud]	**ridden** [’ridn] a călări
to ring [riŋ]	**rang** [ræŋ]	**rung** [rΛŋ] a suna
to rise [raiz]	**rose** [rəuz]	**risen** [’rizn] a se ridica
to see [si:]	**saw** [s□:]	**seen** [si:n] a vedea
to sew [səu]	**sewed** [səud]	**sewn** [səun] a coase
to shake [ʃeik]	**shook** [ʃuk]	**shaken** [’ʃeikn] a scutura, a clătina
to show [ʃəu]	**showed** [ʃəud]	**shown** [ʃəun] a arăta
to shrink [ʃriŋk]	**shrank** [ʃræŋk]	**shrunk** [ʃrΛŋk] a se strânge
to sing [siŋ]	**sang** [sæŋ]	**sung** [sΛŋ] a cânta
to sink [siŋk]	**sank** [sæŋk]	**sunk** [sΛŋk] a se scufunda
to slay [slei]	**slew** [slu:]	**slain** [slein] a ucide
to slide [slaid]	**slid** [slid]	**slid** [slid] a aluneca
to smite [smait]	**smote** [sməut]	**smitten** [’smitn] a lovi
to sow [səu]	**sowed** [səud]	**sown** [səun] a semăna
to speak [spi:k]	**spoke** [spəuk]	**spoken** [’spəukn] a vorbi
to spring [spriŋ]	**sprang** [spræŋ]	**sprung** [strΛŋ] a sări
to steal [sti:l]	**stole** [stəul]	**stolen** [’stəuln] a fura
to stink [stiŋk]	**stank** [stΛŋk] **stunk** [stΛŋk]	**stunk** [stΛŋk] a mirosi urât
to stride [straid]	**strode** [strəud]	**stridden** [’stridn] a umbla
to strive [straiv]	**strove** [strəuv]	**striven** [’strivn] a se strădui

to swear [swɛə]	**swore** [sw□:]	**sworn** [sw□:n] a se umfla
to swell [swel]	**swelled** [sweld]	**swollen** ['swəuln] a jura **swelled** [sweld]
to swim [swim]	**swam** [swæm]	**swum** [swΛm] a înota
to take [teik]	**took** [tuk]	**taken** ['teikn] a lua
to tear [tɛə]	**tore** [t□:]	**torn** [t□:n] a rupe
to thrive [θraiv]	**throve** [θrəuv]	**thriven** ['θrivn] a prospera
to throw [θrəu]	**threw** [θru:]	**thrown** [θrəun] a arunca
to underline [,Λndə'lai]	**underlay** [,Λndə'lei]	**underlain** [,Λndə'lein] a susține
to wake [weik]	**woke** [wəuk]	**woken** ['wəukn] a se trezi
to wear [weə]	**wore** [w□:]	**worn** [w□:n] a purta
to weave [wi:v]	**wove** [wəuv]	**woven** ['wəuvn] a țese
to withdraw [wið'dr□:]	**withdrew** [wið'dru:]	**withdrawn** [wið'dr□:n] a retrage
to write [rait]	**wrote** [rəut]	**written** ['ritn] a scrie

ESSENTIAL VOCABULARY OF ENGLISH
(Vocabular fundamental al limbii engleze)

A. NOUNS

accident
action
actor
addition
address
advantage
advertisement
affair
afternoon
age
agriculture
aid
air
airport
alcohol
ambition
amount
amusement
anger
angle
animal
apparatus
apple
appointment
approval
arch
architect
area
argument
arm
army
arrival
art
article
artist
assistant
atmosphere
attention
attraction
aunt
authority
autumn
avenue
baby
back
bacon
bag
baker's
balance
ball
band
bank
barber's
base
basin
basket
bath
battle
beard
beauty
bed
bedroom
beef
beer
behaviour
belief
bell
bench
bill
bird
birth
birthday
biscuit
bit
bite
blackboard
blade
blanket
block
blood
blouse
board
boat
body
bone
book
booking-office
boot
border
bottle
bottom
box
boy
branke
brach
bread
breakfast
breath
bridge
brother
brush
building
bus
business
butcher's
butter
button
cafe
cake
camera
cancer
candidate
cap
capital
capitalism
captain
car
card
care
carpet
cart
cat
cattle
centre
century
ceremony
chair
chalk
chance
character
chat
cheat
cheese
chemist's
cheer
cheque
chest
chief
chicken
child
chimney
chin
chocolate
church
cigar
cigarette
cinema
circle
city
class
clerk
climate
clock
cloth
clothes
cloud
coal
coast
coat
coffee
coin
collar
colour
comb
comedy
comfort
commander
commerce
committee
communication
communism
communist

company
comparison
competition
composition
compromise
concert
condition
conductor
congratulation
connection
conservative
constitution
consersation
co-operation
copy
cord
corner
cotton
council
country
courage
court
cover
cow
crack
cream
creation
credit
crime
criminal
crowd
cup
cupboard
current
curtain
custom
customer
danger
date
daughter
day
death
debate
debt
decision
defence
delay
democracy
departure
desk
desert
design
desire
detail
detective
development
dictator
difference
difficulty
direction
discovery
disturb
dining-room
dinner
direction
disarmament
discover
discussion
disease
disgust
dish
dispute
distance
distribution
doctor
dollar
door
doubt
dozen
drawer
dress
driver
driving
dust
ear
earth
east
edge
education
effect
effort
egg
election
element
emotion
employee
end
enemy
energy
engine
engineer
entrance
envelope
equality
error
essay
evening
event
examination
example
existence
expansion
experience
expert
expression
eye
face
fact
factory
failure
fame
family
farm
farmer
father
favour
feeling
female
fever
fiction
field
figure
film
fine
finger
fire
fireplace
fish
flag
flame
flat
flight
floor
flour
flower
fog
food
foot
foreigner
fork
framework
freedom
friend
friendship
front
frontier
fruit
fuel
fun
furnace
furniture
future
game
garage
garden
gas
gate
gentleman
gift
girl
glass
globe
glove
goal
gold
good-bye
government
governor
grandfather
grandmother
grass
grip
grocer's
ground
group
growth
guest
guide
gun
hair
hairdresser's
half
hall
ham
hand
handkerchief

harbour
harvest
hat
head
headache
headline
health
heart
heating
helicopter
hen
hill
history
holiday
home
homework
honey
horse
hospital
hotel
humour
husband
ice
ice-cream
idea
illness
improvement
impulse
increase
independence
idustry
information
initiative
ink
insect
instrument
insurance
interest
invention
iron
island
jam
jet
jewel
job
journey
joy
justice
kettle
key
kidney
kidness
king
kitchen
knee
knife
knowledge
laboratory
labour
lady
lamp
land
language
lake
law
leader
leather
leg
lesson
letter
level
liberty
library
licence
life
lift
limit
line
linen
lip
list
literature
liver
lorry
lot
lunch
lung
machine
magazine
maize
male
man
manager
manner
market
marmalade
map
masterpiece
match
material
matter
mayor
meal
measure
meat
medicine
meeting
member
memory
merchant
message
metal
method
middle
midnight
mile
milk
mine
mineral
minister
minute
misfortune
Miss
mistake
model
moment
money
month
moon
morning
motel
mother
mountain
mouth
movement
Mr.
Mrs.
museum
music
mutton
name
nation
nature
neck
neighbour
neutral
news
newspaper
night
noise
noon
north
nose
notebook
number
nurse
nut
observation
occasion
ocean
office
officer
oil
operation
opinion
opposition
orange
orchestra
organization
origin
oven
owner
packet
page
pain
painter
palace
paper
parent
park
parliament
part
party
patient
pavement
peace
pen
pencil
penny
people
person
petrol
photograph
piane
picture
piece

pig
pillow
pilot
pin
pipe
place
plane
plant
plate
platform
pleasure
plum
pocket
poetry
police
politics
population
pork
port
porter
position
post
pot
potato
pound
poverty
powder
power
present
president
price
print
prison
problem
process
product
profit
programme
progress
property
proposal
prose
protest
pump
punishment
pupil
purpose
pyjamas
quality
quarter
queen
question
radio
railway
range
rate
razor
ray
reaction
reading
reason
record
refrigerator
relation
relief
religion
report
representative
republic
respect
restaurant
reward
rice
ring
rival
river
road
rock
roll
roof
room
root
rubber
ruin
rule
sack
salad
salary
sale
salt
sand
satellite
satisfaction
sausage
scale
scenery
school
science
sea
seaside
season
secretary
self-service
sensation
sense
series
servant
sex
shade
sheep
shelf
shelter
ship
shoe
shop
shop-assistant
shopping
shore
shoulder
shower
side
sight
silence
silver
sister
sitting-room
situation
size
skill
skin
skirt
sky
slope
soap
socialism
society
sock
soldier
son
song
sort
sound
soup
south
space
speed
spirit
sponge
spoon
sport
spring
stage
staircase
stamp
star
state
statement
station
steam
steel
stick
stocking
stomach
stone
storm
story
stranger
street
string
structure
student
subject
substance
success
sugar
suggestion
suit
suit-case
sum
summer
sun
supper
system
table
tablet
tail
tap
tax
taxi
tea
teacher
team
technician
telegram
television
temper

temperature
tendency
theatre
theory
thief
thing
thunder
ticket
time
toast
ton
tongue
tool
tooth
top
towel
town
tractor
trade
tradition
tragedy
train
tray
treaty
tree
trial
trick
trip
trouble
trousers
truck
truth
tube
turkey
twist
typist
tyre
umbrella
underground
unemployed
unemployment
unit
university
use
valley
value
vegetable
vessel
victory
view
village
voice
wages
walk
wall
wallet
war
watch
water
wave
way
weapon
week
weight
welcome
west
wheat
wheather
wheel
wife
wind
window
wing
winter
woman
wood
word
worker
works
workshop
writer
writing
year

The Days of the Week

Sunday
Monday
Tuesday
Wednesday
Thursday
Friday
Saturday

The Months of the Year

January
February
March
April
May
June
July
August
September
October
November
December

B. ADJECTIVES

able
absent
active
actual
afraid
alive
ancient
angry
asleep
awake
bad
beautiful
big
bitter
black
blind
blue
brave
brilliant
broad
brown
busy
calm
capitalist
careful
central
certain
cheap
chemical
clean
clear
clever
comfortable
common
cold
complete
conscious
content
contrary
cool
cruel
curious
damp
dangerous
dark
dead
deaf
dear
deep
delicate
delightful
dependent
different
difficult
dirty
dull
dumb
dusty
easy
economic
elastic
electric
empty
equal
exact
excited
fair
false
familiar
famous
fat
fertile

bright
fine
foggy
foolish
free
frequent
fresh
friendly
funny
full
general
gentle
glad
good
grateful
great
greedy
green
grey
guilty
handsome
happy
hard
healthy
heavy
high
honest
hot
human
hungry
ill
important
impossible
independent
industrial
injured
intelligent
interesting
international
joint
kind
large
last
late
lazy
left
little
local
lonely
long
complex
loose
loud
low
lucky
main
many
medical
merry
mild
military
modern
much
narrow
national
natural
nearby
necessary
nervous
neutral
new
next
nice
noisy
normal
nuclear
old
only
opposite
oval
own
pale
past
peaceful
peculiar
perfect
permanent
pleasant
polite
political
poor
possible
powerful
pretty
private
public
quick
quiet
ready
real
direct
reasonable
red
regular
responsible
rich
roast
rough
round
sad
safe
same
satisfactory
scientific
secret
serious
several
sharp
short
sick
silly
similar
simple
sincere
sleepy
slow
small
smooth
social
socialist
soft
solid
sorry
sour
square
stiff
still
stormy
straight
strange
strong
stupid
successful
sure
sweet
tall
terrible
thick
thin
tired
few
thirsty
traditional
true
ugly
useful
usual
valuable
violent
warm
weak
wealthy
wet
white
whole
wide
wild
wise
wonderful
worth
wrong
yellow
young

C. NUMERALS

Numeralele cardinale:

1 – one
2 – two
3 – three
4 – four
5 – five
6 – six
7 – seven
8 – eight
9 – nine
10 – ten
11 - eleven
12 – twelve
13 – thirteen
14 – fourteen
15 – fifteen
16 - sixteen
17 - seventeen
18- eighteen
19 - nineteen
20 - twenty

21 – twenty-one
22 – twenty-two
23 – twenty-three
24 – twenty-four
25 – twenty-five
26 – twenty-six
27 – twenty-seven
28 – twenty-eight
29 – twenty-nine
30 – thirty
31 – thirty-one
32 – thirty-two
33 – thirty-three
34 – thirty-four
35 – thirty-five
36 – thirty-six
37 – thirty-seven
38 – thirty-eight
39 – thirty-nine
40 – fourty

41 – fourty-one
42 – fourty-two
43 – fourty-three
44 – fourty-four
45 – fourty-five
46 – fourty-six
47 – fourty-seven
48 – fourty-eight
49 – fourty-nine
50 – fifty
51 – fifty-one
52 – fifty-two
53 – fifty-three
54 – fifty-four
55 – fifty-five
56 – fifty-six
57 – fifty-seven
58 – fifty-eight
59 – fifty-nine
60 – sixty

61 – sixty-one
62 – sixty-two
63 – sixty-three
64 – sixty-four
65 – sixty-five
66 – sixty-six
67 – sixty-seven
68 – sixty-eight
69 – sixty-nine
70 – seventy
71 – seventy-one
72 – seventy-two
73 – seventy-three
74 – seventy-four
75 – seventy-five
76 – seventy-six
77 – seventy-seven
78 – seventy-eight
79 – seventy-nine
80 – eighty

81 – eighty-one
82 – eighty-two
83 – eighty-three
84 – eighty-four
85 – eighty-five
86 – eighty-six
87 – eighty-seven
88 – eighty-eight
89 – eighty-nine
90 – ninety
91 – ninety-one
92 – ninety-two
93 – ninety-three
94 – ninety-four
95 – ninety-five
96 – ninety-six
97 – ninety-seven
98 – ninety-eight
99 – ninety-nine
100 – one-hundred

101 – a (one) hundred and one
102 – a (one)-hundred and two
103 – a (one)-hundred and three
200 – two hundred (nu se acordă la plural)
350 – three hundred and fifty

1.000 – a (one) thousand
2.000 – two thousand (nu se acordă la plural)
3.000 – three thousand
1.000.000 - a (one) million
2.000.000 - two million
1.000.000.000. - a (one) billiard

Numeralele ordinale:

1 - the first	1st
2 - the second	2nd
3 - the third	3rd
4 - the fourth	4th
5 - the fifth	5th
6 - the sixth	6th
7 - the seventh	7th
8 - the eighth	8th
9 - the ninth	9th
10 - the tenth	10th
11 - the eleventh	11th
12 - the twelfth	12th
13 - the thirteenth	13th
14 - the fourteenth	14th
15 - the fifteenth	15th
16 - the sixteenth	16th
17 - the seventeenth	17th
18 - the eighteenth	18th
19 - the nineteenth	19th
20 - the twentieth	20th
21 - the twenty-first	21st
22 - the twenty-second	22nd
23 - the twenty-third	23rd
24 - the twenty-fourth	24th

25 - the twenty-fifth	25th
26 - the twenty-sixth	26th
27 - the twenty-seventh	27th
28 - the twenty-eigth	28th
29 - the twenty-ninth	29th
30 - the thirtieth	30th
……………………	
40 - the fourtieth	40th
50 - the fiftieth	50th
60 - the sixtieth	60th
70 - the seventieth	70th
80 - the eightieth	80th
90 - the ninetieth	90th
100 - the one hundredth	100th
101 - the one hundred and first	101st
110 - the one hundred and tenth	110th
1000 - the one thousandth	1000th
1000000 - the one millionth	1000000th

D. VERBS

accept	attack	boil	choose
accuse	attempt	borrow	climb
acquire	attend	break	close
act	avoid	breathe	come
add	be	bring	complain
advance	beat	broadcast	confirm
advise	become	build	congratulate
agree	begin	burn	consider
amuse	behave	burst	continue
answer	believe	buy	control
apologize	belong	calculate	cook
appear	bend	call	correct
apply	bind	can	cost
approve	bite	catch	cough
ask	bleed	celebrate	create
astonish	blow	change	cross

cry
cure
cut
damage
dance
decide
defeat
defend
depend
describe
deserve
destroy
develop
dictate
die
dig
disappear
discuss
divide
do
draw
dry
earn
eat
educate
elect
encourage
enjoy
enter
escape
exchange
excuse
explain
exploit
export
express
fail
fall
feed
feel
fight
fill
find
finish
fix
flee
float
flood
flow

fly
follow
force
forget
form
free
freeze
frighten
gather
get
give
go
govern
greet
grow
guard
hang
happen
hate
have
hear
heat
help
hesitate
hide
hit
hold
hope
hurry
hurt
imagine
imitate
import
improve
include
inform
inherit
inspect
intend
interfere
introduce
invent
invite
join
joke
judge
jump
keep
kill

kiss
knock
know
laugh
lay
lead
learn
leave
lend
let
lie
light
like
listen
live
lock
lose
love
make
march
mark
may
mean
meet
melt
mention
mind
miss
mix
move
must
need
note
notice
obey
object
oblige
offer
omit
open
oppose
order
organize
owe
paint
pass
pay
permit
plan

play
please
point
poison
possess
postpone
pour
praise
prefer
pretend
prevent
produce
promise
pronounce
propose
protect
protest
prove
publish
push
put
rain
raise
reach
read
receive
recognize
reduce
regret
reject
relate
remain
remember
repair
repeat
reply
report
represent
request
rest
rise
rob
rub
run
sail
satisfy
save
say
search

see
seem
sell
send
serve
settle
shake
shall
share
shave
shine
shock
shoot
shout
show
shut
sign
sing
sink
sit
sleep
slip
smell
smile
smoke
sneeze
snow
speak
spend
spill
spread
stand
start
stay
steal
step
stop
strike
struggle
study
succeed
suffer
suggest
support
suppose
surprise
surround
sweep
swim
switch
take
talk
taste
teach
tear
telephone
tell
test
thank
think
threaten
throw
tie
touch
translate
transport
travel
trust
try
turn
type
understand
unite
urge
visit
vote
wait
want
warn
wash
waste
wear
welcome
will
win
wish
witness
wonder
work
worry
wound
wrap
write

E. PRONOUNS, DETERMINERS, ARTICLES

I
me
my
mine
myself
you
yours
yourself
yourselves
he
him
his
himself
she
her
hers
herself
it
its
itself
we
us
our
ours
ourselves
they
them
their
theirs
a
all
an
another
any
anybody
anything
both
each
either
else
every
everybody
everything
except
former
latter
neither
no
nobody
nor
nothing
one
this
these
that
those
other
same
some
themselves
who
whose
what
which
somebody
something
such
the

F. ADVERBS, CONJUNCTIONS, PREPOSITIONS

about	clearly	meanwhile	somewhere
above	close	more	still
abroad	down	moreover	suddenly
across	during	naturally	than
after	early	nearly	then
afterwards	enough	never	there
again	especially	no	though
against	even	not	through
ago	ever	now	thus
almost	everywhere	nowhere	till
alone	except	of	to
along	fairly	often	today
already	far	on	together
also	fast	once	tomorrow
although	for	or	tonight
always	formely	otherwise	too
among	forward	out	towards
and	from	outside	under
anywhere	generally	over	unless
around	gently	past	until
as	hard	perfectly	up
aside	hardly	perhaps	usually
at	here	probably	very
away	highly	properly	well
back	how	publicly	when
because	however	quickly	where
before	if	quite	while
behind	immediately	rather	why
below	in	really	with
beneath	indeed	recently	without
beside	inside	seldom	yes
besides	into	simply	yesterday
between	instead (of)	slowly	yet
beyond	just	so	
but	largely	soon	
by	lately	sometimes	

CHEIA EXERCIȚIILOR

Phonetics

Ex.1. a. [ðei], b. [ðis], c. [ðɛə], d. [ðen], e. [mΛðə:], f. [fa:ðə:], g. [ðəu], h. [ðΛs]

Ex.2. a. [ðis iz ə kl□k], b. [ðei a: 'd□ktəs], c. [it iz ðɛə], d. [ðei a: 'fa:məs], e. [ðis iz ə 'flauə], f. [ðei a: mai frends]

Ex.3. Forme literare: [ai əm],[ju: a:], [hi: iz], [ʃi: iz], [it iz], [wi a:], [ðei a:]
Forme contraste: [aim], [juə], [hi:z], [ʃi:z], [its], [wiə], [ðɛiə]

Ex.4. **then – thin** [ðen] - [θin]

Then we meet here [ðen wi: mi:t hiə] Aşadar ne întâlnim aici.
You are **thin**, Dan [ju: a: θin dæn] Eşti slab, Dan.
they – thank [ðei] - [θæŋk]
They are friends. [ðei a: frendz] (Ei/Ele) Sunt prieteni/prietene.
Thank you, doctor. [θæŋk ju: 'd□ktəs] Vă mulțumesc, domnule doctor.
this – three [ðis] - [θri:]
This is a picture. [ðis iz ə 'piktʃə] Acesta este un tablou.
Here are **three** flowers. [hiə a: θri: 'flauə] Aici sunt trei flori.
they – theory [ðei] - [θiəri]
They are farmers. [ðei a: 'fa:məs] (Ei) sunt țărani/fermieri.
It's an interesting **theory.** [its ən 'intristiŋ [θiəri] E o teorie interesantă.
this – think [ðis] - [θink]
This is a big tree. [ðis iz ə big tri:] Acesta este un copac mare.
I **think** he's intelligent. [ai θink hi:z in'telidʒnt] (Eu) Cred că el e inteligent.

Ex.5. 1. He's my son. [hi:z mai sΛn]
2. They're my friends. [ðɛiə mai frends]
3. They are tall. [ðei a: t□:l]
4. An interesting idea. [ən 'intristiŋ ai'diə]
5. Are you tall, Mr. George? [a: ju: tɔ:l 'mistə dʒɔ:dʒ]
6. Nice to meet you [nais tu mi:t ju:]
7. My name's George [mai neims dʒ□:dʒ]
8. It's only a coincidence. [its 'ounli ə ko'insidns]

Ex.8. **Long forms:** [ai əm n□t], [ju: a: n□t], [hi: iz n□t], [ʃi: iz n□t], [it iz n□t], [wi a: n□t], [ðei a: n□t].
Short forms: [aim n□t], [juə n□t], [hi:z n□t], [ʃi:z n□t], [its n□t], [wiə n□t], [ðɛiə n□t].
[ju: a:nt], [hi: iznt], [ʃi: iznt], [it iznt], [wi a:nt], [ðei a:nt].

Ex.9. 1-a, 2-b , 3-c, 4-a

Ex.10. 1-e, 2-h , 3-a, 4-b, 5-c, 6-g, 7-d, 8-f.

Pronouns

Ex.1. they; she; she; they; they; we; he; she

Ex.2. He, it, they, it, we, they, he, she, she, you

Ex.4. we, us, our, ours.

Ex.5. myself, ourselves, himself, herself, yourself, myself, yourself, myself.

Ex.6. its, my, my, our, their, mine, theirs, ours

The noun

Ex.1. 1. They are farmers. 2. They are violins. 3. We are girls. 4. They are trees. 5. They are artists. 6. We are drivers.

Ex.2. clocks; brushes; reports; cups; sandwiches; doctors; maps; trees; touches; farmers; drivers; watches

Ex.3.

flower	floare	flowers	flori
car	maşină	cars	maşini
box	cutie	boxes	cutii
economist	economist	economists	economişti
sandwich	sandwich	sandwiches	sandwich-uri
violin	vioară	violins	viori

Ex.4. 1. men; 2. women; 3. children

Ex.5. a bunch of flowers; a bunch of bananas; a piece of cake; a bunch of keys; a slice of bread; a glass of water; a glass of sugar; a cup of oil; much flour; a little flour; many flowers; a few children; a little sugar.

Ex.8. 1. Have you got a **child**? I have three **children.** 2. He is a **man.** Thy are **men**. 3. She is a **woman.** They are **women.** 4. This **child** is intelligent. These **children** are intelligent. 5. This **man** is tall. These **men** are tall. 6. This **woman** is beautiful. These **women** are beautiful.

Ex.9.

1. Substantivele care se pot număra:

one house	*two houses*	o casă	două case
one child	*two children*	un copil	doi copii
one boy	*two boys*	un băiat	doi băieţi
one girl	*two girls*	o fată	două fete

2. Substantivele nenumărabile:

flour	făină
oil	ulei
sugar	zahăr
salt	sare
water	apă
bread	pâine

Ex10.

<u>Masculin</u>	<u>Feminin</u>
bull calf	**cow** calf
male elephant	**female** elephant
tom cat	**tabby**
cock pigeon	**hen** pigeon
he-bear	**she**-bear
billy goat	**nanny**-goat

Ex.11. a. There are five geese on the pond.; b. A pigeon flight is flying over the orchard.; c. She-bears take care of their cubs.; d. Squirrels have long tails and brown fur.; e. Some wild animals are very dangerous.

Ex.13. b. A two-week delay; c. a six-month session; d. a law-giver ; e. a trouble-maker; f. an embezzlement of a million USD; g. housebreaker; h. housebreaking; i. Crime report.

Adjectives

Ex.1. 4. Este un copac înalt. 5. El este un băiat inteligent. 6. Este un tablou mare. 7. Ea este o artistă importantă. 8. Este o floare frumoasă. 9. Ea este un bun şofer. 10. Sunt inele mari.

Ex.2. good; driver; intelligent; idea; son; beautiful; flower

Ex.3. big, beautiful, interesting, long, dangerous, good, expensive, rich, bad, clever.

Ex.4. new, good, successful, unbelievable, atomic.

Ex.5. 1. Tablourile lor nu sunt frumoase. 2. Copiii noştri au idei interesante. 3. Bunicul meu nu este acasă. 4. Fratele ei este înalt şi blond. 5. Părinţii lui au o maşină. 6. Cafeaua ta/dvs. este gata.

Ex.6. her relatives; my grandmother, his brothers; your sisters; her idea; their uncle; our aunt; my wife.

Ex.7. their; my; your; our; his; her

Ex.8. a. joyful; b. radiant; c. pleased; d. euphoric; e. euphoric; e. thrilled.

Ex.9. a. wily; b. crafty; c. sly; d. cunning; e. shrewd; f. wise, g. sage.

Ex.10.
<u>**at**</u>: indignant, bad/good, astonished;
<u>**about**</u>: right, sensitive, doubtful, pleased;
<u>**for**</u>: responsible;
<u>**of**</u>: capable, ashamed;
<u>**in**</u>: deficient, interested;
<u>**to**</u>: kind, hostile, sensitive, reluctant, thankful;
<u>**with**</u>: discontented, angry, pleased.

a. An entrepreneur must be capable of handling large orders.; b. Next, she should be good at figures.; c. She should also be interested in identifying new target buzzers.; d. She should be kind to her employees.; e. To succeed she should be sensitive about the customers needs.

Ex.11. my, my, my, my, your, your, your, his, his, her, her, its, their, their.

<u>The comparison of the Adjectives</u>

Ex.1. a. Adrian is taller than Dan, even if he is younger than him.; b. Maria is older than me.; c. I am younger than Maria.; d. Father is a physician. He is dark-haired and very sober.; e. Mother is thin and blond-haired.

Ex.2. a. Eu sunt mai mică decât tine.; b. Ea e mai înaltă decât sora ei.; c. Noi suntem mai rapizi decât tine.; d. Tu eşti mai gras decât crezi tu.; e. El este mai mare decât verişorii lui.

Ex.3.

Pozitiv	Comparativ	Superlativ
small	-as small as -not as small as -smaller then	-the smallest
tall	-as tall as -not as tall as -taller than	-the tallest

Ex.4.

Pozitiv	Comparativ	Superlativ
intelligent	-as intelligent as -not as intelligent as -more intelligent than	-the most intelligent
arrogant	-as arrogant as -not as arrogant as -more arrogant than	-the most arrogant

Ex.5. 1. better; 2. less; 3. more; 4. best; 5. worst; 6. more; 7. better; 8. least; 9. most; 10. most.

Ex.7. better – the best, worse – the worst; more – the most; more – the most; less – the least.

Ex.8. a. Today is warmer than yesterday.; b. My room is bigger then the kitchen.; c. Your wife is taller than my sister.; d. Where is the nearest bus stop?; e. The best child in our class is Mihai.; f. My dog is worse than yours.; g. My sister is two years younger than me.

Ex.9. Cu cît studiem mai mult, cu atât ştim mai mult. Cu cât ştim mai mult, cu atât uităm mai mult. Cu cât uităm mai mult, cu atât ştim mai puţin. Cu cât ştim mai puţin, cu atât uităm mai puţin. Cu cât uităm mai puţin, cu atât ştim mai mult. Aşa că de ce să mai învăţăm?

Ex.10. a. beter and better; b. faster and faster; c. more and more; d. digger / mor

Ex.11. a. taller; b. younger; c. older; d. nicer; e. more beautiful; f. shorter, g. more intelligent; h. fatter; i. more common.

Ex.12. a. not as creditable as; b. not as thin as; c. not as modern as; d. not as flattering as; e. not as thick as; f. not as big as.

Ex.13. a. better; b. more; c. less; d. worse; e. more.

Ex.14. a. the most beautiful; b. the fattest; c. the most modern; d. the most intelligent; e. the nicest.

Ex.15.1. funny, funnier; 2. much, most; 3. taller, tallest; 4. cruel, cruellest; 5. more reliable, the most reliable; 6. little, less; 7. good, better; 8. bad, worse; 9. sensible, more sensible; 10. more intelligent, the most intelligent.

Ex.16.1. in; 2. of; 3. on; 4. of; 5. under; 6. in.

Ex.17.a. an amazing little black straw hat; b. bright enormous blue eyes; c. a tall thin young Frenchman; d. an attractive woman with long blond hair.

Ex.18.possible sentences: Dana's clothes are more fashionable. / Traian is as friendly as Dana. / Dana's French is more fluent than Traian's. / Traian is more daring than Dana. / Dana is more patient than Traian.

Ex.20.1. think; 2. agree; 3. wrong; 4. afraid; 5. don't; 6. agree; 7. are; 8. reason.

Ex.21.a. lazier, laziest; b. more comfortable, most comfortable, c. more resolute, most resolute; d. wiser, wisest; e. more reliable, most reliable; f. crueler, cruelest.

Ex.22. a. the best; b. the most intelligent; c. more reliable; d. less impulsive, e. brighter and brighter; f. understanding; g. the more experienced, the better; h. very interesting.

Ex.23. a. dark/red; b. more precious/dearer; c. white/whiter; d. yellow/yellower; e. red/redder; f. wiser/mightier; g. deeper/deeper; wilder/wilder.

Ex.24. a. the highest; b. the largest; c. the longest; d. the quietest; e. the greatest; f. the lowest; g. the most favorite; h. the steepest; i. the most accessible; j. the biggest.

Ex.25. a. of; b. in; c. on; d. of; e. under.

Ex.26.a. rainy; b. hilly; c. beautiful; d. wooden; e. impressive; f. friendly; g. accessible; h. twinkling; i. amused; j. surprising.

Ex.27. 1. dearest; 2. most beautiful; 3. changing; 4. unpredictable; 5. sunny; 6. comfortable; 7. kind; 8. useful; 9. Georgian; 10. thrilling; 11. personal; 12. lucky; 13. fine; 14. topped; 15. lazy; 16. overwhelming; 17. best.

Ex.30. a. away with; b. up to; c. out of; d. out on; e. off with.

Indefinite Pronoun/Adjective

Ex.1. 1. anyone; 2. someone; 3. somewhere; 4. no; 5. anything; 6. somebody; 7. nobody; 8. anything; 9. anywhere; 10. nowhere; 11. something; 12. no one; 13. some; 14. any; 15. nothing.

Ex.2. a. an hour's journey/half an hour's delay/a year's absence; b. a three weeks' cruise/a thirty years' war/a two months' salary.

Ex.3. a. an hour-journey/half an hour-delay/a tear-absence; b. a three week-cruise/a thirty year-war/a two month-salary.

Ex.5. 1. He must have that dictionary.; 2. Dona cannot miss the meeting.; 3. Ileana must come in time.; 4. The girl cannot go there.; 5. She may feel better now.; 6. They might be here. 7. We may leave earlier.; 8. She cannot translate the poem that fast.; 9. Employees must observe the work hours.; 10. We need accompany her.

Ex.6. 1. Need I remind you of the meeting?; 2. Can't you be punctual?; 3. The others must come any time.; 4. Can I join you/have a seat next to you?; 5. Things might/could become/worse/get.; 6. You may use my desk. I'm leaving now.; 7. He might/could go abroad.; 8. How many words per minute can you type?; 9. You mustn't come late for work.

Ex.7. a. may; b. must; c. can; d. may/can; e. must; f. need; g. may/can; h. might/could; i. can't.

Ex.8. a. could; b. can; c. must; d. may; e. may; can; f. could; g. mustn't.

Ex.9. a. May I have a seat next to you?; b. He could make an effort and come in time.; c. They can't be too far. They left 15 minutes ago.; d. I can't understand what you mean.; e. She might come later.; f. You must go and talk to her.; g. "Need I explain it to you again?" "No, you needn't."; h. I recognized the word "tag". It must be German.

Ex.11. 1. like; 2. pick you up; 3. does; 4. that's; 5. with; 6. see; 7. you; 8. fitness club; 9. would; 10. me; 11. I'd; 12. unfortunately; 13. until; 14. see; 15. time; 16. timetable; 17. call; 18. suitable; 19. invitation; 20. around.

Ex12. a-Ø; b-who; c-which; d-Ø; e-which; f-who.9

Definitive and Indefinitive Articles

Ex.1. 1.-; 2. the, 3. -; 4. the; 5. -; 6. -; 7. the; 8. -; 9. the; 10. -.

Ex.2. a. Gossiping is a survival skill.; b. A stolen painting has been founded in a lost property office.; c. A murder mystery has been solved by a dog.; d. The land speed record has been broken.; e. The missing yacht was spotted of Cape Horn.

Ex.3. 1.a; 2.a, 3.a; 4.a; 5. an; 6. an; 7. an; 8. an; 9. an; 10. a.

Ex.4. 1.the; 2.the; 3.a; 4.the; 5.the; 6.-; 7.a; 8.-; 9.a; 10.a; 11.-; 12.a; 13.a; 14.a; 15.-; 16.-

Ex.5. Maria speaks all the time.; 2. The little one wants to play.; 3. I want to become an assistant manager.; 4. I like having a lot of friends.; 5. She is calling a good friend.; 6. I work as a secretary at a private company.; 7. When are you giving him back the dictionary?; 8. The story of the Titanic is true.; 9. There is an empty glass and plate on the table.; 10. You are a very good dancer.;

Ex.6. a) the; b) -/a/-; c) a/-; d) the/the/the; e) -; f) -/the; g) -/the/-; h) the; i) the/-/a/a/-; j) the/a/the/a/-; k) -/the/-/the/-/the/-; l) an/the; m) the/an.

Ex.7. b) - school; c) - boys; d) The Observator; e) the the slowness; f) – English; g) no mistake; h) – animals; i) the USA; j) no mistakes; k) – Harrods; l) – Mount Everest; m) no mistake; n) The Severn.

Ex.8. 1.Once upon a time there was a king and the king had three sons. 2. The tea on the table isn't yours. 3. The rich live in the district. 4. Do the English like the French? 5. I'm not a lawyer, I'm a teacher. 6. He has always known to appreciate the beautiful. 7. Every Sunday grannies goes to church. 8. How was your travel by train? 9. Oxford Street is a place with well-known stores. 10. They were speaking in a loud voice. 11. They have decided to go on a cruise on the Mediterranean stores. 12. He was dirty from head to foot. 13. Tea is the national beverage of the British. 15. He has made a fortune by selling stationery.

Ex.9. 1. La vremea aceea stăteam cu unchiul şi soţia lui. 2. Cel puţin nu eşti scoţian, nici irlandez, nici galez. 3. Nu-mi plăcea comerţul; aş fi fost doar un ratat. 4. Tânărul O'Casey a ascultat limbajul celor săraci, darn u a căutat cadenţele minunate. 5. Am fost în Caucaz şi ştiu ce spun. 6. Romanii au fost cei care la scurt timp după invadarea Angliei, ordonată de împăratul Claudius în 43 d.H., au întemeiat Londra. Ei au construit un pod peste Tamisa şi oraşul s-a dezvoltat în jurul capătului dinspre nord al podului. În cele din urmă, romanii au construit un zid în jurul Londrei şi linia zidului marchează în mare zona pe care astăzi o numim centrul economic al Londrei. În vremea romanilor, Londra era un centru comercial mare şi important, dar când legiunile au părăsit Anglia în 409 d.H. a intrat în declin. Populaţiile anglo-saxone, care au venit între 400 şi 600 d.H., nu au locuit în oraşele romane, ci în sate din afara acestora.

Ex.10. 1) -; 2) a; 3) -; 4) -; 5) -; 6) -; 7) the; 8) -; 9) the; 10) -; 11) a; 12) -; 13) -; 14) -; 15) an.

Ex.11. a) an; b) an; c) a; d) some; e) a.

Ex.12. a) a; a; b) a; c) some; d) a; e) the; f) an; g) the

Ex.13. the teacher; a horse; a horse; the teacher.

Ex.14.

an applea hare an applea boat
an orange a house an eye an umbrella
a herb a coat a horse an empire
a union an honor an ear a yard

Ex.15. a. a book; a pencil and a copy-book; b. a man; a woman and a child; c. a story and an essay; d. a European, an American, an Asian and an Australian; e. a hen and an egg.

Ex.16. a. A noun is a word.; b. A town is a big city; c. A horse is an animal; d. A rose is a beautiful flower; e. A table is a piece of furniture.

Ex.17. a. Cats are animals; b. Flies are insects; c. Table are made of wood; d. Chickens are birds; e. Cakes are sweet; f. Dictionaries are books; g. Dogs eat meat; h. Birds can fly; i. Fish can swim.; j. Men can walk.; k. Houses are buildings; l. Planes are made of metal; m. fountain pens have ink in them; n. Cows give milk.

Ex.18. a. I go to the theatre every week; b. She goes to the Disco every Saturday night; c. Ana is playing tennis now; d. Adrian likes to go for a walk in the park; e. Alexandra is going to the cinema now.

Ex.19. 1. The National Theatre; 2. museums; 3. theatre; 4. cinema; 5. park.

Ex.20. a. the; b. some; c. an; d. some; e. the

Prepositions

Ex.1. 1-b; 2-a; 3-c; 4-c; 5-b; 6-b; 7-a; 8-c; 9-b; 10-b.

Ex.2. 2-on; 3-of; 4-to; 5-for; 6-with; 7-of; 8-with; 9-with; 10-in; 11-to; 12-about; 13-with; 14-against; 15-against.

Ex.3. a - at; b - out; c - in; d – in; e – on; f – in; g – out; h – on; i – in; j – on.

Ex.4. 1-in; 2-on; 3-next to; 4-by; 5-at; 6-behain; 7-under; 8-in; 9-on; 10-from; 11-of; 12-in; 13-at.

Ex.5. 1-a; 2-c; 3-a; 4-b; 5-b,c; 6-a; 7-a,b; 8-a; 9-c, c, c; 10-a, a

Ex.6. 1-C; 2-B; 3-C; 4-D; 5-B.

Adverbial particle

Ex.1. a. write, off; b. takes after; c. cut out; d. plays on; e. laid out; f. has lived through; g. walked up to; h. speak for; i. let off; j. act out; k. keep in; l. was, getting at; m. made for; n. have been turned into; o. put forward.

Ex.4. 1-b; 2-b; 3-a; 4-c; 5-c; 6-c; 7-a; 8-b; 9-b; 10-a.

Ex.5. a-slip through; b-slipped out; c-slips down; d-slipped in; e-slip on; f-slipped up.

Ex.6. a-is working up _______ into; b-work out; c-has been working at; d-work in; e-work off; f-working away at; g- worked up.

Ex.7. 1-b; 2-a; 3-c; 4-b; 5-c.

Ex.8. a-out; b-up; c-for; d-down; e-through.

Ex.9. a. It has been sent up.; b. We've sent for the doctor but he hasn't arrived yet.; c. He's not doing very well. As a matter of fact he was sent down last term.; d. Not many. I sent the invitation out just yesterday.; e. Quite far. I've sent them off in Switzerland.

The verb "To be"

Ex.1. I'm, she's, they're, he's, it's, we're, he's, it's.

Ex.2. are; is; are; are; am; is; are; are

Ex.3. 's; 'm; 're; 're; 're; 're; 's; 're

Ex.4. they; she; she; they; they; we; he; he

Ex.5. 1. Are they friends? 2. Is he right? 3. Is it three o'clock? 4. Is Liza an economist? 5. Are you hungry? 6. It is a box?

Ex.6. 1. My report is not ready. 2. He is not thin. 3. It is not an interesting theory. 4. You are not a good driver. 5. My son is not short. 6. It is not ten o'clock.

Ex.7. 1. They're not my friends. They aren't my friends. 2. it's not an interesting theory. It isn't an interesting theory. 3. You're not economists. You aren't economists. 4. He's not my friend. He isn't my friend. 5. it's not six o'clock. It isn't six o'clock. 6. We're not hungry. We aren't hungry.

Ex.8. 1b; 2a; 3c; 4a; 5b; 6c

Ex.9. 1. George şi Diana are not relatives. 2. You are right. 3. Is Petre at home? 4. It's not three o'clock, it's four o'clock. 5. Are you hungry? 6. It is an important box.

Ex.10. 1. Is Marius in the office?; 2. No, he is not in the office.; 3. Are you at home?; 4. Is she intelligent?; 5. She is not intelligent.; 6. Am I a good dancer?; 7. Yes, you are a very good dancer.; 8. Are they busy?; 9. No, they are not busy.; 10. Who are you?; 11. I am Roxana.; 12. Is it one o'clock?; 13. It isn't one o'clock. It's two o'clock.

The verb „To Have"

Ex.1. 1. has got – El are o maşină. 2. have got – Noi avem patru copii. 3. have got – Am raportul gata/pregătit. 4. have got – Ai/Aveţi o soacră inteligentă. 5. have got – Ei au un fiu şi o fiică. 6. has got – Ea are un nepot care este student.

Ex.2. 1. You've got a good car. 2. We've got a big clock at home. 3. He's got two sandwiches. 4. I've got a very big problem 5. They've got an American car. 6. She's got a nice son.

Ex.3. **I've got** an American friend.; 2. **You've got** a good idea. 3. He**'s got** a difficult problem. 4. She'**s got** a big car. 5. It'**s got** four wheels. 6. We'**ve got** a small farm. 7. They'**ve got** a caring mother-in-law.

Ex.6. a-have got; b-are; c-are; d-is; e-has got; f-have got; g-am; h-have got; i-are; j-is

Ex.7. a. have; b. has; c. has got; d. has got; e. have; f. haven't got; g. does ….. have; h. have ….. got; i. does …….. have; j. doesn't have.

Ex.8. a. is; b. is; c. have got/is; d. are; e. are; f. is; g. has got ; h. are; i. has got; j. have got; k. are; l. is; m. am/be; n. have got; o. is; p. have got; q. have.

Ex.9. 1-has to; 2-have to; 3-have to; 4-has to; 5-have to; 6-don't have to; 7-have to; 8-don't have to; 9-doesn't have to; 10-don't have to.

Expressing time and date

Ex.1. 1. Este ora 11. 2. Noi nu suntem economişti. 3. Cât e ora? 4. Eşti/sunteţi încă pe ora britanică? 5. Ce zici/ziceţi de o ceaşcă de cafea? 6. Este ora opt?

Ex.2. 1. half past six; 2. a quarter to eight; 3. half past eight; 4. half past one; 5. half past five; 6. a quarter to eleven

Ex.3. 1. Fiica mea se scoală la şapte fără un sfert în fiecare dimineaţă. 2. Ei/Ele locuiesc în Arad. 3. Eu iau micul dejun la ora opt şi jumătate dimineaţa. 4. Noi învăţăm engleză în fiecare zi. 5. El se uită la televizor în fiecare seară. 6. Cred că viaţa mea e minunată.

Ex.4. 1. I get up at seven o'clock in the morning. 2. We have dinner at half past eight in the evening. 3. He studies every day. 4. They live in Arad. 5. My sister watches TV every evening, then she reads a book. 6. I go to bed at half past ten in the evening.

Ex.5. 1. It is 10 past 1 a.m.; 2. It is a quarter past 2 p.m.; 3. It is half past 3 p.m.; 4. It is 12 to 8 p. m.; 5. It is 37 past 9 p.m.; 6. It is midnight. 7. It is 4 o'clock sharp. 8. It is half past 7 p.m.

Ex.6. a. It is half past 3 p.m.; b. It is 21 past 8 p.m. c. It is a quarter to 6 p.m.; d. It is 52 past 7 p.m.; e. Ir is half past 9 p.m.; f. It is 27 past 7 a.m.; g. It is 42 past 9 a.m.; h. It is 20 past 10 a.m.

Ex.8. Este unu fără un sfert.; 2. Este unu şi un sfert.; 3. Este unu şi jumătate.; 4. Este patru şi un sfert.; 5. Este patru şi jumătate.; 6. Este cinci fără un sfert.; 7. Este cinci şi jumătate.; 8. Este şase fără un sfert.

Ex.9. 1. Today is the 9th of May. Today is May the 9th.
2. Today is the 30th of June. Today is June the 30th.
3. Today is the 2nd of January. Today is January the 2nd.
4. Today is the 5th of February. Today is February the 5th.
5. Today is the 7th of March. Today is March the 7th.
6. Today is the 21st of April. Today is April the 21st.
7. Today is the 23rd of Jully. Today is Jully the 23rd.
8. Today is the 31st of August Today is August the 31st.
9. Today is the 29th of September. Today is September the 29th.
10. Today is the 15th of October. Today is October the 15th.
11. Today is the 18th of November. Today is November the 18th.
12. Today is the 13th of December. Today is December the 13th.

Ex.10. a. nineteen-hundred; b. seventeen-fifty-three; c. nineteen-ninety-nine; d. two thousand; e. two thousand and three; f. nineteen-eighty-nine; g. sixteen-hundred; h. nineteen-twenty; i. two thousand and seven; j. twenty-three-fifty; k. twenty-twenty-two

Expressing quantity and probability

Ex.2. **a.** Can you lend me a little sugar? b. There is little hope of finding the cat. c. I'm meeting a few friends at the restaurant. d .I have few friends and I feel lonely. e. He hasn't got any friends. f. Have you got some spare copies? g. He never has any many. h. She did it herself without any help. i. I don't have much spare time these days. j. Is there much unemployment in UK? k. Will there be many people there? l. They have come up with many new issues. m. There is plenty of bread for the population. n. A large number of people have become aware of the costs of this convenience.

Ex.3. 1) all; 2) none; 3) most; 4) little; 5) little; 6) more; 7) most; 8) many; 9) some; 10) several; 11) anything; 12) anyone; 13) every; 14) every; 15) each.

Ex.4. a) little; b) many; c) a little; d) much; e) little; f) a few; g) few; h) many; i) much; j) many

Ex.5. a. May I have some juice, please? b. Shall I buy some fruit for the dessert? c. Would you help yourself with some biscuits? d. Is there any news for me? e. She never has any money. F. He did it without any help.

Ex.6. a. If anybody calls, tell them I'm out. b. Nobody knows anything about this matter. c. Is everybody present today? d. Someone has tot tell her the bad news. e. Is anybody in here? f. The book must be somewhere in the house. g. The little boy could be found nowhere. h. I've been looking for the book everywhere but I haven't found it. i. Tell me something I don't know. j. She told me nothing about your trouble.

Ex.8. (1) many, (2) some, (3) more, (4) much, (5) more, (6) fewer, (7) most, (8) less, (9) each.

Ex.10. răspunsuri posibile

a. It's sure/bound to happen as they have already launched many satellites.; b. I wouldn't be surprised if a spacecraft reached the edge of the solar system. c. There's no chance of Astronomy being taught in kindergartens. d. I'm absolutely sure it won't happen. e. Of course it will, that's why they're carried out.

Ex.11. a) crumbs; b) bar; c) pinch; d) rasher; e) scrap; f) speck; g) splinter; h) clod; i) chunk.

The imperative (Imperativul)

Ex.1. 1. Hai să vorbim englezeşte! 2. Ei au trei copii. 3. Ce vârstă/câţi ani are soţul tău/dvs.? 4. Soacra mea este amabilă şi grijulie. 5. Cine eşti/sunteţi? 6. Prietenul/Prietena ei are 12 ani.

Ex.2. 1. Let's start. 2. Our children are not at home. 3. Her brothers are economists. 4. How old is your wife? 5. My violin is small. 6. How old is your aunt?

Ex.3. 1. Hai să ne cunoaştem. 2. Hai să fim prieteni. 3. Hai să vorbim limba engleză. 4. Hai să începem. 5. Hai să ne gândim. 6. Hai să mâncăm. 7. Hai să ne întâlnim mâine. 8. Hai să ne oprim.

Ex.4. a. Come here!; b. Watch out!; c. Please take a seat.; d. Eat an apple - it's much better for you than a biscuit!; e. Open your book.; f. Come in and sit down. Make yourself at home; g. Speak to him. Tell him how you feel. h. Let's have some lunch.; i. Do not walk on the grass.; j. Do be quiet.

Ex.5. a-8; b-4; c-10; d-6; e-5; f-9; g-7; h-2; i-3; j-1

Ex.8. 1-c; 2-b; 3-c; 4-b; 5-b; 6-c.

Ex.10. a. go; b. sit; c. take; d. try; e. call; f. stay; g. open.

Present Simple Tense

Ex.1. 1a; 2b; 3a; 4a; 5b; 6b

Ex.2. lives; watches; gets; speaks; goes; arrives.

Ex.3. 1. He gets up early. 2. He lives in a big house. 3. He speaks English. 4. He watches TV in the evening. 5. He goes to bed early. 6. He has lunch at half past one.

Ex.4. 1. breakfast; half; seven; 2. learn; day; 3. work; morning; 4. always, early 5. think; wonderful 6. have; dinner; clock; evening

Ex.5. 1. I always get up at 6 o'clock in the morning.
2. I usually cook breakfast for my family.
3. We often drink coffee in the morning.
4. Andreea speaks English every day.
5. We seldom learn at night.
6. You never drink coffee in the evening.
7. I go to work every day.
8. We watch TV every evening.
9. My mother cooks every morning.
10. We sleep for 8 hours every night.
11. They have a party every month.
12. We meet every day.

13. She drinks coffee every morning.
14. I read every day.

Present Continuous Tense

Ex.1. being; doing; having; eating; drinking; coming; standing; listening; becoming; behaving; cutting; stopping; talking; making; believing; forgetting; leaving; going

Ex.2.1. am; 2. is; 3. are; 4. are; 5. are; 6. is

Ex.3.1. am writing; 2. is cleaning; 3. is asking; 4. is cooking; 5. is playing, 6. are doing

Ex.5.1. Yes, I am. / No, I am not.; 2. Yes, she is.; 3. Yes we are.; 4. No, it isn't.; 5. Yes, they are.; 6. No, he isn't.

Ex.9.1. I usually get up early.
2. She doesn't usually buy soap.
3. He doesn't usually cook dinner.
4. He doesn't usually fly in a plane.
5. They are not usually doing their homework.

Ex.10. 1. a); 2. b); 3. a); 4. a).

Ex.13. a. Laura is going to her sister this weekend; b. Dana is singing at a pop concert next week; c. I am giving a test paper next month; d. You are flying to Italy tomorrow; e. She is changing her house in a few days.

Ex.15. a. I'm buying a bicycle in a few days; b. Diana is going to the party the next Saturday; c. My cousin from Paris is coming tomorrow; d. Laura is writing her homework's tomorrow; e. Dana is going to the physician in 2 days; f. Andreea is having a difficult exam in a few days; g. Ana is singing at a pop concert tomorrow night; h. Father is repairing the car next week; i. We are having dinner at 6.00 p.m., j; Andreea is calling Florin the day after tomorrow; k. your girlfriend is waiting for you at the station tomorrow; l. Alina is studying French next year.; m. Mihai is getting up early tomorrow; n. Alexandru is having a picnic next weekend; o. Maria is meeting her friend on Friday at 2 o'clock.

Ex.16. a. Ies în oraş să cumpăr nişte îngheţată; b. La ce oră te trezeşti tu de obicei?; c. Tuturor le place vara; d. Toţi elevii din această clasă citesc bine în limba engleză; e. Parcul arată frumos primăvara; f. Prietenul meu mă aşteaptă la colţ; g. Trenul ajunge în Gara de Nord la ora 18,30; h. Am programare la dentist la ora 17.00; i. De ce bei din paharul meu?; j. Nu ştiu ce vrei să spui; k. În timpul săptămâni de obicei ne trezim devreme, dar astăzi ne trezim târziu; l. Bunica mea vine să mă viziteze în această după-amiază; m. El zboară spre Arad mâine.; n. Sper să te văd la petrecere; o. Ce faci acolo? Încerc să găsesc cheia de la uşă.

Ex.17. a. We watch T.V. every evening; b. We are having breakfast now; Mother is drinking coffee, I am drinking orange juice and father is having an omelet; c. Mihai is in his room. He is writing his homework's; d. Your friends are waiting for you at the café round the corner; e. Maria is wearing a nice dress today; f. You don't know how to prepare the tea, do you? g. No, I don't. But I know how to make coffee; h. Why are you being so clumsy today?

Ex.18. a. making; b. running; c. crying; d. swimming; e. building; f. calling; g. traveling; h. stopping; i. hoping; j. blowing; k. flying; l. coming; m. believing; n. being; o. buying.

Ex.19. a. am doing; b. are staying; c. is eating; d. are learning.

Ex.20. a. I am going shopping next week; b. They are visiting their grandparents next month; c. The children are organizing a party tomorrow evening; d. My parents are going to the theatre on Sunday; e. Our neighbors are painting the house tomorrow.

Ex.21. a. Prietenii mei dau o petrecere mâine seară; b. Toţi studenţii lucrează la un proiect nou luna viitoare; c. Formaţia dă un spectacol sâmbătă seara; d. Maria poartă o rochie de mătase la petrecere; e. Fetele merg la plimbare, la sfârşit de săptămână.

Ex.22. a. is going; b. are studying; c. is teaching; d. is making; e. are the children playing football now?

Ex.23. a. acţiune obişnuită, regulată – Present Tense Simple; b. acţiune obişnuită regulată – Present Tense Simple; c. acţiune care se desfăşoară în momentul vorbirii – Present Tense Continuous; d. acţiune care se desfăşoară în momentul vorbirii – Present Tense Continuous; e. acţiune viitoare programată în prezent – Present Tense Continuous.

Ex.24.1. c; 2. a; 3. c; 4. c; 5. c.

Ex.25.1. is; 2. are; 3. do; 4. am; 5. does; 6. is; cooking; 7. is

Ex.26.1. am leaving; 2. knows; 3. goes; 4. are travelling; 5. are; 6. looks; 7. goes; is going.

Ex.27. a. A job interview; b. What a nice dress you are wearing!; c. I usually wear sport-clothes; d. I have a smart dress; e. You look gorgeous in this dress; f. I'm sure you are getting the job in no time; g. I'm a little nervous; h. It is a T.V. advertising; i. I understand now why you are being nervous; j. You are looking absolutely ravishing today; k. Gook-Luck.

Ex.28. a. What are you wearing?; b. How is she looking today?; c. Where is Maria going?; d. What is it?; e. When is she going to the seaside?

Ex.29. a. He is repairing the car.; b. He is digging the flowers.; c. They are playing.; d. She is watching her favorite show.; e. He is working.

Ex.30. a. I'm eating a lot of sweets while I am on holiday.; b. I'm writing a lot of letters while I am on holiday.; c. I'm catching a lot of fish while I am on holiday.; d. I'm reading a lot of books while I am on holiday.; e. I'm watching a lot of movies while I'm on holiday.; f. I'm having a lot of fun while I'm on holiday.

Ex.32. a. This cake tastes sweets.; b. Your teacher look nice.; c. This problem looks difficult.; d. This coffee tastes bad.; e. This soup smells delicious.; f. This song sounds bad.; g. The apple seems fresh.

Ex.33. a. looks like; b. looks like; c. feels like; d. sounds like; e. tastes like.

Ex.34. a. am thinking; b. is seeing, is having; c. am tasting; d. are being; e. am expecting; f. am feeling; g. am thinking, h. are having; are studying.

Ex.35. a. am listening to; b. is writing; c. are having; d. is playing; e. are doing.

Ex.36. a. I am drinking tea.; b. They are watching cartoons.; c. We are going to the seaside.; d. I am going by tube.; e. They are staying at home.

Ex.37. a. are going; b. is traveling; c. are getting married; d. are leaving; e. are coming.

Ex.38. a. She usually wears trousers, but she is wearing a dress today.; b. We are watching a horror movie now.; c. My friends are going out tomorrow night.; d. Mr. and Mrs. Dumitrescu are eating at the restaurant at week-end.; e. I'm cooking and I'm cleaning the house this week because my mother is away.

Revision of the Present Simple and Continuous Tense

Ex.1. 1-c; 2-d; 3-a; 4-e; 5-b.

Ex.2. a) being; b) been; c) are; d) looking; e) being; f) been; g) will; h) too; i) be; j) ever; k) had; l) deed; m) not; n) will; o) been; p) had.

Ex.3. b) been working here for; c) are having a meeting; d) ages since I haven't had; e) arrives at; f) have lost my; g) are you doing on; h) you own this; i) wish you were; j) are you being served.

Ex.4. 1) are putting; 2) stares; 3) are flying; 4) are learning; 5) walk; 6) talk; 7) is following; 8) says; 9) laugh; 10) am talking; 11) does not hide; 12) has changed; 13) think; 14) knew; 15) did; 16) is getting; 17) are run.

Ex.5. a) have changed; b) is coordinated; c) offers; d) are resorting; e) are you typing; f) has been running; g) were; h) are you expecting; i) begins; j) are going; k) has been changed.

Ex.7. 1-have had; 2-have made; 3-comes; 4-is learning; 5-is; 6-own; 7-have (got); 8-has thought; 9-have been here; 10-have not told; 11-are attending; 12-have discovered; 13-halps; 14-have been studying; 15-have made; 16-am working; 17-are; 18-am watching; 19-are being.

Ex.8. a) Mr. Popescu teaches English. He has been teaching English for ten years. b) What books have you read for the paper on new methods to teach English? c) I've been attending this course since spring. I'm attending it to improve my knowledge in English. d) I often borrow video tapes which aren't subtitled. e) She speaks English fluency. She is speaking to a client now. f) More and more people speak English to communicate in an easier way.

Ex.9. a. I'm calling a friend now; b. Dana wants an apartment; c. Toni is cooking dinner now; d. Paul goes to the theatre every week; e. Elena and Mihai are not going to the party now; f. You like sweets very much; g. The children play tennis every day; h. The girls are going for a walk in the park now.

Ex.10. 1. boil; 2. is boiling; 3. opens; 4. am opening; 5. are listening; 6. mean; 7. am seeing; 8. smells; 9. is smelling; 10. is; 11. is being; 12. understand; 13. is having; 14. has; 15. am having; 16. are waiting; 17. am thinking; 18. think; 19. am feeling; 20. is feeling; 21. are looking; 22. look; 23. looks; 24. looks

Ex.11. a. is having; b. is preparing, c. is wearing, d. are ringing; e. opens; invites; f. is opening.

Ex.12. a. I go to work every day; b. I usually go to school by bus, but I'm going by car this week; c. Water freezes at 0^0 C. Woods floats on water; d. I'm drinking coffee now; e. Plane Crushes in the Pacific Ocean!; f. I'm going to France next week; g. Boil some water in a kettle, then pour it into a cup. Take the tea and put it in hot water for 3-4 minutes. Then add sugar and lemon.

The YES/NO, TAG and WH Questions

Ex.1. 1. It is; 2. Am I; 3. Isn't she; 4. Is she; 5. Isn't he; 6. Are you; 7. Aren't they; 8. Aren't we; 9. Is she; 10. Isn't she

Ex.2. 1. Is; 2. Isn't; 3. Is; 4. Aren't; 5. Are; 6. Isn't; 7. Isn't; 8.Is

Ex.4. 1. aren't they; 2. aren't you; 3. isn't it; 4. isn't ; 5. aren't you; 6. aren't; 7. isn't he.

Ex.5. 1. are; aren't they; 2. doesn't; does she; 3. are; aren't you; 4. don't; do you; 5. is; isn't he; 6. isn't; is she

Ex.6. a. did you; b. didn't she, c. did she; c. did you; e. didn't she.

Ex.8.

1. Where is she sleeping?
2. Where do I go every day?
3. Where is Florin playing tennis?
4. Why does she love Dan?
5. Why is the baby crying?
6. What am I writing now?
7. When are they leaving for Paris?
8. When do I have lunch?

Ex.11. 1. Who is cooking dinner? / What is Florin cooking? 2. What does Florin usually have for breakfast? 3. Who has lunch at 12 every day? / What do they have every day? / When do they have lunch? 4. Who is cooking? / What is mother doing? / What is mother cooking for lunch?

Ex.12. b. Whom did girls look after?; c. Where could one see "a little mother"?; d. How old was she?; e. What would she do?; f. What did she nurse?; g. How would she soothe the baby?; h. How often was her attention drawn?; i. Why was she fed up?

Ex.15. a. Where do you go every day?; b. What are you doing now?; c. When do you usually get up?; d. Where does she work?; e. Why is Maria happy?

Ex.16. a. Where did Mircea live last summer?; b. Who walked to the beach yesterday?; c. What did Paul play?; Where did Paul play football.; d. Who did you visit yesterday?; e. What did you decide?

Ex.17. a. Who is already prepared for the day's drive?; b. Where has the garage door been opened from?; c. What is the video disk for?; d. How are instructions provided?; e. What does the disc store?; f. When will the car radio be automatically interrupted?; g. Why will the car radio be interrupted?

Ex.18. a. I would need to know.; b. How many tracks it has.; c. Which image support system is compatible.; d. What the advantages and disadvantages of the tape system are.; e. Whether/if you can record off TV.; f. If/whether you can use a camera for personal filming.; g. What the sound quality is.; h. What an expert recommends.; i. Where you can buy the latest generation of VTC.; j. How a VTC is installed.

Ex.19. b. aren't they; c. doesn't it; d.wasn't it; e. did he; f. isn't it; g. do they; h. hasn't he; i. can't they; j. weren't they; k. is it; l. won't they.

Past Simple Tense

Ex.1. to work – worked; to learn – learned; to cry – cried; to try – tried.

Ex.2. a. didn't do; b. tried; c. studied; d. walked; e. watched; f. Did you listen.; g. played.

Ex.3. a. walked; b. played; c. worked; d. talked; e. listened; f. looked; g. tried, h. did.

Ex.4. a. When did I look into a magazine?; b. What did you do yesterday?; c. What did Dana play last week?; d. Where did she talk to her for an hour?; e. When didn't I look at you?

Ex.5. to play – played; to talk – talked, to walk – walked.

Ex.6. a. I didn't work last month.; b. Did she study in the library last night?; c. Dana tried to talk to him a week ago., d. I stopped him by the traffic light an hour ago.; e. I didn't play tennis last year.

Ex.7. a. El a cântat la pian timp de două ore, seara trecută.; b. Eu nu am studiat franceza anul trecut., c. El a vorbit cu ea o dată, cam acum 2 ani.; d. Nu am vrut să-l trezesc.; e. Ea s-a uitat la televizor sâmbăta trecută.

Ex.8. a. You wanted to buy the flower, didn't you?; b. She didn't try to help him, did she?; c. He talked to her yesterday, didn't she?; d. You didn't listen to the music last night, did you?; e. Dana played the piano on Sunday, didn't she?

Ex.9. a. When didn't I see you?; b. Where did she work last weekend?; Where did she work in the garden?; c. Where did you walk to last month?; d. What did he do the day before yesterday?; e. What did you do two hours ago?

Ex.10. a. Suddenly, Mirela says:; b. We can have a look if you want.; c. Look, there's a table.; d. They always show very nice clothes here.; e. I was mad about sports-wear.; f. I used to wear all kinds of denim clothes.

Ex.11. to learn – learned; to invite – invited, to listen – listened, to talk – talked, to wait – waited; to work – worked; to watch – watched; to look – looked.

Ex.13. a. didn't want; b. cooked, d. invited; d. used; e. watched; f. visited; g. solved.

Ex.14. a. phoned, yesterday; b. traveled, last summer, c. lived, last year; d. played, two days ago, e. received, yesterday.

Ex.15. a. What did you wash yesterday?; b. What happened yesterday?; c. When did you made phone you?; d. Who prepared breakfast yesterday?, e. What did Dan do last week?

Ex.17. a. We moved into a new house last month.; b. Paul helped his brother yesterday.; c. Dana arrived late at school last Friday.; d. The children visited the Village Museum.; e. I watched TV last night. f. Alina played the piano yesterday afternoon.; g. Simona studied French at school last year.; h. Tim talked to Mihai last evening.

Ex.18. a. Eu nu am vrut să urmăresc filmul acela.; b. Ieri ea a ajuns la şcoală la ora 9.; c. Tu nu m-ai văzut la şcoală.; d. Diana m-a ajutat la nişte probleme.; e. Eu am vizitat-o pe bunica mea ieri.

Ex.20. went; had; leave; tell; lost; said; wrote; met; taught; would; stood, run; set; sing; sold; read; made; spoke; eat; drink; feel; drove; break; fell; bring; caught; bought, chose; be.

Ex.21. a. White Fang didn't leave his kennel.; b. He didn't see five women.; c. His Indian master didn't sell him for gold dust.; d. White Fang didn't fight ferocious bear.; e. He didn't feel friendship for Beauty Smith.

Ex.22. a. Did White Fang leave his kennel?; b. Did he see five women?; c. Did his Indian master sell him for gold dust?; d. Did White Fang fight a ferocious bear?; e. Did he feel friendship for Beauty Smith?

Ex.23. a. did it? – No, it didn't.; b. didn't he? – Yes, he did.; c. didn't he? – Yes, he did.; d. did he? – No, he didn't.; e. was he? – Yes, he was.

Ex.24. a. There are five geese on the pond.; b. A pigeon flight is flying over the orchard.; c. She-bears take care of their cubs.; d. Squirrels have long tails and brown fur.; e. Some wild animals are very dangerous.

Ex.25. a. When did you go to work last Monday? (Last Monday) I went to work at 8:30.; b. Who did you meet with three days ago? (Three days ago) I met with my former teacher.; c. What book did you read last week? I read "The English Patient".; d. Where did you spend your holidays last year? I spent my holidays at my grandparents.; e. What was the last cassette you bought? I bought "Celine Dion".

Ex.26. 1. lived; 2. felt; 3. gave; 4. heard; 5. said; 6. was; 7. went; 8. wanted; 9. found; 10. slept; 11. belonged; 12. gave; 13. had; 14. came; 15. woke; 16. liked; 17. gave; 18. bought; 19. took; 20. got; 21. set; 22. sent; 23. sent; 24. got; 25. bought; 26. became; 27. married; 28. knighted; 29. became.

Ex.27. a. give not; b. give off; c. give up; d. give in, e. give back.

Ex.28. a. I guess she/he is right.; b. The window frame was very narrow.; c. I cannot figure out what you're saying.; d. The little boy reached ont his hand for the ice-cream.; e. Try to take hold of the boll.; f. I was rooted to the spot with fear.; g. The prisoner scratched the number of days on the wall.; h. A rescue team looked for survivors.

Past Continuous Tense

Ex.2. a. was talking; b. was standing; c. wasn't doing; d. was passing; e. was trying.

Ex.3. a. Was Dona talking to …; b. Was she standing there …; c. Wasn't she doing …; d. Was anyone else passing by?; e. Was the little girl's mother trying …

Ex.5. Dona came in while Alex was talking over the phone.; b. Dona was walking when she heared a noise.; c. Dona was telling the story when Alex interrupted her.; e. As she was standing speechless, the man came to her.

Ex.7. a. Q: What did the TV set show? A: It showed waving lines.; b. Q: What was father doing? A: He was reading the newspaper/smoking his pipe.; c. Q: Who did mother ask for help? A: Mother asked David to help her.; d. Q: Where did David climb? A: He climbed on the roof.; e. Q: What did David do? A: He straightened the aerial.; f. Q: How did David straighten the aerial. A: He straightened it carefully.; g. Q: Why wasn't the TV working? A: (It wasn't working) Because the dog was sitting on the aerial.

Ex.9. 1-e; 2-c; 3-e; 4-a; 5-b.

Ex.11. a. I was packing my things when the phone rang.; b. While I was packing by things, my mother was making same sandwiches.; c. I was watching TV when I heard a noise.; d. I wanted to watch TV, but it wasn't working.; e. I asked him for help, but he was studying for exams.

Ex.12. cele şapte cuvinte sunt: store, stadium, theatre, agency, hospital, cinema, museum; propoziţia este: Bucharest is a capital city.

Ex.14. 1-d; 2-e; 3-b; 4-g; 5-h; 6-i; 7-a; 8-f; 9-c.

Ex.15. a. had; b. was, didn't, eas; c. had; d. been, didn't; e. would; f. was; g. had, was; h. would; i. had.

Ex.16. a. We meet last year when I was on holiday in Bucharest.; b. They said they would come in time for the show; c. She was studying when I rang her up.; d. Florin didn't use to call on unexpectedly.; e. He had been thinking over and over again till he made up his mind.; f. Hardly had they known each other when he proposed to her.; g. The professor was examining a candidate when the secretary came in; h. If only he had known about the danger, the damage could have been avoided.

Ex.17. noticed, were, was, rushing, became, were standing, came, recognized, had greeted, asked, was happening, told, had caught, had managed, was heading for, met, was carrying, asked, didn't knee, was, had put, entered, went, reached, saw, was, entered, noticed, was missing, had just helped.

Present Perfect Simple Tense

Ex.2. a. have; b. has; c. have; d. have; e. have.

Ex.3. a. driven; b. taken; c. got; d. run; e. come.

Ex.4. a. just; b. yet; c. just; d. already; e. yet; f. recently.

Ex.5. (comentarii posibile) a. A thief has robbed a neighbor's apartment.; b. The Popescu have accepted an invitation.; c. The teacher has asked a question and is now waiting for the answer.; d. Your friend has thanked you for your help.; f. The girls have talked about an evil chance.; e. The mountain climbers have set out on an expedition.; g. Dan and Traian have clinked glasses.; h. Maria has passed an examination with excellent results.; i. My friend has left.;

Ex.6. a. I've parked the car next to the subway station.; b. Have you read in the library or at home?; c. The traffic jam hasn't been cleared off yet.; d. Has he driven a car so far?; e. Haven't you ordered yet?; f. They have replaced the traffic sings recently.

Ex.7. b. A gyrfalcon has travelled by helicopter.; c. A race horse has galloped on motorway.; d. A dog has saved 3 people in a fire.; e. A Brazilian seaman has spent 11 days on a raft.

Ex.9. a. have just finished; b. hasn't she come yet?; c. have forgotten; d. has already failed; e. has driven.

Ex.10. a. so; b. so; c. neither; d. so; e. neither.

Ex.11. 1-c; 2-d; 3-e; 4-a; 5-b.

Ex.12. a. Alex has known Dona for 3 months.; b. The pop concert has lasted for 3 hours; c. Dona's husband has practiced for 2 hours.; d. The pop band has worked with the new manager for one month.; e. The singer has recorded for 3 hours.;

Ex.14. a. since; b. for; c. for; d. since; e. since.

Ex.15. a. They have worked together since they met the new manager.; b. The band has recorded since they came to the studio.; c. I haven't tuned my violin since I dropped it down.; d. The press conference has lasted since the photo session finished.; e. The orchestra hasn't rehearsed since the conductor left.

Ex.16. a. The record company has released a new CD of Tony Amos.; b. Laurențiu Cazan has signed in my autograph book.; c. The writer has changed the lyrics of the song.; d. We've bought it for our friend.; e. Her stylists have designed new clothes for her.

Ex.18. a, c, e.

Ex.19. a) F; b) T; c) T; d) T; e) F.

Ex.20. a. haven't tuned; b. have you played; c. has gone; d. have sent; e. has rehearsed.

Ex.21. a. They've played together since they were's 18.; b. I've enjoyed the lyrics of her song. So have I.; c. She's listened to the same deafening music since she came home.; d. He's hummed the tune for several minutes, but hasn't remembered it yet.

Ex.22. a. On Sunday morning I go swimming.; b. When she was a child, she was very good.; c. I'm looking forward to receiving my birthday presents.; d. They've decided to go hiking.; e. He isn't good/He is bad at writing compositions.

Ex.24. Dona has always sung in public.; Dona has often made chocolate.; Dona has sometimes gone jogging.; Dona has seldom told funny stories.; Alex has seldom gone fishing.; Alex has sometimes sung in public.; Alex has never made chocolate.; Alex has always gone jogging.

Ex.26. răspunsuri posibile; a. ... the most interesting news I've ever watched.; b. ... the most expensive dress I've ever worn.; c. ... the strongest man I've ever met.; d. ... the most amazing story I've ever heard.; e. ... the most boring film I've ever seen.

Ex.27. a. He is the most intelligent/the cleverest pupil I've ever met.; b. "I'm repairing/mending the radio set today. Have you ever repaired/mended it before?"; c. Have you ever traveled abroad?; d. I've never eaten snails.; e. I've seldom/rarely told jokes.

Ex.28. noise: noisy, noisily, noisiness, noiseless, noiselessly, noiselessness.

Ex.29. Propoziții posibile: a. I've never spoken Chinese.; b. It's the first time I've met him.; c. I've seldom gone to the disco.; d. It's the most incredible thing I've ever met.; e. My boy/girl friend has often rung me up.

Ex.30. a. Niciodată n-a mers prin pădure singur.; b. E pentru prima dată când mă sui/cațăr într-un copac.; c. Mereu a spus glume bune.; d. E cea mai amabilă persoană pe care am cunoscut-o vreodată.; e. Ai mai mers atât de departe (până acum)?.

Present Perfect Continuous Tense

Ex.1. a. has been sticking; b. have been talking; c. has been studying; d. has been experimenting; e. has been working.

Ex.2. a. hasn't been lecturing; b. haven't been writing; c. hasn't been looking for; d. hasn't been researching; e. hasn't been gathering.

Ex.3. a. How long have you been reading in the library?; b. What has she been doing since she was a child?; c. Who have been dating for 3 months?; d. What has Mr. Ionescu been giving for 10 years?; e. How long have the students been attending the courses?

Ex.4. răspunsuri posibile: a. I have been looking everywhere.; b. He has been talking for almost 30 minutes.; c. We've been taking exercise.; d. He has been reading through his new lecture.; e. I've been studying for the exams.

Ex.5. a. He has written scores of articles for "The Scientist".; b. Dan has looked up 20 words in the dictionary.; c. They have taken 4 exams for the last month.; d. The committee has discussed 3 topics since 2 o'clock.; e. The professor has examined 10 students for 3 hours.

Ex.7. 1) c; 2) d; 3) e; 4) b; 5) a.

Ex.8. a. I've been here for ... .; b. I've been writing letters.; c. I've written 2 letters.; d. I've been writing to my cousins.; e. I've received 1 letter for them.

Ex.9. a. How long has Alina been reading in her room.; b. She's been writing her graduation paper for half an year.; c. He's been looking for that old atlas since last summer.; d. Dona has taken a lot of pictures so far.; e. How many chapters of the new novel have you written (so far)?

Ex.10. 1. write out ; 2. write in; 3. write up; 4. write down; 5. write back.

Ex.11. a. from time to time; b. all the time; c. at one time; d. in no time; e. in time.

Ex.12. a. Because people have cut down trees for agriculture.; b. Because they have been their homes for centuries.; c. Because many of them have disappeared from Earth.; d. Because there have left very few specimens.; e. Because factories have released sulfur oxide.; f. Because people have released chemicals into the atmosphere.; g. Because the ozone layer has become thinner.; h. Because people have caught too much fish.; i. Because people have caught a lot of tuna.; j. Because people have hunted them near extinction.

Ex.13. 2. I haven't been digging up wild flowers.; 3. I've been taking bottles to the recycling point.; 4. I've/haven't been using recycled products.; 5. I've/haven't been using ozone-friendly sprays.; 6. I've/haven't been using beauty products tested on animals.; 8. I've/haven't been growing my own organic foods.; 9. I've/haven't been reading labels carefully.; 10. I've/haven't been protesting on environmental issues.

Ex.14. 2. Radioactive waste has been poisoning the seas and rivers since the latter half of the century.; 3. Smoke and fumes have already polluted the air.; 4. People have destroyed many forests and lakes up to now.; 5. Wildlife hasn't disappeared completely yet.; 6. Governments have been extracted the Earth's mineral riches for centuries.; 7. The scientific community has often warned against the danger.; 8. The public opinion has been challenging the forces of destruction since the 80s.; 9. Environment organizations have always protested against abuses to environment.; 10. Their actions have shocked governments lately.

Ex.15. a. inflatable; b. whales; c. ban; d. aware; e. depleted; f. recycles; g. dumping; h. wastes.

Ex.18. a. since; b. for ; c. for; d. since; e. for.

Ex.20. (possible answers) a. Because I've been cleaning the house. b. Because I've been jogging in the park. c. Because I've been mending the roof. d. Because I've been sorting my letters. e. Because I've been painting the fence.

Future Continuous and Future Perfect

Ex.1. At 9 o'clock he will be seeing his dietician. From half past nine to half past eleven he will be training. At half past eleven he will be doing experiment son the gravitational field. At half past twelve he will de reading and interpreting the results. A tone o'clock he will be having lunch with his crew. At half past two he will be giving a speech at a junior school. At five o'clock he will be discussing the results with Professor Smith for the Physics Department. At six o'clock he will be having a medical check-up at the health centre. At seven he will be jogging with Mike. At eight he will be talking to Sally about school.

Ex.3. a. Indefinitely were space shuttle missions postponed while NASA set out to design a space shuttle for safety.; b. Dramatically did Apollo 11 achieve America's goal to walk on the Moon.; c. Never had a human being traveled in space around the Earth before Juri Gagarin did it in 1961.; d. Permanently will a space station serve as an orbiting scientific laboratory.; e. Little have the outer planets changed since they were formed.

Ex.4. a. will/shall have built; b. will be circling; c. shall/will be establishing; d. will be watching; e. will have increased.

Ex.5. 1. f; 2. c; 3. a; 4. g; 5. b; 6. d; 7.e; 8. i; 9. h.

Ex.7. 1. go; 2. will agree; 3. will have bought; 4. will have been traveling; 5. am driving; 6. will peopople be traveling; 7.does the plane take off; 8. will give.

Ex.8. a. I'm going to talk to him about the project when I see him. b. Tomorrow I am driving the children to school. c. The road network will be substantially improved. d. The delegation arrives at the airport a tone o'clock. e. This time tomorrow I will be seeing the new Programme Manager. f. It's late and my car is broken. I'll take the taxi. g. By the end of this year, the rural roads will have been modernized. h. Slow down! The car is going to skid on this slipper road.

Ex.9. 2-b; 3-e; 4-a; 5-d.

Ex.10. (întrebări posibile) a. Will I meet my friends?; b. Where will the party be?; c. Will there be any barbecue?; d. Who will help you? E. Will I be able to dance?

Ex.11. a. She isn't going to work any more. B. He's going to give a party; c. They're going to paint/white wash the walls.; d. I'm going to take a day off.; e. He's going to ask her out.

Ex.12. a. am going to study; b. will call; c. will come; d. are going to; e. will visit.

Ex.14. When will you redecorate your house?; b. I'll talk to her as soon as she opens the letter.; c. Will you stay with us for a long time?; d. I'm going to invite all my friends.; e. The first exam session starts in January.; f. If you apply/use light colors, the house will look brighter.; g. The Smith are going on a trip on Saturday.

Ex.16. a. will graduate; b. will phone/am getting; c. am going to spend; d. takes place; e. are coming back.

Ex.17. a. takes; b. am taking; c. takes; d. is traveling; e. starts; f. are attending.

Simple Past vs. Perfect Present

Ex.1. a. have given; gave; b. has added; added; c. have been talking; talked; d. has held; held; e. has attended; attended.

Ex.2. a. Yes, I have. I had it 10 minutes ago.; b. Yes, They have. The people for "Xerox" did.; c. Yes, she has. She drew them yesterday.; d. Yes, I have. I gathered all the information I needed.; e. Yes, I have. I saw him one hour ago.

Ex.3. a. yesterday; b. for the past months; c. by now; d. recently; e. when they heard the news.

Ex.4. a. He studied Economics from 1985 to 1989. After that he worked for A & B Ltd. In 1995 he taught evening classes in a state school. Next year he contributed to "The Economist" / wrote articles for "The Economist". The same year he became the director of a local youth club. In January 1998 he came in Romania to work as a Manager Assistant for an A & B Brach. b. He has studied Economics. He has worked for A & B Ltd. He has taught evening classes. He has contributed to "The Economists". He has been the director of a local youth club. He has been working in Romania since January 1998.

Ex.5. a. has made; came; b. has learnt; c. has been taking; d. has helped; e. bought.

Ex.7. a. read; b. action; c. letter; d. ago; e. break.

Ex.8. 1-d; 2-e; 3-a; 4-c; 5-b.

Ex.9. a. sayings; b. healthy; c. takes exercise; d. made sport of; e. was in for.

Modal Verbs

Ex.1. a. He can play football.; b. I can mend radio sets.; c. Mirela can play the piano.; d. The boy can ride a horse.; e. We can skate.

Ex.2. a. Paul can't solve the problem.; b. You can't sing.; c. They can't speak English well.; d. She can't cook.; e. She can't take pictures.

Ex.3. a. Can you dive in deep water?; b. Can you draw portraits.; c. Can they play chess?; d. Can Mirela make pancakes.; e. Can Dona knit a pullover?

Ex.5. răspunsuri posibile: a. Robert can act wonderfully.; b. Florin can play tennis very well.; c. Dan can play the guitar perfectly.; d. Dana can dance and sing very well.; e. Petre can rule a people powerfully.; f. Cristi could paint strange portraits.; g. George could compose interesting music.; h. Nicu could play the violin skillfully.; i. Marian could sing wonderful songs.; j. Robert could write beautiful sonnets and plays.

Ex.6. b-can't/can; c-can/can't; d-can/can; e-can/can; f-can/can.

Ex.7. a. He could climb trees, so he was able to rescue the little boy.; b. She could use a computer, so she was able to edit the text.; c. He could understand difficult problems, so she was able to pass the examination.; d. The woman could remember people's names, so she was able to identify the baby-sitter.; e. She could play the piano, so she was able to give a charity concert.

Ex.8. a. I shall be able to speak French.; b. Alex will be able to speak Italian.; c. Her children will be able to solve their Maths problems.; d. I shall be able to knit.; e. The team will be able to win the competition.

Ex.9. a) 1. Dona managed to persuade Alex.; 2. Dona succeeded persuading Alex., b) 1. How did you manage to survive?; 2. How did you succeed in surviving?; c) 1. Mihai managed to decipher the code.; 2. Mihai succeeded in desiphering the code.; d) 1. Alex didn't manage to finish the race.; 2. Alex didn't succeeding finishing the race.; e) 1. The students managed to solve the equation.; 2. The students succeeded in solving the equation.

Ex.11. a. My students can't understand the theory of relativity.; b. Andrei can comment on the Romantic poetry.; c. Professor Brown can lecture on post – war economics.; d. Miss Alice can demonstrate how to use the electronic analyzer.; e. Freshers sometimes can't adapt themselves to university life.

Ex.12. a. He solves difficult algebra exercises so he will teach me.; b. He managed critical situations so he was able to advise me.; c. He explains abstract notions simply so he is able to help me understand philosophy.; d. He read the score so he was able to play the musical piece.; e. He draws accurately so he will be able to win the first prize.

Ex.13. a. Irina has managed to translate for the conference.; b. They managed to get to the Louvre.; c. Professor Brown didn't manage to arrive in time.; d. I will not manage to understand the theory.; e. He has managed to discover a new cure.

Ex.14. c. Would you mind if I left earlier?; d. Do you mind letting me use the laboratory of the university?; e. Can I use your word processor?; f. Would you mind if I quote your in my paper?; g. Can I take your car for a drive in the country?

Ex.15. a. up; b. off; c. down; d. out; e. up; f. down; g. off.

Ex.16. a. can/will be able to; b. can; c. managed; d. do, mind; e. wasn't able to; f. would, mind.

Ex.17. a. She may watch late TV programmes.; b. He may drive his father's car.; c. I may buy whatever I want.; d. They may come home at 11 p.m.; e. She may listen to loud music.; f. Your daughter may wear miniskirts.

Ex.19. răspunsuri posibile: a. might not buy it.; b. might not go to get late.; c. might stay with her.; d. might not enter his office.; e. might not go to the disco.

Ex.20. She'll allowed to wrote.; She'll allowed to get a driving license.; She'll allowed to get married … .; She'll allowed to drink alcohol … .; She'll allowed to get a full-time … .; She'll allowed to have a say … . ; She'll allowed to join a party.; She'll allowed to adopt children.; She'll allowed to make use … .

Ex.22. a. out; b. on; c. away; d. up to; e. in; f. off; g. for; h. after.

Ex.23. 2-e; 3-d; 4-a; 5-f; 6-b.

Ex.24. 1. You may burn yourself.; 2. You may slip.; 3. He may get tired.; 4. A rash may appear/You may have a skin rash.; 5. You may make an indigestion.; 6. You may fall over.; 7. You may strain your back.

Ex.26. You needn't know it. I'll come straight home.; b. He needn't. My boyfriend is driving me back home.; c. You needn't. I understand you.; d. You needn't. I can take care of myself.; e. You needn't. I'll do as you say.

Ex.27. a. Need I look for it?; b. Need I come to take you?; c. Need I type the letter?; d. Need you get up earlier?; e. Need I come with you?

Ex.30.a. had to; b. need; c. must; d. will have to; e. mustn't.

Ex.31.a-irritation; b-perceived; c-pushy; d-straight; e-hasty.

Ex.32.a-must; b-must; c-does-have to; d-needn't; e-didn't have to; f-shall have to; g-must not.

Ex.33.a. I Must be at school at 8 o'clock every morning.; b. I had to help him because he didn't know the answer.; c. I've bought bread. You won't have to buy any.; d. "Need you call your parents each time you're late?" "No, I needn't."; e. You needn't translate. I can speak English.; f. No one must enter the laboratory.

Ex.35. 2. I have to do more physical work; 3. I have to avoid unhealthy food; 4. I don't have to lose weight; 5. I have to improve my posture; 6. I don't have to sit at my desk all day long; 7. I don't have to sit in an armchair all the time.

Ex.37. (possible answers); a. … you are putting on weight/you are growing fat; b. … I am going to the gym three times a week; c. … it can damage your muscles and joints; d. That's the reason why you're lost your vitality; e. … she is slender.

Ex.38. a. spot; b. check-up; c. fill in; d. surgical; f. implies; f. workout; g. posture.

Ex.39. a. foot; b. hand; c. guts, d. skeleton; e. heels.

Ex.40. a. over; b. for; c. after; d. in; e. off.

Ex.41. 1. You could get ill.; 2. You might faint.; 3. It could have good results.; 4. She might burst into tears.; 5. Her condition might be worse.

Ex.42. 1. Without that syrup, my cough might not relieve my chest.; 2. Without that gargle, the soprano might not sing.; 3. Without the health insurance, my grannies might not pay for the cure.; 4. Without that antidote, the venom might damage his brain.; 5. Without the family's help, the patient might not overcome this critical moment.

Ex.43.1. He cannot be a beginner/novice.; 2. You cannot have a cold.; 3. It cannot be far from here.; 4. You cannot miss it.; .

Ex.44.1. You can damage your sight.; 2. You can catch a cold.; 3. You can hurt yourself.; 4. You can fall off the ladder.; 5. You can lose weight.

Ex.45. 1. It could be in the bathroom.; 2. It could be more serious.; 3. It could close at 8 p.m.; 4. It could have good results.; 5. It could stop gradually.

Ex.46.1. It must be a nervous breakdown.; 2. It must be rheumatism.; 3. It must be overworking.; 4. It must be food poisoning.; 5. It must be insomnia.

Ex.47. a-3; b-1; c-5; d-4; e-2; f-6.

Ex.48. a-C; b-I; c-P; d-P; e-P.

Ex.49. a. can't; b. could/might/may; c. must; d. could; e. could; f. can.

Ex.50. b. possibility; c. certainty; d. necessity; e. obligation; f. permission; g. possibility; h. lack of obligation; i. obligation; j. permission.

Ex.51. 1. can; 2. must; 3. can't; 4. can't; 5. have to; 6. must; 7. may; 8.can; 9. needn't; 10. have to; 11. should.

Ex.52. 1. Can you make custard?; 2. I can't use a computer. Can you help me?; 3. I can't hear you because of the noise.; 4. You will be able can (to) resume your training when your health improves.; 5. Yesterday they quarreled again, so Maria may not come; 6. "You may kiss the bride now"; 7. He may be the perfect match for you.; 8. You needn't marry him if you don't love him.; 9. Yesterday I had to order other invitation cards. I didn't like the old ones.; 10. "You must love and cherish your wife."; 11. "You should talk to your husband about this."; 12. You must be very much in love with him if you can't see what is as plain as daylight.

Ex.53. a. I can't believe my best friend is cheating on me.; b. I may go to Monaco for my honeymoon.; c. You must know what you're doing.; d. You might be wrong.; e. He/She may not attend wedding.

Ex.54. 1. love; 2. success; 3. marriage; 4. divorce; 5. married; 6. couples, 7. partner; 8. husband; 9. marry; 10. relationship.

Ex.55. 1. may; 2. are likely; 3. might; 4. must; 5. can; 6. is probable; 7. should; 8. could, 9. might; 10. are certain; 11. perhaps.

Ex.56. 1-may; 2-haven't been able; 3-can; 4-should ; 5-could ; 6-may; 7-may; 8-is not allowed ; 9-must ; 10-shouldn't; 11-can't; 12-mustn't; 13-can; 14-may ; 15-should.

Have to / Should

Ex.1. a. He should report to the supervisor; b. You should stop seeing her/him.; c. He should convince his friend not to tell his parents; d. He should talk to the supervisor; e. You shouldn't accept the invitation.

Ex.5. (possible answers) 1. My parents don't let me go.; 2. There are two many boys.; 3. Yesterday I came home late.; 4. Dan and I walked for a while.; 5. How should I do that?.

Ex.6. a. tolerant/severe; b. rude/polite; c. reckless/sensible; d. obedient/prankish; e. lenient/authoritarian.

Ex.8. 1. on the contrary; 2. despite; 3. even so; 4. at the same time; 5. on the other hand; 6. whereas; 7. all the same.

Used to / Would

Ex.3. b. would ask for advice; c. would arrive; d. would go picnicking; e. would play; f. wouldn't work.

Ex.4. a. used to drive; b. was working; c. used to offer; d. used to be; e. didn't use to; f. were showing.

Ex.5. a. Poor women used to work as maids to help their large family.; b. When I called on him, he was working on his new novel.; c. She used to be one of the best of my students.; d. Where were you when I called?; e. She didn't use to complain about hard work because she was strong.; f. He used to read all advertisements in the newspapers with the hope of a job.; g. I was reading the last chapter of the novel when some one knocked on the door.

Ex.6. a. down; b. up; c. into; d. over; e. out; f. off; g. to; h. on

Ex.7. a. Poor women used to work as servants.; b. Men would earn more than women.; c. She didn't use to read the newspaper in the morning.; d. They used to have their own tutor.; e. As a child she would look after her younger brothers.

Conditional sentence – type 1

Ex.1. a. You'll keep yourself up-to-date if you use a database.; b. You'll learn better, faster and easier if you buy a multimedia CD-ROM.; c. Imaginary life will develop if computer companies produce electronic novels.; d. If you buy an extra floppy disc, you'll find information on the author's life.; e. Interactive fiction will emerge as a new genre if more and more educational institutions are receptive to it.

Ex.2. a. if you see / you will believe; b. if you play "Sea world" / you will ride; c. if you use / you will feel; d. if you want / you'll spend; e. if you enjoy / you will take part.

Ex.4. a. If there isn't enough space, people will build towns under sea.; b. Telepathy will become an ordinary means/way of communication if scientists prove that each person has such qualities.; c. People will control weather when stationary satellites revolve around the Earth.; d. People will eat synthetic food if the food shortage increases.; e. If people contact/get in touch with intelligent beings, the fear of aliens will disappear.

Ex.6. True; a, b, e, g; False: c, d, f, h.

Ex.7. a. don't use; will damage; b. have already used; won't have; c. won't be allowed; works; d. am waiting for; have received; e. won't be; discover.

Ex.8. a. He won't develop his mind in he uses a calculator all the time.; b. You can read in the library unless you enjoy computer games.; c. I will buy a new video game for you, provided it isn't too expensive.; d. We will use the new medicine when we are sure there are no outside effects.; e. As soon as I receive the message, I'll let you know.

Ex.9. b. The estate agency will sell more houses if the prices go down.; c If you hide it discretely, you won't spoil the rural feeling.; d. She won't feel alone if she shares it with someone else; e. If you plant grass, your grannies will enjoy the view.; f. I'll feel comfortable if I take out some furniture.

Ex10.a-prepare, will decorate; b-cuts, will peel; c-will hover, move; d-tidies, will clean; e-will buy, helps; f-organize, will make; g-looks, will let; h-will play, bring; i-will mix, gives; j-do, will be.

Conditional Sentence – type 2

Ex.1. a. If he watched TV less, he would study harder.; b. You would hear me if you turned down the radio.; c. If you were interested in Economics, you would buy economic magazines.; d. Dona would ask more interesting questions if she were the interviewer.; e. Mihai would take good pictures if he had the chance to see exotic places.; f. If Traian wanted, he could win the Pulitzer Prize.; g. If it weren't so much violence in the media, the young people would be protected.; h. If they knew more, they would learn how to take care of themselves.

Ex.2. (possible answers): a. I'd watch it if it weren't so violent!; b. I'd listen to it if the language weren't so aggressive.; c. I'd answer if it weren't so difficult to understand.; d. I'd have nothing to object if soap operas weren't so melodramatic.; e. The series would be less boring if it weren't so long., f. I would understand if the speaker didn't speak so quickly.; g. I could answer the questions if they weren't so difficult.; h. I'd let them watch if it weren't so immoral.

Ex.3. a. I wish/if only they changed the programme.; b. I wish/if only I were here for you show.; c. I wish/if only the interview turned out better.; d. I wish if only our newspaper sold well.; e. I wish/if only I didn't miss this opportunity.

Ex.4. a. The script may not be a good one.; b. Our audience may become larger.; c. New ideas may help.; d. Younger characters may appeal to our public.; e. A happy ending may be a solution.

Ex.7. a. Dacă ați avea o sumă mare de bani, cum ați cheltui-o?; b. Articolele tale ar fi mai bune dacă te-ai strădui mai mult.; c. Dacă n-ar fi călătoria de documentare, n-ar putea să scrie cartea.; d. De-am obține subvenția!; e. Concluziile tale pot să fie greșite.; f. Vânzările ar putea să crească dacă am schimba formatul.; g. Aş vrea să se vândă mai bine ziarul.

Conditional Sentence – type 3

Ex.1. 1-d; 2-a; 3-c; 4-b.

Ex.3. a) The bank wouldn't have approved the loan if she hadn't been determined enough; b) I wouldn't have joined the venture if the business hadn't been convincing; c) The organization wouldn't have commissioned the poll if I hadn't trusted you; d) The staff would have supported her if they hadn't received positive signals from the market; e) She would have failed in business if she had been more flexible.

Ex.4. a. If she had the opportunity, she would have studied international trade.; b. The failure of the business would have been prevented/avoided if you had resorted to a consulting company. c. If she had known to seize the opportunity, now she would have run the company's office abroad.: d. If you should need any help, don't hesitate to call me.; e. You would help me very much if you would agree tom y holiday.

Ex.5.a-want; b-will help; c-choose; d-will arrange; e-wanted; f-would have to; g-caused.

Ex.6.a.-would have improved, had kicked; b.-had jumped up, would have caught; c.-had passed, would have had; d.-would have prevented, had marked. e.-had run, would have scored. f.-had won, would have moved; g.-had seen, would have awarded; h.-would have been, had trained; i.-had been, would have won; j.-would have become, had sent.

Ex.7. 1. had studied, would have passed; 2. had asked, would have helped; 3. had gone, would have seen; 4. had spoken, would have understood; 5. had listened, would have been; 6. would have written, had had ;7. had not broken, would have taken part; 8. had not started, would have walked; 9. would have swum, had not been; 10. had taken, would not have arrived.

Ex.8. 1. used, would not have got; 2. had not rained, would have played; 3. had not cheated, would not have phoned; 4. had eaten, would not have caught; 5. had checked, would not have broken; 6. had waited, would have seen; 7. had spoken, would have understood; 8. had gone, would have had; 9. had bought, would have tasted; 10.had been, would have played;

Ex.9. 1. had explained, would have done; 2. had not driven, would not have crashed ; 3. had not been, would have watched; 4. had taken, would have arrived; 5. had asked, would have emailed; 6. had not switched off, would have known, 7. had come, would have arrested; 8. had used, would not have got; 9. had learned, would have written; 10. had not stopped, would have reached.

The Passive Voice

Ex.1. 1. Glasses are being raised.; 2. The waiter's being called.; 3. Orders are being taken.; 4. The wine list is being brought.; 5. Food is being smelt.; 6. The cutlery is being used.; 7. Dan are being paid for.; 8. Music is being played?; 9. Voices are being heard.; 10. Tables are being cleared out.

Ex.2. 1. The banisters has been polished.; 2. The stair steps have been swept.; 3. The tables and chairs have been dusted.; 4. The glasses have been washed up.; 5. The menus have been laid on the tables.; 6. The pictures have been hung on the walls.; 7. The walls have been white washed.; 8. The parquet has been waxed.; 9. The flowers and glasses have been arranged on shelves.; 10. The height bulbs have been fitted up.

Ex.3. First the banana is sliced. Next the banana pieces are put in a blender. After that some yoghurt is added. Then a spoonful of honey is poured into the blender. Finally the milk is added and everything is mixed for ten seconds. When it is ready portions are made and poured into four glasses.

Ex.4. 1. What would you like to drink?; 2. Are you sure you don't want something stronger?; 3. Why aren't you trying?; 4. What do you like drinking?; 5. Can I buy on one?

Ex.5. 1-b; 2-a; 3-c; 4-b; 5-a.

Ex.6. 1. A kettle is filled with water.; 2. The water is boiled.; 3. A teaspoon of tea is put in the teapot.; 4. Boling water is powered into the teapot.; 5. The tea is left to brew fot three minutes.; 6. A cup, saucer, teaspoon and sugar are taken.

The Infinitive Mod

Ex.1. (possible answers): a. to sent an expedition to the Southern Pacific Ocean; b. to obey the orders?; c. not to know anything; d. to sail further south; e. to settle in Australia.

Ex.3. a. The merchant made the crew unload the merchandise.; b. The supervisor made them carry the boxes to the storehouses.; c. The captain didn't let the crew carry the merchandise.; d. The merchant let the sailors make a suggestion.; e. The merchant let the sailors have small amounts of spices.

Ex.4. a-for; b-over; c-up; d-out; e-up to, f-up for.

Ex.5. (possible answers): a. to join the crew; b. to raise the crew's pay; c. to reach the shore safely; d. to tell the truth; e. to revenge his father's death.

Ex.6. a. James Cook promised to discover new territories for the British Crown.; b. The government decided to send the convicts to Botany Bay.; c. Sometimes, the convicts threatened to rebel.; d. Ordinary people hoped to start a new life/turn a new leaf.

Ex.8. a. I expect to be able to use a PC. b. Of course I hope to finish sooner. c. Mark refused to print the document. d. Now you are learning how to erase useless information. e. I'd like to attempt a computer course. f. Did you try to get advice?

Ex.10. a. I'd love you to connect me to the local network; b. I'd prefer Paul to scan the pictures today; c. I'd don't want you to change the password; d. I'd like Maria to access my e-mail box; e. I' wish you to buy the new accounting programme.

Ex.12. a) Marius was glad to receive her message. b) Traian was afraid to lose important information. c) Petre was upset not to find the disk. d) Andrei was excited to get a PC as a birthday present. e) Traian was proud to win the competition.

Ex.13. a. Can you tell me how to get there. b. Show me where to put this parcel. c. Do you know where to buy it from. d. I didn't know where to come for Ionut the party. e. She explained clearly what to do with these things. f. He wondered whether to go or stay.

Ex.14. a. I regret to say it. b. Although they've promised to come, I have my doubts. c. She's explaining to me how to use this device. d. Bogdan was pleased to find her among the guests. e. I don't want you to meet them any more. f. It's advisable to see a doctor.

Ex.16. (răspunsuri posibile); a. I could be supporting your view.; b. The police could be following them.; c. He could be staying with his parents on the ranch.; d. She could be persuading her
husband.; e. Their hippy friends could be coming.

Ex.17. a. He can't be selling the orchard.; b. You can't be thinking of going on an expedition in the Alps.; c. She can't be telling the truth.; d. She can't be going to the disco by herself.; e. You can't be showing them the secret passage.

Ex.19. a. They may be examining the critical environmental problems at the moment.; b. They may be looking for a solution to garbage dumping.; c. Nowadays, pollution may be threatening the survival of the human race.; d. Ordinary people may be unconsciously contributing to the disaster.; e. Today garbage dumping may be degrading larger areas of soil than ever.;

Ex.20. a. We could be implementing the new method these days.; b. You can't be doing such a reckless thing.; c. He may be holding the press conference now.; d. Who could I be talking to find sympathy?; e. I might be going on a short holiday.

The Infinitive and the Present Participle

Ex.1. a. They saw strange things happen.; b. They believed it to be a practical joke.; c. They allowed their son to leave the house.; d. They expected their neighbors to laugh at them.; e. It didn't make them appear insane.

Ex.2. a. They believe it to have a connection with young people's personality.; b. They know teenager's life to be more hectic.; c. They reckon poltergeists to be young playful spirits.; d. They suppose energetic entities to come and visit kindred spirits.; e. They think the visible and the invisible to communicate.

Ex.3. a. It is believed to have a connection with young people's personality.; b. Teenager's life is known to be more hectic.; c. Poltergeists are reckoned to be young playful spirits.; d. Energetic entities are supposed to come and visit kindred spirits.; e. The visible and the invisible are thought to communicate.

Ex.4. a. They heard a noise of footsteps coming from the attic.; b. They felt the floor quaking under their feet.; c. They sensed a danger approaching.; d. They watched the furniture moving all over the place.; e. They saw the water was bursting from the tap.

Ex.5. a. I know her to be intelligent.; b. I'd like you to join us.; c. I suspect (guess) him/her to get scared easily.; d. Don't let him play a trick on you.; e. I heard two people talk.; f. The phenomenon is believed to be wider.; g. He was seen to enter the basement.; h. He/she felt his/her heart throbbing.; i. While I was driving, I saw a light coming from ahead.; j. A flat object was noticed moving away at an unthinkable speed.

Ex.6. a. L-am auzit vorbind.; b. Aş vrea să rămâi.; c. Îl consideră cel mai bun prieten al ei.; d. L-au declarat apt pentru postul acela.; e. Vizitele spiritelor gălăgioase au loc ... ; f. Băiatul a fost văzut venind.; g. Se aşteptau ca ea să cîştige.; h. Au văzut obiecte zburând în jur.; i. Au auzit pe cineva tropăind.

Past Simple Tense and Present Perfect Simple Tense

Ex.1. A-1, 4, 6; B-2, 3; C-5.

Ex.2. a. in her teens; b. as a high school student; c. for seven years; d. since she was 19; e. so far.

Ex.3. a. Have you ever attracted people's attention? / Yes, I have. / Where did you attract their attention? / I drew their attention at Palm Beach.; b. Have you ever won a swimming contest? / Yes, I have. / When did you win? / I won two years ago.; c. Have you ever trained at night? / Yes, I have. / When did you train? / I trained at night in my teens.; d. Have you obtained your certificate? / Yes, I have. / When did you obtain it? / I obtained it last year.; e. Have you worked at this pool for a long time? / Yes, I have. / When did you start? / I started six month ago.

Ex.4. died; detected; have been; got, began; has been; has probably been; has become.

Ex.5. A: Ce s-a întâmplat? B: Doi alpinişti nesăbuiţi au încercat să urce versantul de vest. A: Când au plecat/pornit? B: Acum o jumătate de oră comunicarea cu ei a fost întreruptă. A: Nu a sosit încă echipa de salvare? B: Sunt pe drum.

Ex.6. (possible answers): 1. How do you feel/What do you think/What's your opinion; 2. if you ask me/in my view/opinion/I believe that; 3. do you think/believe that?; 4. you don't have any intimacy/it is stressful to be closely watched.

Ex.7. a. glamorous; b. rescues; c. prevent; d. suntanned; e. training.

Ex.8. A) a. have washed away; b. washed up; c. haven't washed out; B) a. water under the bridge; b. keep his head above the water; c. get into deep waters.

Ex.9. a. have been; b. has worked/graduated; c. was/trained; d. has already made; e. have you rescued/did you make/was.

Past Perfect Simple and Continuous Tense

Ex.1. b. when; c. when; d. than; e. when; f. than; g. when; h. when; i. when; j. than; k. when.

Ex.3. (possible answers): a. That reminds me of a similar story.; b. Did I ever tell you about my first boy friend/girl friend?; c. To get back to the story my first night out was a total failure.; d. To cut a long stories short, I and my boy friend/girl friend decided to elope.

Ex.4. a. households/families; b. consented; c. friar/rancor; d. stabbed/banished; e. potion; f. vault/poisoned/coffin; g. dagger.

Ex.5. a. act up; b. acted for; c. act out; d. act up to them; e. acted on.

Ex.6. a. had been; b. had put; c. had taken; d. had seen; e. had left.

Ex.7. a. Hardly had Juliet appeared at the window when Romeo was enthralled.; b. No sooner had Juliet said the first words than Romeo didn't know what to do: to listen more or to speak:; c. Barely had Romeo sworn by the moon when Juliet stopped him.; d. Scarcely had Romeo and Juliet confessed their love to each other when the nurse called her.; e. No sooner had Juliet gone inside than she returned to the window.

Ex.10. A) a. I hadn't been writing down my dreams; b. I hadn't had reasonable explanations for my fears; c. I hadn't been familiar with relaxation techniques; d. I hadn't discovered the healing power of conversations before I met Dr. Zen; B) a. After I had been talking to someone about my fears; b. After I had met people with similar problems; c. After I had been on a short holiday; d. After I had started a diary, I felt more relaxed.

Ex.11. I dreamt that I was trying to clib a steep hil. The hill was covered in brambles and I kept getting caught and scratched by the thorns. I began to cry because I wanted to reach the top. Syddenly, I found that I was flying up in the sky over the top of the hill. The sun was shining and I felt light and happy. I landed on the other side of the hill in a huge orchard full of many trees. There was a ladder reaching up into one of the trees. I climbed the ladder into that tree and I found that I was surrounded by ripe yellow lemons. I began to pick and eat the lemons. They tasted sweet.

Ex.12. 1-was reading; 2-was reading; 3-was; 4-had escaped; 5-wasn't; 6-was riding; 7-ran; 8-carried; 9-began; 10-disappeared; 11-was; 12-tried; 13-appeared; 14-turned; 15-attacked; 16-began; 17-was bleeding; 18-had given up; 19-stopped; 20-cleared up; 21-ran off; 22-had stopped; 23-had disappeared; 24-stoop up; 25-looked; 26-had got; 27-was stretching.

Reported Speech. Statements.

Ex.2. a. He told that he was feeling very weak.; b. He said that he couldn't walk at all.; c. He said that he was too faint to go hunting.; d. He told that he was going to stay in his den that day.; e. He said that he was sure he would feel better the following day.

Ex.3. a. ... England was a nation of shopkeepers.; b. ... the report of his death had been an exaggeration.; c. ... he though, therefore he was.; d. ... that was one small step for a man, one giant leap for man kind.; e. ... he had come, seen, conquered.

Ex.4. .a The stranger said he would give him/Mick that bottle in exchange.; b. He told him/Mick that the bottle was worth all the cows in Ireland.; c. The stranger noticed that hi/Mick's cow might die before he got to Cork.; d. Mick hoped Molly wouldn't be angry with him.; e. The stranger said she would be surprised at what that bottle could do.

Ex.5. 1. "I'll soon see about that."; 2. "I'm going to lie... ."; 3. "I'll also put ... ."; 4. "I've had a horrid night."; 5. I was hardly able to close my eyes the whole night.; 6. "Heaven knows what was in my bed, but there was something hard under me and my whole body is black and blue with bruises."; 7. "I can't tell you what I've suffered."

Ex.7. 1-c; 2-e; 3-a; 4-b; 5-d.

Ex.8. a. up; b. down; c. in; d. out; e. into; f. off; g. by.

Ex.9. A. a. The genie said that he couldn't allow him to go.; b. The fisherman told that he must ask him/the genie something first.; c. The fisherman noticed that he could hardly believe him/the genie had fitted in the vase.; d. The genie said he would swear it.; e. The genie told him/the fisherman that the Sultan would give him more money than he had ever had in his life.; B. a. "I'll give the princess common sense."; b. "I don't think much of that gift. All she needs is charm."; c. "I must have a princess to devour or I will breath out my fiery breath and destroy the kingdom.; d. "I'm thinking of advertising for a knight to slay the dragon. This is generally done in these cases."; e. "We don't have time. The dragon has only given us until tomorrow morning."

Ex.10. a. The boy wished her a Happy Easter.; b. Maria greeted Mrs. Ionescu.; c. His mother complained that he never listened.; d. The student thanked for the help.; e. His sister disagreed with her.; f. The clerk apologized for being late.; d. Dana refused his invitation.; h. Traian advised her not to join him.; i. Andrei invited her to the disco.; j. Mother told him not to do that again.

Ex.11. 2. that was fireworks; 3. they were colorful and bright; 4. going upstairs to see better; 5. it was a great idea; 6. sit on the window sill; 7. she might fall over; 8. sit next to her; 9. were enjoying the fireworks; 10. was going to the square; 11. to join him; 12. his invitation; 13. him; 14. was waiting for them downstairs; 15. keeping him waiting; 16. they had put on warmer clothes; 17. didn't mind it; 18. Maria an apple; 19. took/accepted; 20. getting started not to miss the show.

Ex.13. 1. church; 2. Friday; 3. Sunday; 4. buns; 5. cross; 6. eggs; 7. good; 8. presents; 9. parts; 10. look; 11. holiday; 12. fine; 13. picnic; 14. popular; 15. days; 16. Christmas; 17. end; 18. spring.

Ex.14. a. failure; b. plot; c. effigy; d. complexion; e. traitor.

Ex.15. a. down; b. in; c. in for; d. off; e. on.

Ex.16. Florina greeted Mirela and said she was glad they had met. Mirela answered and asked if she could be of any help. Florina told her it was not about helping and she added that she was giving a small Mother's Day party. She invited Mirela at her party. Mirela thanked her saying she would love to go. Florina also told her to put on something casual because only their closets friends would be there. Mirela wanted to know if Florina had finished the preparations and offered to come earlier to help. Florina appreciated her offer, but everything was already arranged.

Ex.19. a. He say that he didn't know anything about the plans of the Local Council.; b. He admitted he had always done that.; c. The minister stated that he would take severe measures against his employees.; d. The man didn't know whom he should address for his problem.; e. He wanted to know where the information office was.; f. They questioned him if he had been in touch with anyone else.; g. The spokesperson said that the minister would wave a press conference.; h. They told me not to make any statement.; i. The journalist remarked that the MP avoided to give a clear answer.; j. He said that they had already sent a group of experts to look into the matter.

Ex.20. He said that in the last decade out country had changed for the better.; b. He remarked that every election was a time for decision.; c. He added that election would decide whether they put their resources to good use.; d. He asked what their main goals were.; e. He wanted to know if they really wanted to make a destination of their own.

Let/Make/Have/Get

Ex.1. a. They are going to have the leading actress changed.; b. The director is having the most difficult scene shot by his assistant.; c. We should have the lines shortened.; d. They plan to have the score played by a famous band.; e. He always has dangerous stunts done in his films.

Ex.2. a. Get the spotlights turned on!; b. Get light intensity checked!; c. Get some filters added!; d. Get the scene shot again!; e. Get the ending changed!; f. Get your make-up refreshed!; g. Get some background noise recorded!; h. Get the setting fixed!

Ex.3. a. I'll have it revised.; b. I'll have the stunt done by a stunt-artist.; c. I'll have them altered.; d. I'll have him replaced.; e. I'll have it done by a hair stylist.; f. I'll have the expenses cut down.

Ex.4. Today he is getting her best dress cleaned/car serviced/audition postponed/fitting rescheduled/the new script delivered. Tomorrow she'll have her eyes tested/a film developed/her hair done/a speech written/a stand-in replaced.

Ex.6. a. The merchant made the crew unload the merchandise. ; b. The supervisor made them carry the boxes to the storehouses. ; c. The captain didn't let the crew carry the merchandise. ; d. The merchant let the sailors make a suggestion ; e. The merchant let the sailors have small amounts of spices.

Ex.9. 1-a; 2-b; 3-c; 4-b; 5-a; 6-b; 7-c; 8-b; 9-a; 10-b.

The ing form and the gerund

Ex.3. a. Do you mind closing the door? b. He suggested going out. c. Has he finished writing the report? d. Just imagine living in the country side! e. I'll never forget visiting Paris! F. I stopped smoking two months ago. g. I can't help feeling that this is wrong. h. Her husband helped her moving all the furniture. i. They need sorting out. j. I don't feel like going on the party.

Ex.5. a) After I leaving the hotel, I went to the station. b) She is very good at drawing. c) I enjoy staying in hotels. d) I'm looking forward to meeting him. e) She's used to walking long distances. f) The landscape is magnificent. It's worth going there. g) Its no use pretending you love him.

Present tenses in the passive voice

Ex.1. a) are demanded; b) is born; c) be said; d) have been loved; e) be forgotten; f) am being driven.

Ex.2. a) In the nursery the baby is being fed.; b) In the bedroom grandpa is seen by the doctor. c) In Mary's room music is being played loud.; d) In the kitchen snacks are being prepared.; e) In the back yard the fence is being mended..

Ex.5. a. Parents-children relationship has been changed by social conditions lately.; b. Water in the swimming pool is changed weekly.; c. The placement of the furniture is being changed now.; d. The course of events cannot be changed,; e. I want to be told the truth.

Ex.6. a. have been persuaded; b. aren't changed; c. is being heard; d. be eaten; e. to be carried.

Ex.7. a. Children are treated equally by their parents. b. At present people move away from their home town to work, and so the family is being scattered. c. Some of these changes have been caused by new laws. d. I want everything to be arranged before mother is coming. e. About 750,000 of old people must be taken care of.

The suffixes

Ex.1. a. papery; b. recyclable; c. saver; d. wasteful, e. glassy; f. useful; g. pollution; h. carrier; i. metallic; j. package.

Ex.2. a. wedding; b. married; c. betrothal; d. marriage; e. wedded; f. betrothed; g. engagement.

Ex.3. 1. selfish; 2. reliable; 3. senseless; 4. sympathetic; 5. witty; 6. passionate; 7. caring; 8. impulsive; 9. assertive; 10. decisive.

Ex.4. a. -ly; b. –ness, c. –ness; d. –ward; e. –less; f. –ism; g. –en; h. –eous; i -ly.

Ex.5. a. lionesque; b. lioness; c. lionized; d. lion-hearted; e. lionet.

Ex.7. supernatural/unnatural; natural; naturally; natured; naturism; naturalness; naturalism; naturalistic; naturalist; naturalize; naturalization; a-natural; b–naturalized; c-naturalism; d-naturally; e-naturalist.

Ex.8. a-stardom; b-emanation; c-galactic; d-solar; e-planetary; f-spatial; g-navigator; h-starry; i-astronomer; j-orbital.

Ex.9. a. agonize, b. grievous, c. confidence, d. fearful, e. threaten, f. desperate, g. solidarity.

Ex.10. 1 - communication; 2 - advertising; 3 - technological; 4 - practiacally; 5 - information; 6 - possibilities; 7 - endless; 8 - instantly; 9 - development; 10 - amazing.

Idioms and Iiomatic Expressions

Ex.1. 1-d; 2-g; 3-a; 4-i; 5-j; 6-b; 7-h; 8-c; 9-f; 10-e.

Ex.2. a. before the mast; b. learn your lesson; c. as fit as a fiddle; d. keep an iron rod over; e. by heart; f. get on like a house on fire; g. as right as rain; h. to nip in the bud; i. a storm is brewing; j. err on the right side.

Ex.4. a. paper; b. oil; c. can; d. breath; e. glass; f. hatchet; g. drain; h. rubbish.

Ex.5. a-carpet; b-linen; c-bag; d-whistle; e-chest.

Ex.6. 1-c; 2-d; 3-a; 4-b; 5-e.

Ex.7. a. doesn't beat about the bush; b. above board; c. mince his words; d. lay his cards on the table; e. call a spade a spade; f. pull their punches; g. has come clean.

Ex.8. 1-mast; 2-boat; 3-board; 4-colours; 5-air; 6-mind; 7-oar.

Ex.9. 2- … you should tell me; 3- Just tell me …… ; 4- …… clearly unable to say a word; 5- … before she has a chance to tell anyone/the police about us; 6- …. Ever saying what the press attributed to her; 7- I'm afraid to say what I'm thinking; 8- …. Now that I've told you everything; 9- I can't say a world; 10- …. What he'll say next.

CUPRINS